The

Jerusalem

Problem

The Struggle for Permanent Status

Menachem Klein
translated by Haim Watzman

University Press of Florida
Gainesville/Tallahassee/Tampa/Boca Raton
Pensacola/Orlando/Miami/Jacksonville/Ft. Myers

In association with the Jerusalem Institute for Israel Studies
Jerusalem, Israel

08 07 06 05 04 03   6 5 4 3 2 1

Library of Congress Cataloging-in-Publication Data
Klein, Menachem.
The Jerusalem problem : the struggle for permanent status /
Menachem Klein.
p. cm.
A revised ed. of: Shovrin Tabu : ha-maga'm le-hesder keva'
Includes bibliographical references and index.
ISBN 0-8130-2673-3
1. Jerusalem—International status. 2. Arab-Israeli conflict–1993–Peace.
I. Klein, Menachem. Shovrim Tabu. II. Title.
DS109.95.K54 2003
956.94'42054—dc21 2003050727

The University Press of Florida is the scholarly publishing agency
for the State University System of Florida, comprising Florida A&M
University, Florida Atlantic University, Florida Gulf Coast University,
Florida International University, Florida State University, University
of Central Florida, University of Florida, University of North Florida,
University of South Florida, and University of West Florida.

University Press of Florida
15 Northwest 15th Street
Gainesville, FL 32611-2079
http://www.upf.com

Contents

Maps

Preface

Some of the material from this book has been taken from *Jerusalem: The Contested City,* with the kind permission of its publisher, C. Hurst of London. I am grateful to Christopher Hurst and Michael Dwyer for their permission. That material has been updated in accordance with developments since the publication of that book.

My colleagues at the Jerusalem Institute, Ora Ahimeir, Avraham (Rami) Friedman, Yisrael Kimchi, and Reuven Merhav read the manuscript of this book, as did Ron Pundak of the Economic Cooperation Foundation and Col. (Res.) Sheul Ariel, the head of the Peace Administration in the office of the Israeli prime minister. As always, their precise readings enlightened me and greatly improved the original manuscript. Similarly, I am grateful to a number of Israeli and Palestinian experts and statesmen who shared their impressions and memories with me yet preferred to stay anonymous. No less helpful were Avi Shlaim from Oxford University and Benny Morris from Ben-Gurion University. David Matz from the University of Massachusetts and Joel Migdal from the University of Washington read the manuscript carefully and helped me to improve its shape. However, I alone bear the responsibility for the book's contents. I do not presume to have made no mistakes. On the contrary, the very fact of dealing with such a current subject means that errors lie in ambush. Therefore, I would be grateful to my readers for informing me of any factual errors, while distinguishing them from disagreements they may have with my analysis or conclusions.

The translation into English has been accomplished professionally, as always, by Haim Watzman. Both the readers and I owe him gratitude for the fluency of the text. Of course, I alone bear responsibility for errors.

Introduction

The eyes of the world were on Jerusalem in the year 2000. The pope visited the holy city as the climax of the Holy See's millennium celebrations. At the same time, the city—both its holy places and its political future—was at the top of the Israeli and Palestinian agendas. The situation reached a climax in July of that year, when President Bill Clinton, Prime Minister Ehud Barak, and Chairman Yasir Arafat met at the Camp David summit with the aim of reaching a historic final status agreement between the Israelis and the Palestinians.

No agreement was forthcoming. Shortly after the summit ended, a second Palestinian uprising broke out, beginning at the holiest Muslim shrine in Jerusalem. That holy site gave the uprising its name: the al-Aqsa Intifada.

This book outlines the major developments in the efforts of Israel, the Palestinian Liberation Organization (PLO), and the United States to reach a permanent status agreement, with a focus on the discussions of the future of Jerusalem. Unlike the memoirs that have been published by Israelis, Palestinians, and Americans who have been active at various stages of the peace process, this book uses research methods to cover the process from all sides, from 1994, shortly after Israel and the PLO signed a Declaration of Principles calling for a peaceful resolution of their conflict. Based on Arabic, Hebrew, and English primary sources as well as the author's personal experience in the official and informal talks between the two sides, this book reassesses current knowledge and disproves a number of claims made by the Israeli and Palestinian actors involved in the process.

During the negotiations about Jerusalem, all three parties' long-held preconceptions about how the issue would be resolved were shattered. The talks, which reached their most intensive stage during the Camp David summit in the summer of 2000, did not end in an agreement. Quite the contrary: while they were still in progress, a new Palestinian Intifada broke out. In addition to recounting and analyzing the negotiations, this book also seeks to explain why the dialogue ended in an outbreak of violence rather than a settlement.

This is a current history rather than a work of history in the classic mode. The latter would require the analysis of more extensive memoirs about and documents from the negotiations before, during, and after the Camp David summit than have yet been published. Moreover, neither side ever drafted a single definitive document setting out what was understood and said at Camp David. Each side has, in fact, several versions. There is no official record of the talks that has been certified by all sides. The discussions at the talks alternated between questions of principle, which the leaders were expected to decide, and questions of secondary importance, which were dealt with by other participants. It should be recalled that a number of leaders from the uppermost echelons participated in the Camp David summit, and each sought to go down in history as having played a decisive and important role. The formal channels of communication, the negotiating teams headed by Oded Eran of Israel and Yassir ʿAbd Rabbu of the PLO, had ceased to exist prior to the conference, leaving communication between the parties to improvised channels. These factors prevented any agreement on a single document or protocol. The Americans tried to draft such a document after the summit ended, but for some reason the Israelis and Palestinians remembered the talks differently than did their American hosts.

At the same time, there is a wealth of information that has already been published and may not be disregarded. This book analyzes existing knowledge and is based solely on generally available sources of information, which it classifies and organizes into a meaningful form. The profusion of political events and the rapid pace at which they have unfolded require that they be synthesized into a clear picture that will indicate the reasons for the failure to reach a permanent settlement on Jerusalem as well as other unresolved issues, such as the future of the Palestinian refugees from the 1948 war. Such an understanding is vitally important in light of the violence that, since late-September 2000, has once again come to characterize Israeli-Palestinian relations. Were the talks on a permanent status agreement commenced too early for one or both sides? Was the push for a final settlement the caprice of three or four senior decision makers? No less important, what remains of the talks? Has the cycle of violence turned the clock back, or did the sides pass the point of no return during their discussions, with the ideas raised now shaping consciousness even if not actualized? I hope that what follows will provide answers to these and other questions and will be a useful aid to the public, institutional, and academic discourse on Israeli-Palestinian relations.

In the Oslo agreement, Israel and the PLO for the first time recognized each other and committed themselves to finding a peaceful solution to the Israeli-Palestinian conflict. Israel agreed to hand to PLO control the city of Jericho and nearly all of the Gaza Strip and to allow the Palestinians in the West Bank and Gaza Strip to elect a leadership that would negotiate with Israel over its withdrawal from further territories that would be governed by the Palestinians. As such, it transferred the Israeli-Palestinian conflict from the existential plane, where the two sides each fought for their exclusive right to exist, to the plane of a dispute over the territories Israel had conquered in 1967. Why, then, did the attempt to settle the territorial dispute ultimately end in violence? One of this book's central arguments is that the peace process foundered on the negative dynamic created by the process itself, especially from May 2000 onward. In other words, the outcome was neither inevitable nor completely determined by the personalities of its participants. Metahistorical and all-inclusive explanations have become popular since hostilities recommenced and escalated after September 2000. So have arguments that failure can be attributed to Arafat's mendacious character or Barak's high-handed style (Drucker 2002; Ben-Ami 6 April 2001; Benziman 23 March 2001; Shavit 14 September 2001; Sher 20 March 2001; Sher 2001; Morris 13, 27 June 2002).

What is required, however, is a historical, prosaic, concrete, and complex explanation that takes into account all the parties involved as well as the context in which the official talks originated. In short, this book seeks to compile a balance sheet. The Oslo process turned dysfunctional because of a deficiency in interaction. The Israeli and the Palestinian sides interacted destructively, as did the negotiators and leaders on each side among themselves. In addition, the American interaction with each side was detrimental.

In their comparative study of peace efforts, John Darby and Roger MacGinty identify five essential criteria for a successful peace.

1. The protagonists must be prepared to negotiate in good faith. Once such a conscious choice has been made, the success or failure of a peace process is determined by the management of the tension between the negotiators' needs both to cooperate and to compete with each other.

2. The key actors must be included in the process. They are existing governments, paramilitary groupings enjoying significant sup-

port, and elements that have the power to bring about the downfall of an agreement (veto holders).

3. The negotiations must address the central issues in dispute.

4. The negotiators must not use force to achieve their objectives. A peace process cannot progress if any of the participating parties continues to be systematically involved in political violence.

5. The negotiators must be committed to a sustained process. (Darby and MacGinty 2000a: 7–8)

As I will demonstrate, except for the third item in this list, all other criteria were missing or deformed in the Israeli-Palestinian permanent status talks.

In their research on Northern Ireland, Darby and MacGinty found the following key factors brought the peace process to its successful conclusion:

1. The British and Irish governments developed a close, institutionalized working relationship.

2. By the mid-1990s both governments were successful in establishing a paradigm and outlining the parameters of future agreement. They made clear that no alternative framework was acceptable.

3. Both governments were successful in establishing themselves as the process's gatekeepers and timekeepers.

4. Imposition of a deadline helped to move the parties from rhetoric to substantive discussion.

5. The political parties linked to paramilitary organizations were involved. Furthermore, these organizations, as well as security agencies and branches of government, were given time to acclimatize to anticipated changes. (Darby and MacGinty 2000b: 85–86)

None of these elements was present in the Israeli-Palestinian final status talks. When the talks seemed to be going nowhere, relations between the two sides moved toward confrontation.

The case of South Africa is no less important for understanding the faults in the Israeli-Palestinian peace process. According to Pierre du Toit, when talks in South Africa recommenced in 1993, innovative negotiating rules prevented another breakdown.

The concept of "sufficient consensus" was used by each side to bring on board a maximum number of its respective subgroups. According to this principle, each side offered all its subgroups, including the radical ones, an opportunity to participate in the discussions in which the side's negotiating position was considered. However, the subgroups in the discourse had to accept that decisions would be made within the group by a consensus that might not be endorsed by all the subgroups. These opposition subgroups would not have veto power to prevent their side from taking stands that received sufficient but not unanimous consensus. Their dissent would, however, be recorded, and they could remain within the process and try to influence it from the inside.

When there were fundamental differences of opinion, the sides withdrew to a retreat in a remote area, away from the pressure of media and audiences, where they could break deadlocks, debate matters of principle, or design new plans.

A deadlock-breaking mechanism was established in advance. It consisted of a planning committee with the specific task of preventing deadlocks from slowing the process's momentum. A committee of two members met behind closed doors, no minutes were taken, and its membership was never altered. The two met every day to consider problems, to anticipate others, and to initiate new ideas.

The negotiators dealt with the problem of an imbalance in institutional bargaining power, not by making use of external third-party mediation but by creating new institutions geared to managing the transition from minority white to majority black rule.

The symbolic importance of historical experience and the pain it produced was not ignored. The two sides addressed their past by forming a Commission on Truth and Reconciliation in 1995. The commission, chaired by Archbishop Desmond Tutu, published its report in 1998 (du Toit 2000: 29–31).

Unfortunately, these elements of the South African process were missing from the Israeli-Palestinian peace process, as were other elements I learned about in a trilateral retreat convened and chaired by President Thabo Mbeki of South Africa in January 2002.

In South Africa, the African National Congress (ANC) leadership understood that no solution could be imposed by an outside power, no matter how much sympathy and international support the ANC enjoyed. Furthermore, the ANC decided not to torpedo the talks by setting a large number of demanding preconditions. Both sides agreed to continue negotiations even though not all black prisoners were released by the government and even though bloodshed continued on both sides (note that this violated one of the five necessary conditions for successful negotiations laid out by Darby and MacGinty, yet the negotiations in South Africa succeeded). The leaders of the black majority also understood that apartheid would not end before an agreement was reached. Instead of making the termination of apartheid a precondition, it became the final goal of the black majority. Even though the South African government was more powerful militarily, the ANC viewed itself as the stronger side. Its power lay in the moral strength of its claims, its demographic majority, and its international support—despite the fact that the South African government was more powerful militarily. The truly powerful side, the ANC realized, must create space for the weaker side, the white minority. In order to help their partners regain legitimacy and public support, the ANC decided not to resist elections based on apartheid laws. The ANC also realized that the agreement would have to guarantee minority rights if it were to be durable (Klein 23 January 2002).

As in Northern Ireland, each side in South Africa built its own peace coalition in order to include in the process a maximum number of groups. A network of agencies and organizations operated on each side, conducting dialogues and updates within its constituency on subjects discussed and progress made in the talks. The principle of sufficient consensus helped to achieve an understanding without giving veto power to radicals on either side. Thanks to this mechanism, the radicals' power was minimized as the negotiators made progress. Aside from bringing on board as many participants as possible and preventing an angry reaction once a compromise agreement was signed, this discourse opened the discussion on national identity in the postagreement era.

Finally, the security and intelligence establishments played a key role in pushing the South African apartheid government toward an agreement. Once the highest echelons of these organizations became convinced that conventional military thinking was no longer appropriate and that the regime could not decide the conflict in its favor through the use of force, they openly brought this message before the political leadership. This debate helped those in the regime who believed that old concepts had to be jettisoned and that negotiations had to be opened with the ANC (Klein 23 January 2002).

Of course, there are fundamental differences between the conflicts of South Africa and Northern Ireland and the Israeli-Palestinian conflict. Yet there is much in common, and some of the elements cited could have been but were not part of the Israeli-Palestinian interaction during the permanent status talks, as I will show.

The Israeli-Palestinian permanent status talks did not end with a comprehensive agreement because of reasons that originated in the process itself. I will provide details in the chapters that follow, but here I wish to relate the most important of them in a general way.

First of all, the parties did not choose negotiating techniques that had proved to be successful in other difficult negotiating situations. Second, there was disharmony between the internal interactions of the parties and the Israeli-Palestinian interaction. Third, the negotiators inappropriately touched on matters of national ethos and myth: the Palestinians demanded that the refugees who fled Israel in 1948 be given the right to return to Israel, and the Israelis demanded sovereignty on the Temple Mount/al-Haram al-Sharif. Instead of launching a public debate on the need to make concessions and reach a compromise on these issues, both sides recommitted themselves to their respective national myths and symbols. Fourth, for different reasons neither leadership followed the South African and Northern Ireland models, failing to construct a broad inclusive peace coalition, either in its civil society or inside its own establishment. Groups with a variety of worldviews remained outside the scope of necessary consensus, as did most bureaucrats. "Bureaucratic and political institutions—who shared years of mutual hostility and distrust, deeply rooted in an organizational culture of conflict—were kept out of the picture. . . . By not involving these institutions in the process they would not be prepared for the change, neither mentally nor functionally. In particular, the Israeli Defense Forces did not undergo a substantive learning process on the possible constructive role of military apparatuses in times of peace" (Javetz 2002). A few external experts and think tanks were brought in, but their involvement was limited. The negotiating approach was mainly top-down; the bottom-up approach was neglected. No less destructive were two discrepancies in expectations. One was between Palestinian political and national expectations and actual institutional capability. This was a by-product of an asymmetry that existed between Israel and the state-in-making Palestine in their levels of institutionalization, legal system, and commitments to formal texts, bureaucratic orders, and procedures. The second discrepancy was between the Israeli expectation that the agreement would end the conflict and the relatively low price it was prepared to pay for a conflict-ending agreement.

This is not a book about Jerusalem as a holy city or about the Israeli-Palestinian interim agreements (Oslo I 1993, Oslo II 1995, Wye Plantation memorandum 1998, Sharm al-Shaykh memorandum 1999). Rather, it is about the permanent status talks. My intention is not to compare the Israeli-Palestinian case to other abortive or successful peace negotiations. Nor do I view the subject through a theoretical lens with the intention of presenting a simplistic theoretical analysis of a complicated and elusive reality. I use instead a positivist current-history method to present a detailed study of what happened in the first Israeli-Palestinian permanent status talks. Such a reading is a prerequisite for any comparative or theoretical analysis.

The book's structure is mainly chronological, putting the official negotiation of the years 2000 and 2001 in focus. My intention is to collate the considerable amount of information that is available but not yet collected and ordered and to analyze it in a more rigorous way than has been possible up to now.

The first chapter charts the path that led to the opening of the official Israeli-Palestinian permanent status talks and the obstacles that had to be removed along the way. Its presentation is threefold: it covers actions on the ground, tracks the two sides' diplomacy from 1994 onward, and provides an account of the preparations on both sides, both within and outside their establishments.

Chapter 2 addresses the Camp David summit of July 2000 and its aftermath. It provides an account of the diplomatic negotiations but also gives attention to the Israeli and Palestinian public discourses. It includes the outbreak of the Palestinian Intifada in September 2000 and describes how the new wave of violence connected with diplomatic events. The chapter ends with an analysis of the Taba talks of January 2001, where the two sides negotiated over the ideas President Clinton presented to them in December 2000.

The changing facts on the ground since the adjournment of the Camp David summit, and especially after the eruption of the Intifada, open the discussion in chapter 3. Based on the detailed discussion of the previous chapters, this one is devoted mostly to analyzing the dysfunctional peace process. The dysfunctional elements, as noted, are failed interactions between the sides, within each side, and in the American mediation effort. I analyze the negotiating strategy used by each side in the official talks. The prevailing strategies included the declaration of red lines that could not be crossed and a style of bargaining characteristic of an oriental bazaar. This approach was introduced by Israel and adopted by the United States. Though the Palestinian leadership was unhappy with this approach from the beginning, it did not suggest an alternative. The red-lines strategy and bazaar-style bargaining created a negative dynamic that stymied negotiations.

This book is based on primary sources published by actors affiliated with one party or the other in the peace talks. A cautionary note is in order: by nature, the accounts provided by participants in the process are subjective, partisan, and of polemic intent. However, their articles and memoirs and interviews granted to the media contain important data. Over time, as each actor has read the accounts of others, the consensus among them about the basic facts of what happened has grown larger. Finally, several official documents and maps published or given to me by Israelis, Palestinians, or a third-party mediator have helped me to establish my conclusions on firmer foundations. I have included the most important of the papers in the appendixes.

My firsthand observation of the process has helped me in two ways. First, it taught me how to navigate among the myriad news items, articles, speeches, accusations, and counteraccusations coming from all sides. Much of this information was leaked to the media during the negotiations in order to serve the interests of one side or the other. I have used the memoirs published in the wake of the talks to check the accuracy of these pieces of information. My involvement in the process also helped me to evaluate accounts and reports published on web sites by experts who had access to official information.

Of course, my own judgment and preferences are open to criticism. To enable critical evaluation of my analysis, I have provided full references to my source material in a reader-friendly academic note style, at the end of each discussion of an issue. Where there is no reference, the information is my own and should be counted as a primary source.

The information presented in chapter 2 on the negotiations over Jerusalem's future is based in part on what I learned during my participation in the track-two talks and my position as a scholar at the Jerusalem Institute for Israel Studies think tank, which was involved in preparing proposals for the talks. I have not provided an account of all track-two meetings, only those in which I participated or about which I received firsthand information. This section of the book should also be taken as a primary source.

Some of the researchers at the Jerusalem Institute for Israel Studies served, as I did, as outside experts at various stages of the talks concerning Jerusalem, or as volunteer members of teams of advisers. In 2000, I served as an external expert adviser to the minister of internal security and minister of foreign affairs, Shlomo Ben-Ami. Between October 2000 and February 2001 I was also a member of the political advisory team that operated in the bureau of Prime Minister Ehud Barak under the auspices of Gilad Sher, the bureau director. Sher and Ben-Ami led the contacts with the Palestinians during the tenure of the Barak government. I hope that the perspective from which I occasionally observed the political processes has helped rather than hindered my ability to deal with the subject discussed here. I was not, at any stage, a member of the negotiating team or a government employee; this has enabled me, I hope, to remain a sufficient distance from the subject to research it objectively.

My participation in these advisory forums was in fact a product of my activities as a scholar, and not vice versa. My two books, *Doves over Jerusalem's Sky* (1999 in Hebrew) and its updated English version, *Jerusalem: The Contested City* (2001), extensively discuss the urban and metropolitan reality of Jerusalem as well as the connection between this reality and the negotiations over the future of the city. These research projects were carried out in the framework of an independent brainstorming team associated with the Jerusalem Institute for Israel Studies that examined several alternatives for a permanent arrangement in Jerusalem. This book should be read as research performed in the context of the constraints mentioned, rather than as political reportage. Let me reiterate that this essay is not the official version of the State of Israel. It is rather my own attempt to understand the events.

The Road to Official Talks

Focus on Jerusalem

The negotiations between Israel and the PLO over a permanent arrangement commenced three times. They first opened on 6 May 1996, at an official ceremony in Taba. The ceremony, coming toward the end of the term of the government in Israel that had signed the Oslo accords with the Palestinian leadership, marked the parties' formal adherence to the timetable set by those agreements. It was clear to both sides that they would not be able to accomplish more than a formal ceremony just before the Israeli elections. During the election campaign, the opposition Likud Party accused Prime Minister Shimon Peres of seeking to divide Jerusalem and hand a part of it over to the Palestinians. The ploy worked: voters convinced he would do so tipped the election, by a narrow margin, to the Likud candidate, Binyamin Netanyahu. The change of government in Israel later that month put the negotiations on a permanent status agreement into deep freeze.

Talks were renewed only when Ehud Barak won the prime ministership in 1999, and then not immediately. At first Barak chose to concentrate on the Syrian track, believing he could quickly achieve a peace treaty with Israel's northern adversary. Barak assumed that the Israeli public would be willing to accept an agreement involving far-reaching concessions, but only if the agreement terminated the conflict with the other side. He displayed antipathy toward interim accords in general and to the Oslo agreements in particular, preferring to make a deal with a full-fledged state like Syria rather than an autonomous authority (Agha and Malley 2001). Barak rejected the approach that advocated swift implementation of the agreements signed with the Palestinians and intensive negotiations over the permanent settlement (Pundak 2001). From the Palestinian perspective, Barak's noncompliance with existing agreements was aimed at pressuring and isolating them, lowering their expectations, and humiliating them by ignoring them in favor of Syria, an enemy of the Palestinian leadership (Agha and Malley 2001). Only when the Syrian track proved to be a dead end did Barak turn his attention to negotiations with the Palestinians.

He commenced a search for an envoy to represent him to the Palestinian leadership. In the meantime, another opening ceremony was held in October 1999. Israel was represented by Foreign Minister David Levy, who replaced Uri Savir, a former foreign ministry director general, as Israel's official representative to the talks with the Palestinians. Abu Mazen, the secretary-general of the PLO Executive Committee, continued to represent the Palestinian side. A third ceremony was held in December 1999, when the negotiating delegations effectively began their discussions, with Oded Eran, a former Israeli ambassador to Jordan, heading the Israeli delegation and Yassir 'Abd Rabbu, minister of information of the Palestinian Authority (PA), representing the PA. This ceremony was held five months after the negotiations were to have ended according to the original timetable set by the Oslo I accords of September 1993. The Oslo timetable was, in fact, seldom observed. This, of course, neither added credibility to the process nor increased trust between the two sides. One got the impression that the sides found it hard to part with the existing situation and preferred it to creating a new dynamic.

This impression was reinforced on the Palestinian side because the interim agreements were not fully implemented. Following the Oslo II agreement of September 1995, the parameters of the last Israeli redeployment on the West Bank, which was to have taken place prior to the talks on the permanent status agreement, were never settled. According to the Oslo agreements, Israel was to complete its redeployment in the West Bank and Gaza Strip prior to the opening of the final status talks, remaining only in settlements and security locations. In addition, the Palestinians demanded the implementation of other provisions, such as the release of prisoners. It was not until Barak's government came into power in July 1999 that Israel carried out other commitments it had made to the Palestinians, among them the opening of the safe-passage route connecting the West Bank to the Gaza Strip, operation of the airport near Rafah, and construction of a seaport on the Gaza Strip. Israel, for its part, claimed that the Palestinians had violated the interim agreements by engaging in violence, stockpiling illegal arms, enlisting more policemen than permitted under the agreements, sponsoring anti-Israel incitement, and acting with insufficient determination against terrorism. A kind of ritual developed. Each time Israel was supposed to redeploy its forces on the West Bank, it would insist on restricting the extent of the redeployment. The Palestinians would then claim that the spirit, if not the letter, of the Oslo accords required Israel to withdraw from about 90 percent of the territory.

The Palestinians' calculation was based on the presence of settlements on some 2 percent and Israel Defense Forces (IDF) bases on some 8 percent of the territory of the West Bank and Gaza Strip. But Israel did not want to let go of areas it saw as bargaining chips for the permanent arrangement. As with his predecessors, Rabin, Peres, and Netanyahu, this was Barak's personal preference and not just a position imposed on him by hawkish coalition partners. In order not to expose itself to Palestinian demands in Jerusalem and on the question of the 1948 refugees, Israel tried to delay or restrict its withdrawal in the West Bank. Close examination reveals that at the beginning of 2000 the argument over the extent of the Israeli redeployment on the West Bank prior to the permanent arrangement became linked to the discussions on the Jerusalem question, and the target dates set for the talks on both issues overlapped. In other words, the Israeli-Palestinian dialogue became focused on the Jerusalem area. This was a kind of prelude to the talks that would be held at Camp David and afterward on the city itself and on its historical and religious heart.

Too Little Change on the Ground In and Around Jerusalem

The Oslo II agreement defined three kinds of territorial status in the West Bank. Areas under full Palestinian control were called Zone A; areas remaining under Israeli civilian and military control were called Zone C. In areas defined as Zone B, the Palestinian Authority controlled civilian affairs but Israel retained ultimate security powers. In the framework of the argument over the Israeli withdrawal and over the percentage of territory it would cover, the Palestinians began in January 2000 to demand that the status of the villages Abu Dis, al-ʿAzariya, and Sawahreh al-Sharqiyya be upgraded from Zone B to Zone A. These three villages are located outside of the Jerusalem municipal boundaries set by Israel in 1967 and have effectively become suburbs of East Jerusalem. On 20 March 2000, the Barak government approved a withdrawal from 6.1 percent of the territory of the West Bank, including these three locations. However, pressure from the opposition and some members of his government (the ministers of the National Religious Party [NRP], Shas, and Yisrael Be'aliya) caused Barak to reverse his decision. A part of Abu Dis overlooks the Temple

Mount and contains a building that Palestinian Authority officials have designated unofficially as the seat of the Palestinian parliament. This has increased its value in the eyes of the hawks in the Israeli governmental coalition and of the opposition, who worry about the significance of this step for the future. As an alternative, Barak proposed to reclassify ʿAnata, a suburban village located north of al-ʿAzariya, from Zone B to Zone A. However, the hawks in the government claimed that under Palestine military control ʿAnata would endanger the adjacent Jewish Jerusalem neighborhood of Pisgat Ze'ev. The prime minister was then forced to abandon that idea as well.

Barak then proposed that he commit himself to changing the status of Abu Dis, al-ʿAzariya, and Sawahreh al-Sharqiyya at some future date as an "advance" on the next withdrawal and as proof of his sincerity. In return, he demanded immediate Palestinian consent to a postponement of the deadline for the framework agreement of the permanent status arrangement from January to May 2000. The framework agreement was to be a document in which the two sides would agree on the basic parameters of the permanent status agreement before all the detailed issues were resolved. The Palestinians were suspicious of the concept of negotiating a framework agreement prior to the permanent settlement but consented to give it a try (Agha and Malley 2001). In the meantime, Israel withdrew from the area of Ubeidiya, which borders on Abu Dis to the south. In other words, Barak promised to enlarge the Palestinian Zone A to the north in the future, while immediately enlarging it to the south. According to the Palestinians, fulfillment of the promise to hand over Abu Dis and the other two suburbs was deferred three times, while at the same time construction in the settlements was sped up.

Unlike the policy pursued by the Netanyahu government (1996–99), during the Barak government Israeli-Palestinian competition was not focused within Jerusalem's municipal boundaries. Instead, it took place alongside those boundaries. The Netanyahu government took action against Palestinian institutions and operations in East Jerusalem, confiscated identity cards from Palestinians who moved outside the municipal territory, demolished illegal structures, decided to build the Har Homa neighborhood and open the Western Wall tunnel, and encouraged private Jewish settlement in Palestinian neighborhoods. Other projects, such as the paving of an eastern ring road, were kept on a low flame (Klein 2001: 271–78). According to an estimate made by the city, 1,500 illegal buildings were built in East Jerusalem during 1998, while in 2000 about a thousand were built. But the number of demolitions carried out by the city was miniscule: thirteen in 1998, sixteen in 1999, and eleven in 2000. The relevant ministers in the Barak government approved only some of the demolitions requested by Mayor Ehud Olmert's administration in Jerusalem. Olmert has attributed this to political considerations (Shragai 13 June 2000).

At the beginning of 2000, Israel's national planning authorities approved the Jerusalem eastern ring road project. The road is to run through Palestinian suburbs such as Sur Baher, 'Isawiyah, Abu Dis, and al-Tur, and in some places it will circumvent them to the east. Construction of the highway and its access roads require expropriation of 685 dunams (171.25 acres) of land from Arab owners. The expropriation proceedings began in March–April 2000, in parallel with the Israeli-Palestinian discussions of the upgrading of Abu Dis, al-'Azariya, al-Tur, and Sawahreh al-Sharqiyyah from Zone B to Zone A (*Ha'aretz* 15 March, 6 April, 21 September 2000; *Kol Halr* 24 March 2000). The eastern ring road was aimed at diverting Bethlehem-Ramallah traffic away from Jerusalem. This is an objective reason why the road is needed. But the Palestinian side also took stock of the context in which the Israeli plan was placed. Was it part of Israel's enterprise of expanding settlements and paving roads in the West Bank? Was the road aimed at detaching East Jerusalem from the interior and thus perpetuating Israel's annexation of the Arab city? In the context of a permanent settlement and full Palestinian rule over the suburbs through which the road runs, the answer is negative. When the diplomatic process and the transfer of the three villages were delayed and Israeli operations in the Jerusalem periphery increased, Palestinian fears became more profound. The Palestinian side did not believe that Israel's intention was to pave a road that would serve the Palestinian population and not Israeli rule. On several occasions during the year 2000, the Palestinian side expressed to Israel its displeasure with the preparation work for the road, but it also believed there was a possibility of reaching a permanent settlement according to the timetable that Prime Minister Barak had declared (Beilin 2001: 74–83, 91).

The Barak government reached tacit agreements with Faisal Husseini, who held the PLO's Jerusalem portfolio and coordinated Palestinian activities in the city out of his office in Orient House in East Jerusalem. The agreements set the parameters of Orient House's activities in East Jerusalem and the Islamic Waqf's activities on the Temple Mount, subjects that had been under dispute during the Netanyahu government (Klein 2001: 252–54). The bottom line was that Orient House resumed the activities it had engaged in under the Rabin and Peres governments of 1992–96. In general, during the Barak government's tenure, diplomatic meetings at the senior level were not held at Orient House but rather at East Jerusalem churches and hospitals or at the American Colony Hotel. The speaker of the European Parliament met with Husseini at St. Anne's Church, which is French property, and the president of the European Commission met with him at the Evangelic School (*Ha'aretz*, 24, 29 February, 3 March 2000).

The Barak government's policy was a cause of concern for the Jerusalem municipal authorities. The municipality took several actions in April–May 2000 aimed at reinforcing the Jewish foothold in Arab areas and preventing their transfer to Palestinian administration and perhaps even sovereignty. First, it prepared a plan for renovating the compound surrounding the tomb of Simon the Just in the Shaykh Jarah neighborhood, close to the homes of five Jewish families and several single men. In response, the Palestinians fenced in the site. The dispute ended up in court, with the judge finding in favor of the city. Second, the municipality pressed forward with a plan to build a Jewish neighborhood of 200 housing units in Abu Dis. Third, Mayor Olmert declared that he wanted to revise the policy of his predecessor, Teddy Kollek, who had envisioned a Jerusalem composed of a mosaic of separate Jewish and Arab neighborhoods. Only about 1,500 Jews live in the Arab neighborhoods of East Jerusalem, which are home to 200,000 Palestinian Arabs (*Ha'aretz* 15 February, 30 April, 23 May 2000; Shragai 13 June 2000). In parallel, settler organizations increased their efforts to purchase real estate in East Jerusalem's Arab neighborhoods. The Palestinian security apparatuses tried to frustrate the deals, but, as in the past, the actions of the various Palestinian agencies were not coordinated and were random and intermittent. Furthermore the Arabs of East Jerusalem did not honor some of the instructions issued by the Palestinian Authority that were aimed at overseeing the sale of homes and land in Jerusalem and preventing their transfer to settlers via straw men (*Kol HaIr* 28 July 2000).

Too Much Change on the Ground: Settlement Expansion versus Palestinian Construction

It was Yitzhak Rabin who decided to build extensively in "Greater Jerusalem"—that is, in those Israeli settlements in the Jerusalem vicinity. These settlements were to remain, according to his plan, under Israeli sovereignty after the permanent status agreement. Annual population growth during the 1990–2000 decade in all Israel's settlements in the territories was between 7 and 8 percent, twice the rate of natural increase (*Ha'aretz*

1 May 2001). During Barak's tenure, the pace of construction accelerated. In the first half of 2000 there was a 44 percent increase in construction in the settlements as compared to the equivalent period in 1999, at the end of the Netanyahu era. Barak's administration issued 3,500 construction tenders for the settlements between the middle of 1999 and the summer of 2000. Furthermore, during Barak's term in office, there were building starts for 2,830 housing units out of the 19,190 commenced since the first Oslo agreement (September 1993). Of these 2,830 housing units, some 1,800 were public housing and the rest were by private contractors. These building starts came in addition to the housing units commenced during the Netanyahu period. In 1998, for example, there were 4,210 building starts in the territories. This was the largest number of building starts since 1991 (*Ha'aretz* 1 May 2001). During 2000 there were in all more than 5,000 housing units in various stages of construction in the settlements. Moreover, a further 30 outposts (unauthorized settlements) were added to the 145 official Israeli settlements established in the West Bank and Gaza Strip after June 1967. These outposts were set up during the Netanyahu period, and less than a third were dismantled by the Barak government.

It should be emphasized that Israel made a special effort to construct housing for Israelis in the Jerusalem area. These were concentrated in four blocks of settlements. One is the Giv'on block in the northwest with 3,400 residents, and the second is the Kokhav Ya'akov–Tel Zion block in the northeast with 2,700 residents; these two blocks contain 6,100 settlers in an area in which 35,700 Palestinians live. The Ma'aleh Adumim block in the east has 29,050 people with borders extending over some 69,500 dunams (6,950 hectares), an area almost fifteen times larger then the current built-up area in this block. By having such a large territory this block affects the lives of 27,700 Palestinians, mostly living in Jerusalem's suburbs, adjacent to the city's municipal boundaries. The Etzion block in the south is inhabited by 12,500 Israelis. Near the Etzion block lies the municipality of Betar Illit, with 15,800 residents. Excluding the nearby Palestinian cities of Bethlehem and Bait Jala, 21,500 Palestinians live in villages and refugee camps close to the Etzion block and Betar Illit.

The Jerusalem area thus contains two types of settlements. There is Ma'aleh Adumim, large in territory and relatively far from Palestinian population concentrations, and the other three blocks, which are all very close to Palestinian residential locations. Unlike other West Bank areas that remained in IDF hands, the lands that Israel seized control of in Ma'aleh Adumim and Etzion block have been attached to one of these settlement municipal councils (B'tselem May 2002: 80–101; *Ha'aretz* 14

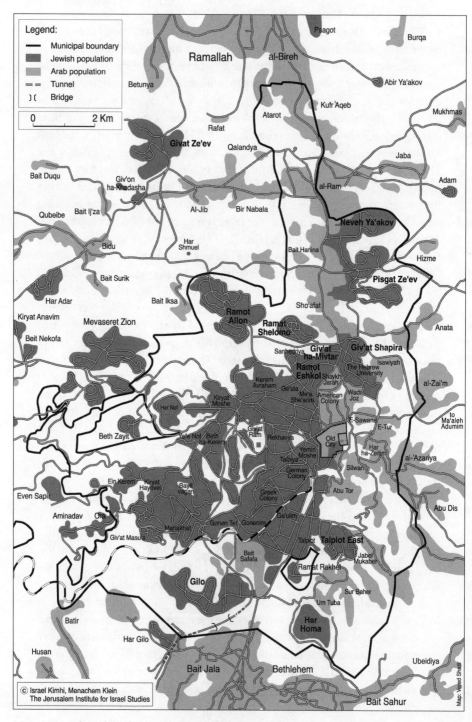

Map 1. Jewish and Arab populations in Jerusalem, 2000

May 2000). As I will show, these facts shaped the positions of both sides in the debate over settlement block boundaries in the Taba talks, when they exchanged maps for the first time.

During 2000, building permits were issued for 1,184 new housing units, of which 529 are in the Jerusalem area (Peace Now 3 December 2000; *Ha'aretz* 16 January 2000, 5 March 2001). On paper, there is also a plan to double the number of housing units in the urban residential areas around Jerusalem. At the beginning of 2000, these contained approximately 12,000 units housing some 66,000 residents (*Ha'aretz* 9 January 1998, 21 February 2000; Shragai 18 January 1998). This goal is to be attained, in part, by establishing an ultra-Orthodox city northeast of Jerusalem called Tel Zion, on which construction commenced in 1999. Another city, Geva'ot, is planned for the national-religious public in the Gush Etzion area south of Jerusalem and is to contain 6,000 housing units (*Ha'aretz* 23 March 2001). During the years 2000–01 the housing ministry began marketing the land designated for these plans to the private contractors who were actually to construct the homes. In 2000, the land for 2,800 housing units was sold (*Ha'aretz* 10 April 2001). Furthermore, in March 2001 earthwork commenced for the expansion of the Har Gilo settlement to the west of Jerusalem by the addition of land purchased from the Arabs of the village of al-Walaja, a village that spans the Green Line, Israel's pre-1967 border. Part of al-Walaja is in Jerusalem and part in the West Bank, classified as Zone C (*Ha'aretz* 20 March 2000).

The goal of the Israeli government, and of the municipality of Jerusalem, is for implementation of those construction initiatives, together with the other provisions of the plan "to strengthen Jerusalem" to bring about a demographic balance of 70 percent Jews and 30 percent Arabs in Greater Jerusalem as a whole, and not just within the present city limits. In the mid-1990s, this demographic balance became the benchmark for the Israeli planning authorities, replacing the former goal of an ideal balance of 75:25, formulated in 1975 (*Ha'aretz* 21 January, 3 May, 1999; *Kol HaIr* 22 January 1999). The plan may well be no more than wishful thinking. Concurrently with the Israeli plan, the Palestinians have increased their own hold in the Jerusalem area. According to the Palestinian Bureau of Statistics, in addition to some 220,000 Palestinians living under Israeli jurisdiction, some 120,000 Palestinians live in the suburbs adjacent to East Jerusalem. This does not include the Palestinian cities of Ramallah and al-Bireh north of Jerusalem, and Bethlehem, Bait Sahur, and Bait Jala to the south. From the social, urban, political, and economic points of view, life in these communities is similar to living in East Jerusalem under Israeli control. This larger community is far from complacent. The Palestinian Authority encourages building in order to create continuity among the Palestinian neighborhoods in the northern part of the city and to connect these to Ramallah, with the goal of preventing Jewish settlements from surrounding Palestinian neighborhoods and populated areas. Moreover, the construction is meant to strengthen the connections between East Jerusalem and the areas held by the Palestinian Authority and to foil the Israeli plan to physically connect Ma'aleh Adumim to Jerusalem (Plan 1E) (Klein 2001: 271).

Between 1997 and 2000, the Palestinian Authority issued 1,777 building permits in the Palestinian Jerusalem district. During this period 2,977 requests for building permits were submitted to the Jerusalem district governor in the Ministry of Local Government and Municipal Affairs (data from Orient House and the Ministry of Local Government). The Israeli Ministry of Construction and Housing issued tenders for the construction of 3,000 housing units during this period (Klein 2001: 271). Thus, carrying out the tenders for construction in Greater Jerusalem, including the establishment of the new ultra-Orthodox city of Tel Zion northeast of the capital, will not change the demographic balance in metropolitan Jerusalem in Israel's favor. Not counting Ramallah, al-Bireh, Bethlehem, Bait Sahur, and Bait Jalla, and even including Israeli settlements within a radius of twenty kilometers from Jerusalem, the demographic balance is presently 56:44 percent in Israel's favor (calculation according to the 1998 *Statistical Yearbook for Jerusalem*).

The spatial reality in the Jerusalem metropolitan area on the eve of the Camp David summit was summed up by geographer Elisha Efrat. There is, he noted, a fundamental difference between Jerusalem's Palestinian periphery and its Israeli periphery. The Palestinian periphery is characterized by its adherence to the city's boundaries. It is territorially contiguous and is settled in most places. The inhabitants of the Palestinian periphery maintain a daily link with East Jerusalem. In contrast, the Jewish periphery has a narrow arterial structure, without depth. Its population is scattered and restricted, and only a part of it maintains a daily link to Jewish Jerusalem (Efrat 31 May 2000).

A picture of construction activity during the Barak era emerges from the following data as well: there were 1,943 public building starts in the settlements during 2000, as compared with 1,367 in 1999. This is the largest number of building starts in the settlements since 1992. No less significant is the fact that the settler population grew by some 8 percent in 2000, and during Barak's tenure by some 12 percent, as compared to a natural increase of only 1.7 percent in Israel (Peace Now 3 December 2000; *Ha'aretz* 16 January 2000, 5 March 2001). The Palestinians did not distinguish between private and public construction, or between a tender legally issued during the Netanyahu period and implemented during the tenure of the Barak government and a tender issued by the Barak government. Neither did they see any difference between settlements near Jerusalem that were considered as within the Israeli "national consensus" and those in other areas that were more controversial to the Israelis. Similarly, the Palestinians did not distinguish between older Israeli plans, such as Plan 1E, drafted in the 1980s and approved by Defense Minister Moshe Arens at the end of May 1999 (*Ha'aretz* 28 May 1999; Klein 2001: 256–57), and newer plans. To the Palestinians, the result was the same: the loss of territory, Israeli control over water sources and planning, and frustration and disappointment. They came to the conclusion that Israel had misled them and exploited its territorial control in order to create facts on the ground prior to the conclusion of the permanent status agreement. The Palestinians hoped to regain what they had lost or were about to lose in the negotiations over the permanent status of the West Bank and Gaza Strip.

According to Agha and Malley, "All these external political events surrounding the negotiations, in fact, had critical implications for the negotiations themselves. The U.S. administration felt so at the time, seeking on countless occasions before, during, and after Camp David meetings to convince Barak to change his approach, precisely because the administration feared his tactics would harm the prospect for a deal . . . critical Palestinian constituencies had turned decidedly sour. . . . Israeli actions that strengthened those trends further narrowed the Palestinian leaders' room to maneuver and accentuated the sense of paralysis among them" (Agha and Malley 13 June 2002).

A Limited Clash on the Ground

The Israeli government approved the change of status for Abu Dis and al-'Azariya on 15 May 2000, despite the threat of the hawkish factions to resign from the coalition. Barak took this initiative because he expected the talks on the permanent status agreement on the Stockholm track (to be discussed later in this chapter) to lead to a summit conference and the inevitable resignation of the hawkish factions from his government. Neither could Barak continue to procrastinate without severely undermining Palestinian confidence in his actions and intentions. Furthermore, Clinton, who had closely monitored the contacts and had passed on to Arafat

Israeli assurances about withdrawing from the two villages, was starting to express concern about Barak's postponement of the withdrawal (Agha and Malley 2001; *Ha'aretz* 27 April 2000; *al-Ayyam* 12 May 2000).

The implementation of the Israeli decision was frozen due to the events of Naqba Day on 15 May 2000 ("Catastrophe Day" in Palestinian parlance—the anniversary of the day the British evacuated Palestine in 1948). Naqba Day also marked the end of Prisoners Week. This was a week of violent demonstrations all over the West Bank and Gaza Strip, demanding the release of Palestinians imprisoned in Israel. All the Palestinian organizations, including the opposition organizations in the PLO and Hamas, participated in Prisoners Week and Naqba Day, during which more than 100 Palestinians were injured in confrontations with Israeli forces. Prisoners Week and Naqba Day were organized by local branches and the apparatus of the Fatah movement (the Tanzim) (Baskin 2000). Public servants, police, and armed members of the Fatah apparatus also participated. These events occurred during a time when the atmosphere was already tense. The lack of diplomatic progress and the agitation over the expansion of the settlements caused many Palestinians to conclude that the Oslo accords had brought benefits only to Israel and to a handful of Palestinians with Israeli connections ('Abdul Hadi 2000, in English).

Israel's unilateral withdrawal from southern Lebanon on 24 May, just a few days later, added to the turmoil. Many Palestinians concluded from that move that Israel understood only the language of force. To these Palestinians, the strategy of the Hezbollah and al-Amal movements in southern Lebanon, which consisted mainly of guerrilla actions against soldiers in order to maximize Israeli casualties, was the appropriate way to bring about an Israeli withdrawal from the West Bank as well. Demonstrations sanctioned by Arafat—whether tactically, to let off steam and release internal pressures, or as a strategy for obtaining Israeli concessions— along with others that were not approved by him, spun out of control for awhile. According to Israel, the Fatah militia and members of the Palestinian Authority's security forces initiated shooting at Israeli soldiers. The Palestinian Authority regained control after a relatively short time, and the Israeli reaction was restrained. Six Palestinians were killed and some 400 Palestinians and twenty-six Israeli soldiers and civilians were wounded in the exchanges of fire between Israeli soldiers and Palestinian police in some of the cities of the West Bank (*Ha'aretz* 16 May 2000).

Paving the Way through Track-Two Channels

Since 1994, more than thirty Israeli and Palestinian groups have discussed the parameters of a permanent status agreement in Jerusalem, in what are called track-two channels, negotiations conducted usually secretly, parallel to and separate from the official talks. These Israeli-Palestinian contacts created a common professional discourse and program founded on a base of data that was more or less agreed upon. Sometimes the participants stopped at that point, and sometimes they went beyond it in an attempt to find a political structure that would encompass and give direction to the points on which the experts reached consensus. Some of the groups dealt with the city and the metropolis only, and some included Jerusalem in a wider framework and discussed all of the issues of the permanent status agreement. Sometimes there were many participants in the meetings, and at other times only small delegations. As far as is known, most of the groups met under West European auspices (Sweden, Denmark, Norway, Great Britain, France, Holland, Italy, Portugal, Greece, Cyprus, Spain, Belgium, and the European Union), sometimes under the sponsorship of governmental institutions and sometimes at the initiative of nongovernmental organizations (NGOs). A Palestinian participant in many track-two meetings summed them up as follows: "The Dutch and Swedish track sponsored issues related to planning, zoning and infrastructure for the whole city in times of peace, while the British track focused more on the political dimension of the conflict in Jerusalem. The Spanish track sponsored the religious dimension of the Holy City, and the Greek track focused on the discussion of general issues in preparations of the final talks" (Kassisiyyeh 2002).

The U.S. government was influenced by the Israeli taboo against any discussion of the future of Jerusalem. In American government slang, the letter *J* signified the zone that Washington bureaucrats were forbidden to enter. Washington did not initiate informal channels for talks on a subject that could have impinged on internal U.S. politics through the Jewish vote and the Jewish lobbies. Perhaps even more than Israeli citizens, U.S. Jews lived the myth of a united Jerusalem and the miraculous Israeli victory of 1967. For them, Jerusalem was a national and religious symbol and not a complex and tension-filled city. It was Teddy Kollek, Jerusalem's mayor for almost three decades (1965–93), who brilliantly marketed Jerusalem to American Jewry as a symbol of day-to-day coexistence and as a city containing a mosaic of religious beliefs.

It would be difficult to exaggerate the importance of the informal channels and their contribution to the negotiations. They prepared the professional and political infrastructure and created a common language between the two sides. Through them, several breakthroughs were made and creative ideas formulated that were later brought to the negotiating table. These ideas included new concepts of sovereignty: suspended, joint, and divine sovereignty; a common economic regime for Jerusalem and al-Quds; territorial exchange by mutual agreement; a Jewish-Muslim-Christian religious council that would coordinate management of the holy places; cooperation between the Israeli and Palestinian police and the creation of a joint police force for the seam zone between East and West Jerusalem; and the concept of the holy basin (Hassassian 2001; Kassisiyyeh 2002).

The back channels, though, had their own shortcomings. They were conducted almost exclusively between professionals. Insufficient effort was made to bring together community leaders representing the two peoples who would have to live side by side from the day a peace accord was signed. Second, government officials and bureaucrats rarely participated. True, a few highly placed decision makers on each side were briefed about the issues discussed, but they were content to remain outside the track-two meetings. Their attitudes toward the back channels varied. Some of them underestimated the potential of track-two talks for creating understanding, let alone an acceptable agreement. Others evinced apathy, while others used the back channels to float experimental balloons without incurring political costs.

Thus, when the official track was about to commence and as it proceeded, mutual dependency produced relationships between officials and professionals. The taboo that prevented the officials from adequately preparing their brief for negotiations over Jerusalem forced them to open their minds to understandings reached and ideas exchanged in the track-two talks over the capital city. For their part, the track-two professionals were eager to inject their insights, ideas, and proposals (whether fully thought out or half-baked) into the official talks. On both the Israeli and Palestinian sides, however, official-professional dialogue was shaped by the decision makers' selectivity, preferences, and limited attention spans. Individual officials chose which professional voices they would listen to, and they placed time limits on professional involvement. The outsider professional was called in either intermittently or when the talks faced a deadlock and serious crisis. The leader also decided which level of official the professional would meet, and could limit access to chief decision makers and to the negotiating team. The officials' decision about which professionals to listen to was not dependent solely on the skills and excellence of those professionals. The officials tended to prefer mainstream, levelheaded voices, as well as people who appeared to be loyal to them, to their negotiating goals, or to their administration. Former civil servants and experts who maintained open channels with the administration had a great advantage as well. Furthermore, the selection of decision makers was influenced by "packaging" considerations. The influence of the professionals increased to the extent that their ideas were consistent with other components of the deal the political leader had prepared or already offered. Finally, in choosing their negotiating strategy and tactics, the leaders' approach was shaped also by political and public relations considerations. The decision maker did not share those considerations with the former establishment professionals, only with close and loyal assistants.

Consequently, ideas created or understandings reached in track two were rarely adopted by the official negotiators in their original form. Such ideas were either rejected completely or revised or put in a different context. It goes without saying that they were presented in a style very different from that used successfully by the track-two professionals to achieve acceptance by the other side. This is not to say that decision makers went beyond their authority and responsibility or to conclude that the Israeli-Palestinian case is unique—quite the opposite. However, a comparison of the creative ideas and understandings produced on track two with the positions taken by the decision makers during the official talks can help us understand the parameters that shaped the official talks and limited the influence of track two.

The groups that discussed the subject of Jerusalem in the unofficial negotiations may be divided into two basic categories. In one category were the groups that did not dare to raise political issues and contented themselves with discussing professional subjects of a technical nature; in the other were groups that reached understandings on political issues as well. (The output of some of the informal channels may be found in the following sources: Hirschfeld 2000: 212–17; Yuchtman-Yaar and Hermann 2000; Maoz and Nusseibeh 2000; Chazan 1991; Shatayyeh 1998; 'Abdul Hadi 2000; Hirschfeld 1998; IPCRI 1999; Cingoli 2001).

The first category includes discussions conducted in 1996–97 between the Jerusalem Institute for Israel Studies and the Arab Studies Society, whose office is located in Orient House. The International Peace and Cooperation Center (IPCC), which split away from the Arab Studies Society in 1997, was also included. Talks between experts at the Truman Institute of the Hebrew University of Jerusalem and the Palestine Consultancy Group (PCG) in 1993–94 also belong to the first category. This kind of discussion was based on the preparation of professional papers, some by joint Israeli-Palestinian groups and some by each side separately. These covered urban and metropolitan subjects such as transportation, the environment, water and sewage, economics, planning and construction, holy places, and the preservation and restoration of historical sites. Also covered were subjects such as planning for the urban space and its environs and models for running cities as parts of metropolitan areas (Kassisiyyeh 2002). The participants in this track did not want to assume the statesman's mantle and restricted themselves to preparing the ground professionally for coexistence in the common area of Jerusalem and for cooperation on various levels.

This model is important for the long term—for a reality that will exist after a political arrangement has already been reached—more than for the short term, when the two sides are directing their efforts principally toward attaining an agreement. In the long term, the content of the model, molded by the experts to fit the framework created by the statesmen, is important. It preserves the division of labor and professional expertise between politicians and experts. The danger is that the two will become disengaged. The framework of the political arrangement may be determined without or indeed in contradiction with professional input. Political considerations may override professional necessities, and the absence of professional experts from the principal discussions will later cause trouble for the statesmen when they are required to find solutions to the problems raised by the political framework. Similarly, professional recommendations may be made without any political input or overview. The statesman and the expert may not understand each other's language.

The statesman's role was played by the participants in the second category of informal channels. These channels were opened in order to make political breakthroughs and to provide tools to the decision makers if and when the negotiations over Jerusalem would take place. Professional dialogue alone is not enough—that was the concept that guided the participants in this track. Professional dialogue should be placed within a political framework. These participants also agreed that without a political framework for the talks, the professional dialogue could not go very far. Naturally, most of the attention in these channels was devoted to political principles, and very little to clearly professional questions.

In January 2000, a joint statement on the principles that were to guide the negotiations on Jerusalem was published following discussions held under the auspices of the University of Oklahoma and the Rockefeller Foundation. Israelis, Egyptians, Jordanians, Palestinians, and Americans who had met several times over the previous two years signed the statement. This channel was unique in seeking to have an influence on Arab and Jewish public opinion no less than on the decision makers. Of the informal channels, this was the only one whose participants went public, announced their position, and submitted their paper to the heads of the relevant states. The other channels remained secret; for example, the Madrid channel established in 1996 between Israeli and Palestinian intellectuals had access to their political establishments (Hass 28 September 2000). This channel was directed by representatives of the European Union and the Spanish government and dealt with all the issues of the permanent status agreement. It collected ideas that were raised in parallel channels. Because the participants were frank with each other and developed relations of mutual trust, and because they took an inclusive approach, they were able, in March 1999, to agree on a paper; this document remains classified. It was one of the more successful of the informal channels.

The Madrid and Oklahoma channels represented completely opposite approaches to informal channels that discussed political subjects. The Oklahoma channel was directed at the public and public opinion, and when the media's interest waned, it lost most of its influence. The Oklahoma paper helped shape public opinion but not policy. In contrast, the Madrid paper was aimed at the political elite. The Israeli and Palestinian Authority political leadership found it difficult to accept the Madrid paper because of its comprehensiveness. Moreover, the paper was ahead of its time—there was no public or institutional legitimization for the positions expressed there. The political leaders who were the patrons of the Madrid channel did not fully adopt the paper it produced. They were not willing to be identified with the paper, nor were they willing to bring it into the public discourse or put it on the political agenda.

In all these aspects, the Beilin–Abu Mazen paper (discussed at length in the next section) differed from the Madrid paper. Between September 1993 and September 1995, two teams under the guidance of Deputy Foreign Minister Yossi Beilin and PLO Executive Committee member Abu Mazen prepared a draft of principles for a final status settlement between Israel and the Palestinians, including the resolution of the Jerusalem issue. Unlike the authors of the Madrid paper, the Israeli team that directed the Beilin–Abu Mazen contacts relied on a staff of professionals. Most of the work was done by this panel of experts, assisted by scholars who voluntarily attended professional discussions conducted by the staff. In order to help the Israeli public assimilate the main concepts of the Beilin–Abu Mazen understanding, the paper's principles were carefully injected, in a mild form, into the Israeli public discourse, four years before they were published in full. The result was that Abu Mazen not only denied the existence of the paper but actually declared himself opposed to the version of the paper that was presented to the Israeli public. Yossi Beilin, however, associated himself with the paper and was willing to pay the political price for it.

There was also a mixed model, in which politicians and experts from both sides took part. An interesting meeting took place in Italy on the subject of Jerusalem in December 1999 under the auspices of the Italian Center for Peace in the Middle East. Participants on the Israeli side included experts such as Ron Pundak, as well as members of the Knesset representing both the governing coalition—Colette Avital and Avshalom Vilan—and the opposition, such as Nahum Langental and Meir Sheetrit. Palestinian participants included Orient House experts and members of the Legislative Council such as Khatim 'Eid and Hussam Hader. Two other meetings adopting this model were held in July 2000 and were devoted to examining the religious aspects of the agreement on Jerusalem. One meeting was held in Milan and the other in Escorial in Spain. At both meetings, the delegations from each side included academic experts and religious figures.

This model created a dialogue on three levels: between Israelis and Palestinians, between experts and religious figures, and between experts and politicians. While the dialogue between the experts and politicians had already been going on for years, that with the religious figures was only beginning. Too few informal channels were opened between the experts and religious figures, and between Jewish-Israeli and Palestinian Muslim and Christian religious figures. At the Milan and Escorial meetings, an attempt was made to move the discussions from slogans and religious sermons to open and frank talks. Various proposals were raised at these talks as to the management of the holy basin and holy places. Additionally, theoretical questions were examined, such as the issues of national sovereignty and holy places in general and, in particular, holy places over which two religions and national movements are struggling.

The Israel/Palestine Center for Research and Information (IPCRI) is a unique organization, both in its structure and in its mode of operation. It is an Israeli-Palestinian NGO jointly run by an Israeli, Gershon Baskin, and a Palestinian, Zakaria al-Qaq. Located in Tantur, between Bethlehem and Jerusalem, it operates in the open space between the Israeli and Palestinian political establishments. Since November 1989, the center has organized a series of meetings between researchers at which the Jerusalem question was discussed. Two basic assumptions guided these gatherings. One was that a Palestinian state would be established alongside Israel; the other was that Jerusalem would serve as joint capital of the two states. On the basis of these assumptions, the organizers wanted to arrive at an understanding that would produce a jointly written declaration of principles to be signed by Palestinian and Israeli representatives. Not a single one of these initiatives ended in agreement. The ideas that emerged from the discussions were, however, collected in IPCRI's publications, mostly under Baskin's name (IPCRI 1992; Baskin, ed. 1994; Baskin and Twite 1993; Baskin 1994).

As far back as 1990, Baskin had suggested a form of division of Jerusalem as a way of solving the conflict over the city. His ideas were before their time and did not find an audience within the Israeli establishment when they were published. As the negotiations progressed, however, willingness to listen to IPCRI's ideas increased. In May 2000, on the eve of the Camp David summit, three meetings were held at IPCRI's initiative between Israelis and Palestinians on the subject of Jerusalem. Participants included experts, politicians, and members of the establishment with access to senior decision makers on both sides. The talks did not result in agreement, but they served as a channel for clarifying the positions of both sides' leaders on the eve of the conference. When the al-Aqsa Intifada broke out at the end of September 2000, this channel was used in an attempt to restore calm and achieve a cessation of the violence, but without success.

Most of the Palestinian participants in the IPCRI meetings were from the West Bank, though in July 1992 the London representative of the PLO attended one of the meetings. Following the establishment of the Palestinian Authority, its representatives have been participating in IPCRI seminars. IPCRI has not addressed itself to Israeli or Palestinian public opinion. Its starting point has not been the narrow interests of Israel or the Palestinians but rather the question of what should most appropriately be done for peace. Lacking political solutions, IPCRI's ability to influence decision makers depends on its access to the centers of political power. The organization has worked with any and every party in power, including the Netanyahu government. Knesset members from the Likud as well as representatives of the Israeli foreign ministry and defense establishment have taken part in IPCRI activities. IPCRI offered the Israeli authorities channels of communication with the Palestinian authorities, and vice versa. Just how important these channels of communication were became clear when the formal channels were blocked during Netanyahu's tenure as prime minister, or when they became difficult to use due to the outbreak of the second Intifada in September 2000. The political establishment on each side has viewed IPCRI as a mechanism by which it could keep in contact with the other side in order to lower tensions, take the other side's pulse, and check out different ideas. IPCRI, for its part, has exploited its channels of communication with the authorities in order to promote its own ideas. The authorities needed the channels IPCRI opened and therefore agreed to read its directors' papers on how best, in their opinion, to solve the Jerusalem question or overcome the problems that came up during the negotiations over the future of the city. More than it wanted IPCRI's products, though, the Israeli authorities wanted to use the organization to reach their Palestinian interlocutors. This contrasted with their interest in the research and position papers produced by the Jerusalem Institute for Israel Studies and the Economic Cooperation Foundation (ECF).

Most of the meetings of the informal channels on the subject of Jerusalem were coordinated on the Palestinian side by the local Jerusalem establishment headed by Faisal Husseini. Starting in the 1990s, Orient House was the seat of the most important and active local political establishment. With the opening of the talks on the permanent status agreement, Orient House coordinated the staff work and the Palestinian preparations for the talks on Jerusalem. It mobilized Palestinian experts, mostly from Jerusalem and Ramallah but also from abroad, and organized joint seminars with Israeli experts. A small nucleus of Orient House experts participated in most of the informal channels, and thus the institution could collect ideas in a coordinated manner and work relatively efficiently. Starting in 1999, the growth in the number of informal channels and conflicts within Orient House over the management of these channels and their funding damaged this aspect of its activity. In Israel, on the other hand, there was no coordination among the various teams that participated in the informal channels. Only in a few cases did participants move from one informal channel to another. The variety of Israeli participants caused some basic assumptions to be reexamined each time anew and increased the number of participants in the dialogue.

The various papers that were prepared and the discussions that were held helped the Palestinian side to gather information on the city and to become more familiar professionally with its problems. Through the seminars with Israeli experts, the Palestinians tried to overcome their lack of access to open information possessed by Israel. Since they had the status of permanent Israeli residents but not citizens, and since they are part of a different civil society, they did not enjoy the same access to the Israeli bureaucracy and the information in its possession as do Israeli citizens. Through these seminars the Palestinians also verified the information they had gathered on their own, prepared the Palestinian establishment to negotiate over Jerusalem, and prepared the professional infrastructure for building local governing institutions.

The Palestinians who coordinated the talks on Jerusalem through the informal channels were directly connected to the Palestinian political establishment (Kassisiyyeh 2002). In contrast, the Israeli side consisted of academics and professionals who did not represent their government at the talks. In the few channels in which Israeli politicians participated, most of the time they were from opposition parties that included both supporters of the Oslo process and opponents. An unusual attempt to bring together two delegations that included both professionals and politicians was made at a seminar organized by the Economic Cooperation Foundation and the Italian Center for Peace in the Middle East. Communication took place there through two channels. The professionals listened to the politicians, and vice versa. Each of these two groups was cognizant of the Israeli-Palestinian dialogue between their professional or political colleagues. Unfortunately, this mixed model of Israeli-Palestinian meeting only rarely took place.

Through these contacts, the Israeli side examined its own ideas as well as the possibility of reaching a common professional understanding with its Palestinian interlocutor. This understanding helped some of the participants in the informal channels to market their ideas to the Israeli decision makers and to present them as ideas that the Palestinians listened to and even agreed with to a certain degree. In the absence of official legitimization or a green light from the Israeli authorities to prepare to negotiate over Jerusalem, build a database, prepare position papers, draw maps, propose alternatives, and conduct simulations, the informal channels took on great importance in preparing the way to the Camp David summit. The informal professional channel laid the infrastructure for the talks conducted at the summit on Jerusalem as an urban area. Additionally, joint Israeli and Palestinian study of Jerusalem from the professional perspective of urban planners, geographers, economists, engineers, political scientists, and historians brought about a demystification of the city. Jerusalem was perceived in its real dimensions as a living and developing urban area.

However, these informal professional channels did not give enough attention to Jerusalem as a religious city. They treated its status as the holy city with appreciation and respect but also with apprehension. It was easier to discuss the preservation and renovation of historical buildings in the Old City than the connection between political sanctity and religious sanctity in the historical and religious heart of Jerusalem. Only a few of the meetings dealt with religion, and only a very small number of religious leaders took part in them. Besides the two meetings mentioned above, which took place in the summer of 2000, there were two other initiatives that addressed religious issues. In the summer of 1997, experts from the Jerusalem Institute and rabbis met with experts from the Arab Studies Society and Palestinian religious figures in Toledo, Spain, but there was no follow-up to this initiative. At the Toledo talks, the question of whether the status of the holy places in Jerusalem was only an Israeli-Palestinian issue, or whether it was an international issue in which other parties would also be involved, was not fundamentally examined, either internally by the Palestinians or between them and the Israelis.

The second initiative consisted of a series of seminars on religious subjects conducted since 1998 at PASSIA (the Palestinian Academic Society for the Study of International Affairs) in East Jerusalem. Most of the seminars were not dedicated to dialogue between Israeli Jews and Palestinian Muslims or Christians but rather to internal Palestinian discussion. The PASSIA discussions were held in an academic framework, and most were not published, nor were the ideas raised there passed on to decision makers or negotiators. The absence of a deep and intensive religious discourse on two levels—within each of the relevant religions and among them—would later leave its negative imprint on the Camp David summit, where the national-religious complex would suddenly awaken and take its place at the heart of the conflict.

The Beilin–Abu Mazen Understandings

In secret negotiations conducted in 1994–95, Israeli and Palestinian teams formulated an unofficial statement of understanding on the parameters of the permanent agreement. Their goal was to finish the job by May 1996, the official opening of the permanent status talks. At that time, according to the plan, this framework agreement would be produced and initialed by both sides. Israel would hold national elections that would also serve as a national plebiscite on the framework agreement, making it possible to reach a full agreement within a short time (Beilin 1997: 180). Most of the discussions were conducted between the Israeli team that had originally been involved in the Oslo initiative—Ron Pundak and Yair Hirschfeld, under the direction of Yossi Beilin, while the Palestinian team included two academic figures from England, Ahmed Khalidi and Hussein Agha, under the direction of Abu Mazen. Khalidi and Agha, Fatah members since the 1960s, had been members of the advisory team to the Palestinian delegation to the Madrid conference, and Khalidi had also participated in the negotiations at Taba over the Oslo II agreement (Beilin 1997: 183, 195). In these talks, Jerusalem was one of the issues on the agenda, but not the most important or most fundamental of them. The difficulty of reaching agreement on Jerusalem was no greater than that of agreeing on the future of Israel's settlements in the territories. Even when agreement was not reached on various constituent questions of the Jerusalem issue, it did not keep the teams from progressing toward solutions to other questions (Beilin 1997: 174, 193, 200).

The concluding session of the discussions on the document took place on 30 October 1995. It was not an official agreement but rather an academic and nonbinding understanding formulated with the knowledge and under the direction of Beilin and Abu Mazen, from which the political leadership could continue with the negotiations (the original document was printed in *Ha'aretz* 29 September 2000 and in *Newsweek* 17 September 2000). The first section of the document deals with the establishment of a Palestinian state, which had, for the Palestinians, become a touchstone for which they were prepared to pay with other issues, including Jerusalem. The Beilin–Abu Mazen understandings expanded Jerusalem's borders and redivided the expanded territory into five political-municipal areas: the capital of Israel, the capital of Palestine, the Temple Mount, the Old City, and the Arab and Jewish neighborhoods on the east side of the city. In these five areas there was a variable, differential level of Israeli and Palestinian sovereignty.

The proposal was to expand the city's territory and establish an umbrella municipality for the Jerusalem area. The umbrella municipality would be administered by a Jewish majority and would be headed by a mayor. Two submunicipalities would function under the umbrella municipality: a Jewish submunicipality, which would provide services to and be responsible for all the Jewish neighborhoods in the west and east of the city, including in the Old City, and an Arab submunicipality, which would provide identical services to the Arab residents in the new and expanded part of Jerusalem. The jurisdiction of this submunicipality would extend over areas not currently part of Jerusalem's municipal territory: al-

'Azariya and Abu Dis alongside the rest of the more distant suburbs of East Jerusalem. This submunicipality would be called al-Quds and would be the capital of the Palestinian state. The Israeli part of the city would include West Jerusalem and Ma'aleh Adumim and Givat Ze'ev, which would be annexed to the city. Each side would recognize the other's capital. Israel's recognition of the capital of Palestine, after long years of denying the Palestinians' nationality and their ties to Jerusalem, would be a historic achievement. Palestinian recognition of West Jerusalem as the capital of Israel would allow the Arab and Islamic states and the rest of the world's countries to follow suit and recognize Israel's capital, which most countries now refuse to do. East Jerusalem as it is now defined—the Arab and Jewish neighborhoods on the east side of the city, with the exception of the Old City—would remain an area that both sides would continue to claim for themselves and over which Israel would be prepared to negotiate. In practice, however, this area would continue to be under Israeli sovereignty until such time as the two sides reached an accommodation. Israel would argue that there had been no return to the 1967 borders, in Jerusalem in particular, and that Jerusalem was not under divided sovereignty, since the Palestinian capital would be established outside the current borders of the city in an area that is now under the rule of the Palestinian Authority. The Palestinians could claim that their recognition of West Jerusalem as the capital of Israel was acknowledgment of an established fact and that they had by negotiation succeeded in removing East Jerusalem from Israel's hands and annulling its annexation, even though they would not receive full sovereignty over the area that Israel had occupied in 1967.

The question of sovereignty was deliberately left undecided. The sovereignty that would prevail in the current East Jerusalem would be, in Palestinian eyes, a temporary and unrecognized continuation of the forced annexation of 1967. The Palestinians would continue to demand that the zone be transferred to them, and a joint commission would deliberate the issue without setting a deadline for finishing its job. Israel saw this as a long-term solution, in the framework of which the question of sovereignty would remain without any final resolution. In the meantime, the existing situation would continue to prevail, and Israel could continue to manage the affairs of this area. Israel would claim that the retention of the status quo meant that Israel was sovereign, because the Israel police would continue to keep public order; the Palestinians, for their part, could present the establishment of the commission and its mandate to address the issue as an Israeli retreat from the annexation of East Jerusalem. This arrangement would not include the Old City, which would receive a special status; complete and absolute freedom of worship would be guaranteed to the members of all religions at their respective holy sites, with preservation of the status quo with regard to Jewish worship on the Temple Mount.

According to the understandings reached by the two teams, the Palestinians would be allowed to raise their flag over al-Haram al-Sharif as an expression of the Palestinian Waqf's autonomous administration of the site, and the compound would be declared to be of extraterritorial sovereignty. Administration of the Islamic holy sites by the Palestinians would not denote their sovereignty, but at the same time Jordan, Saudi Arabia, and Morocco, for example, would not gain a status equal to that of the Palestinians. Any participation by them in administering the site would be subject to Palestinian approval. Of course, the Palestinians would have right of access to the Islamic and Christian holy sites in the Old City, and for this purpose they would be given a corridor between al-Quds and al-Haram al-Sharif. In an effort to reduce the expected opposition from Jewish extremists, it was proposed orally in the talks that the Palestinians agree to set aside a small and defined place on the edge of the compound for Jewish prayer, in the area that orthodox Jewish religious law states is undoubtedly outside the ancient Temple Mount, but this proposal was not included in the written document, which emphasized the preservation of the status quo. Unlike the Temple Mount, the Church of the Holy Sepulcher would fall under the jurisdiction of the Palestinian submunicipality and would not be declared an extraterritorial zone.

In actuality, the Beilin–Abu Mazen understandings would expand the bounds of the Old City beyond the area inside the walls and include the Jehoshaphat Valley and the Mount of Olives, with their sites holy to the three monotheistic faiths. Sovereignty over this area would remain in practice in Israeli hands, a kind of continuation of the current situation, but daily life would be managed jointly with the Palestinians. Of course, the Palestinians would not recognize Israeli sovereignty in principle. Moreover, it was possible that there would be equal Israeli and Palestinian representation on the administering body. The zone would be declared a holy zone and designated for preservation not only because of its sacred and historic sites but also in order to prevent national and religious competition over it.

With the exception of the holy area, the entire Jerusalem region would be administratively restructured into a framework of boroughs that would have independence in municipal administration. The boroughs of al-Quds would comprise its submunicipality, and the boroughs of Jerusalem would comprise its submunicipality. The boroughs would be geographic, functional, and national-ethnic units. Palestinians and Israelis would each elect the mayor of their own submunicipality. It is important to mention that the Arab residents of East Jerusalem would participate in the election of the mayor of al-Quds, thus expressing their distinct identity. These areas, such as the neighborhoods of Shaykh Jarah and Wadi Joz, would be administered as a borough of the al-Quds submunicipality, even though they would not be under Palestinian sovereignty. In this they would be unlike al-'Azariya and Abu Dis, in which both day-to-day administration and sovereignty would be Palestinian. The understanding that the present residents of East Jerusalem would vote for the mayor of the Palestinian submunicipality was a Palestinian gain. Unlike the current situation, in which they are annexed to Israel and can only participate in the elections to the Israeli municipality, under the Beilin–Abu Mazen understandings they would be able to vote for and be elected to the al-Quds municipality. The Palestinians would see this as an expression of their national sovereignty over East Jerusalem, while Israel would claim that the matter was undecided and that the elections signified only day-to-day administration.

Above the submunicipalities would be the umbrella municipality, with a city council containing one representative from each of the city's boroughs. This body would choose the mayor. Representation in the umbrella city council would be by borough. The number of Jewish and Palestinian boroughs would reflect the current two-to-one balance in Israel's favor, meaning that the mayor of Greater Jerusalem would almost certainly be Israeli. (The document did not provide a mechanism for updating the demographic balance in accordance with an agreed-on timetable and periodic census. Therefore, representation would not reflect changes in population, meaning that Israel's upper hand would be institutionalized. This would not, however, have prevented the demographic race from continuing, just as the un-updated 1932 census in Lebanon did not prevent Muslim frustration and a civil war in 1975.) The umbrella municipality would assume authority over matters affecting both the submunicipalities, such as master development plans, main roads, sewerage, and so on. Finally, the Palestinians would be able to use the Atarot (Kalandia) airport without passing through an Israeli border check.

The beauty of the Beilin–Abu Mazen document is its integration of different elements. It includes achievements that both sides share equally as well as mutual recognition of each other's capitals. It unpacks the Jerusalem issue into its principal separate components and sets up a game of give-and-take between the sides. In this game, each side can stand firm on an important principle while the other side agrees to compromise on a principle that is, for it, less important, and vice versa. Thus, for example, there would be no Palestinian sovereignty within the boundaries of Jerusalem as established by Israel in 1967, nor on the Temple Mount, while the Palestinians could fly their flag over the Islamic holy sites. Certain municipal functions now exercised by the Israeli municipality of Jerusalem would be transferred to the al-Quds municipality, and the Arabs of East Jerusalem would participate in the election of the al-Quds city council, thus connecting them to the Palestinian capital—unlike the current situation, in which they are allowed to vote only for the Israeli city council and mayor on the local level and for the Palestinian Authority on the national level. In exchange, Israel would enjoy control of the umbrella municipality. Furthermore, the Beilin–Abu Mazen understandings used a range of means to mitigate the dispute over Jerusalem. For example, they would postpone the resolution of sovereignty over the annexed part of Jerusalem, declare a holy zone so as to prevent extremists from using religious fervor to ignite a nationalist conflagration, and blur the meaning of the term sovereignty, distinguishing between its legal-official aspects and its political, symbolic, and functional ones. Each one of the characteristics of sovereignty is divided differently between the sides in the Jerusalem region.

The understandings also made extensive and sophisticated use of the functional approach, focusing on the particular arrangements required for day-to-day life rather than seeking overarching decisions and resolution on the symbolic level. But it is important to emphasize that the understanding achieved by Beilin and Abu Mazen did not neglect the symbolic. However, instead of allowing this aspect to be dominant and to determine the lines of the arrangement, there is a hierarchy of institutions and solutions providing symbolic satisfaction as needed. In other words, the Beilin–Abu Mazen understandings also used the differential approach, distinguishing between partial and full realization of rights, aspirations, and symbols and different levels of municipal administration and definition of the municipal space (on the conceptual basis of the document, see Hasson 1993).

The Beilin–Abu Mazen understandings can be seen as preserving the city's unity on a variable basis, yet also as demarcating different levels of the division of Jerusalem. Neither side would fulfill all its dreams, but neither would either side be forced to abandon its viewpoint, which would be realized in some way. Here is the balance sheet for each side: Israel achieves recognition of its capital. There is no Palestinian sovereignty over East Jerusalem as Israel defined it in 1967, nor is there a return to the 1967 borders in Jerusalem. Jerusalem is not divided physically or divided with regard to sovereignty. There is no Palestinian sovereignty on the Temple Mount but rather a de jure confirmation of the de facto status that has prevailed since 1967. The umbrella municipality is under Israeli control and the mayor will be Israeli; Ma'aleh Adumim and Givat Ze'ev, outside Jerusalem's municipal borders, are annexed to Israel with Palestinian consent. The Palestinians, for their part, achieve recognition of their capital. Israel consents to reexamine the annexation of East Jerusalem, thus placing a question mark over Israeli sovereignty there. A Palestinian flag flies over al-Haram al-Sharif and the Palestinians receive a preferential position there, taking from Israel the power to grant any sort of status to other Arab and Islamic states. There is a safe passage between al-Quds and the al-Haram al-Sharif compound and joint administration of the Old City. East Jerusalem Arabs participate in the al-Quds municipal elections, and the al-Quds submunicipality runs the day-to-day municipal affairs of the Arabs, in coordination with the umbrella municipality.

The agreement on the outline of the framework and the guiding principles allowed Abu Mazen to make an optimistic assessment that it would take only a month for Rabin and Arafat to approve the document and its accompanying maps. The assassination of Prime Minister Yitzhak Rabin on 4 November 1995, and the election of a Likud government in May 1996 prevented the plan from being realized. Beilin and Abu Mazen separately presented the plan to Prime Minister Shimon Peres and to Chairman Arafat a week after the assassination. Arafat and Peres, each for his own reasons, did not accept the document. Peres did not want a quick agreement with the Palestinians—for electoral reasons he preferred to defer negotiations. He believed that the document was premature and that Israel's citizens were not yet prepared to consent to it. He thus rejected Beilin's position that the document should be incorporated into Labor's election platform and that it would help Labor win a majority. Peres preferred to receive a general mandate from the Israeli citizenry for conducting negotiations, rather than approval of a specific plan. Instead of intensifying the discord in Israeli society, he preferred to try to heal the wounds created by the conflict between the supporters of the peace process with the Palestinians and its opponents in the national-religious right.

To this should be added the huge responsibility that fell on Peres after Rabin's murder. This was the first time in the country's history that a prime minister or cabinet member had been assassinated, and that after a campaign of defamation, divisiveness, and animosity by his political and ideological opponents. After Rabin's assassination no Israeli prime minister could be anything but apprehensive that political murders might prolifer-ate. This was not just a personal consideration—the damage another as-sassination was liable to cause to Israeli democracy also had to be taken into account. As for the document itself, Peres felt that it left the issue of sovereignty over East Jerusalem too open, and he also opposed allowing a Palestinian flag to fly over the Temple Mount. Furthermore, Peres sought a way to include Jordan in the permanent settlement. He wanted to give it an institutionalized and agreed status on al-Haram al-Sharif. Over and beyond all this was the question of electoral timing (Beilin 1997: 210–18; Galili 4 August 1996; *Ha'aretz* 19, 22 February, 31 July, 1, 2 August, 10 October 1996, 7 March 1997). The news reports in Israel in August 1996 on the Beilin–Abu Mazen understandings roused the anger of the Palestin-ian establishment in Jerusalem (Sokol 4 August 1996) and embarrassed the Palestinian national establishment. Since the new Israeli government elected in Israel in June 1996 considered the document irrelevant, even Abu Mazen disassociated himself from it, denying its very existence in a meeting of the Fatah central committee that convened at the beginning of August 1996 (Sokol 4 August 1996).

The document was tailored for Yitzhak Rabin and the political realities he faced. After his murder, political circumstances changed and it was necessary to update the document. Since 1996, a revised version of the Beilin–Abu Mazen plan has been discussed unofficially by academics from both sides, who have reported their discussions to their respective political leaderships. According to this "improved" proposal, a network of roads, tunnels, and bridges will tie all the pieces of al-Quds together. The major innovation in the revised plan is a call for Israel to allow Palestinian sov-ereignty in the Arab neighborhoods within the current Jerusalem bound-aries, alongside the Arab suburbs now outside the city. In return, the Pal-estinians will consent to leave vague or defer the issue of sovereignty in the holy basin—the Old City and the surrounding sacred and historical areas. Special arrangements will be made for the holy basin, including the option of allowing both sides to display their respective national symbols (*Jerusa-lem Report*, 28 February 2000).

Furthermore, it was necessary to translate the fundamental principles of the Beilin–Abu Mazen document into a plan of action designed by professionals. To this end, the London channel began functioning as a channel for talks among Israeli and Palestinian experts. The Beilin–Abu Mazen document was not officially presented as a framework for the London talks. But the fundamental assumptions on which the document was based were in the air during discussions of municipal management in the Jerusalem area, the Jerusalem economy, interpolice cooperation, the meaning of the term *open city,* and the price that would have to be paid for openness in various areas.

Prenegotiation Talks and First Steps

The permanent status negotiations opened on 6 May 1996. Israel's official position was the plan that Rabin had presented to the Knesset in early October 1995, according to which Jerusalem, in its current borders, would remain united under Israeli sovereignty, with Israel respecting the rights of all the city's religious faiths. Furthermore, Israeli settlements in the Greater Jerusalem area would be included in its borders: Ma'aleh Adumim, the Etzion block, Efrat, Betar Illit, and Givat Ze'ev (*Ha'aretz,* 6 October 1995).

In mid-1997, Prime Minister Netanyahu presented his government with his plan for a permanent settlement, according to which Greater Jerusalem was much larger than it had been in the Labor Party plan. Netanyahu stretched the Greater Jerusalem boundary northward to Ramallah in order to include the settlements Pesagot and Beit El, and on the west he significantly broadened the Jerusalem corridor, the narrow strip of land that had, before 1967, linked Jerusalem to the rest of Israel. The result would have been that the Jerusalem area would stretch from the Dead Sea to Israel's coastal plain, effectively bisecting the West Bank. With regard to the Islamic and Christian holy places, Netanyahu suggested adopting a functional solution that would provide free access along agreed routes in exchange for parallel passage to those Jewish holy places located in the 40 percent of the West Bank that would be under Palestinian rule (*Ha'aretz* 29 May, 5 June 1997).

The Barak government's rise to power in May 1999 did not immediately accelerate the Israeli-Palestinian peace process. The new prime minister sought first to make improvements on the Wye accords signed by his predecessor. As a result, the first agreement the new government reached with the Palestinian Authority, the Sharm al-Shaykh memorandum, was signed only in September. This memorandum set two new target dates. The two sides agreed to sign a framework for the final status agreement by the end of January 2000. This framework would lay out the general outline of a permanent settlement without going into details. The idea, which originated with Barak, was that the two sides would have an easier time reaching an agreement about general principles if they did not get bogged down in specific details and that this would create momentum for resolving those details in further negotiations. A full final status agreement would then be signed by 13 September 2000, the seventh anniversary of the first Israel-PLO agreement of mutual recognition. Barak decided, however, that reaching agreement with Syria should take priority over reaching one with the Palestinians. Putting negotiations with the Palestinians on a back burner unsurprisingly led to their failure, and by January 2000 no framework agreement had been concluded.

The two sides agreed in March to set a new target date for concluding a framework agreement: May 2000. Both sides also promised that by July 2000 they would reach an agreement on implementing the outstanding provisions of the Oslo II accords signed in September 1995. That agreement had stipulated that Israel would carry out a three-stage redeployment of its forces in the West Bank. This redeployment, when completed, was to restrict the Israeli presence there to settlements and army bases. However, it left determination of the precise extent of the withdrawal in Israeli hands. Israel had made only the first two of these staged withdrawals, and the goal now was for Israel to complete the third before the signing of the final agreement in September. Of course, both sides seized the opportunity to violate this timetable as well.

In April–May 2000, Barak turned his attention to the Palestinian track. It had become clear that he would be unable to reach agreement with Hafez al-Assad; moreover, almost a year after taking office Barak could show no real diplomatic achievements, despite his far-reaching ambition to establish Israel's permanent borders to the north and east. The Israeli media, as well as some members of his own government, were criticizing the prime minister for setting overly ambitious target dates and for neglecting the negotiations with the Palestinians. Consequently, he consented to the establishment of the Palestinian track.

In fact, in November or December 1999, Abu Mazen had already suggested to Israel that they conduct secret negotiations via Hussein Agha and Ahmad Khalidi, who had represented him at the talks over the understandings with Beilin. An emissary from Barak, apparently Gilad Sher, met with them, but without results. The Palestinians discovered that the Israeli prime minister was prepared for a Palestinian state that would extend only over 66 percent of the West Bank. Furthermore, Barak did not want to conduct negotiations with scholars, as Abu Mazen had proposed and as had been the case at Oslo. He wanted his representative to meet a person with formal standing and authority (Sher 2001: 63).

From the end of December 1999, three informal channels were functioning in parallel: Minister of Tourism Amnon Shahak with Abu Mazen,

Oded Eran with Yassir 'Abd Rabbu alongside the official contacts, and Minister of Internal Security Shlomo Ben-Ami with Abu 'Ala, the speaker of the Palestinian Legislative Council. The informal channels were, in January 2000, conveying to Israel the impression that the Palestinian position was as follows: the Palestinians would agree to the annexation of about 3.5 percent of the West Bank, on which some 70 percent of the settlers resided. This area was divided into three blocks: around Jerusalem, Gush Etzion, and Gush Ariel. In exchange for this annexed territory, the Palestinian state would receive territory of an identical size adjacent to the Gaza Strip. No Palestinian would be annexed to Israel and the security arrangements between the two sides would not seriously infringe on Palestinian sovereignty. The Palestinians would not concede on the recognition of the right of return, but its practical application would be in the form of a range of solutions that would make the return to the state of Israel a negligible possibility. The boundaries of Jerusalem would be broadened, and the Palestinian capital would be established in East Jerusalem. The two cities would be open to each other (Beilin 2001: 93). In January 2000, Arafat met with Clinton and brought three documents that contained the Palestinian position: the draft of a framework agreement, a relatively flexible position paper, and a paper containing concessions that Arafat intended to deposit with the American president. The president would pass these concessions on to Israel at the appropriate time. In the end, however, Arafat did not submit these papers because the meeting did not go well (Beilin 2001: 94). Between April and July 2000, that is, between the Stockholm talks and Camp David, Israel's information indicated that President Clinton had received a deposit from Arafat in the form of an agreement to the annexation of 2 percent of the West Bank to Israel (Shavit 14 September 2001). In April 2000 the Ben-Ami/Abu 'Ala channel became the Stockholm channel.

Barak had had his reservations about the Oslo accords and interim arrangements from the start. Like Netanyahu before him, he preferred to arrive directly at a permanent status agreement. Until then, Barak wanted to keep a maximum of territorial assets in Israeli hands (Sher 2001: 20). In October 1999, in a personal conversation with Yossi Beilin, Barak said that he was willing to see a Palestinian state on only 50 percent of the West Bank, the parts of which would be connected by bridges and tunnels. The Israeli army and settlements would remain on the Jordan until, in his words, peace became instilled in Palestinian hearts (Beilin 2001: 83–86).

When Oded Eran began negotiations with Yassir 'Abd Rabbu in December 1999, he offered the Palestinians, in Barak's name, a state on about

60 percent of the West Bank to begin with, and another approximately 20 percent in the form of security zones. The remaining 20 percent would remain under Israeli sovereignty and would include the "Jerusalem shell"—from Givat Ze'ev, Ofra, and Beit El in the north to Gush Etzion in the south, and from Kalia on the shores of the Dead Sea in the east to West Jerusalem. There would be no exchange of territory involving sovereign Israeli land within the borders of the state (Beilin 2001: 107; Shavit 14 September 2001; Sher 2001: 68). Beilin and Sher each have their own version of this map; I have presented Sher's. According to Barak's map, which was submitted to the Palestinian delegation to the permanent status talks once again in May 2000, the Jerusalem shell area would later be connected near Kalia to the territory that would remain in Israeli hands along the Jordan Valley. To the west, the Jerusalem area would be connected near Har Adar to a strip to be annexed by Israel along the 1967 lines, up to Qalqilya (*Yedioth Aharonoth* 19 May 2000; *Ha'aretz* 29 May 1997). The Palestinians rejected this map outright.

The Stockholm Track

According to Abu 'Ala, beginning in April 2000 he had seventeen sessions with Ben-Ami in the framework of the secret channel between them. These culminated in meetings in Stockholm under the auspices of the Swedish government. In retrospect both Ben-Ami and Abu 'Ala emerged from the Stockholm talks with positive impressions, claiming that the talks achieved some progress on the issues of territory and refugees (Susser 16 July 2001; Kershner 16 July 2001).

In these talks, Israel presented a map in which Israel was to annex 13.3 percent of the West Bank. Palestine would encompass 76.6 percent, while 10.1 percent, in the Jordan Valley, would remain in Israeli hands for twenty years for defense reasons. Israeli forces would be stationed permanently along the Jordan River, and there would be no territorial exchange. Israel demanded that those of its settlements located in territory designated to become Palestinian would be subject to Israeli administration and law and that the safe-passage corridor connecting the West Bank and Gaza Strip would be under Israeli sovereignty. Furthermore, Israel demanded a set of east-west roads in the West Bank for military use. Israel expressed a willingness to take in 10,000–15,000 Palestinian refugees in a multiyear process, but not under the rubric of the right of return.

The defense concept presented by Israel was rejected by the Palestinians. They opposed both the dimensions of the Israeli annexation and the demand that islands of Israeli sovereignty remain within their country. Furthermore, they proposed that the safe-passage corridor be extraterritorial. Abu ʿAla consented to Israeli warning stations in the West Bank and international forces in the Jordan Valley, but not to the presence of Israeli ground troops there. In the contacts conducted by Ben-Ami before the Camp David summit was convened, he heard Abu ʿAla voice a willingness to accept an Israeli annexation of 4 percent of the West Bank, in exchange for the Palestinians receiving an equivalent amount of territory out of Israel proper. In response, Ben-Ami, speaking for himself, reduced the Israeli demand to 8–10 percent. According to Ben-Ami, Abu ʿAla agreed in Stockholm to Israeli control of the West Bank's airspace, under certain conditions.

The dispute in principle over the refugee issue was not resolved. Israel refused to mention UN General Assembly resolution 194, approved in 1948, which mandated the return of individual refugees to Israel under certain conditions. Furthermore, Israel refused to accept responsibility for the creation of the 1948 refugee problem, fearing that such an acknowledgment would open it up to a flood of lawsuits over property. However, the participants in the Stockholm channel agreed to the establishment of two bodies, one of which would register the refugees and the other of which would deal with compensation. Registration of refugees would be based on data from UNRWA (the United Nations Relief and Works Agency), the UN refugee agency having responsibility for the Palestinian refugee camps. The body that would oversee the financial compensation of refugees, the rehabilitation of the refugee camps themselves, and the resettlement of the refugees would have as members the states hosting the refugees and the countries that would contribute funds for this purpose. The projects would be carried out by a professional fund and not by the states involved. It was also agreed that each family could submit a single claim to property (Shavit 14 September 2001; Sher 2001: 95, 99, 102, 107–14, 221, 225).

The Jerusalem issue came up only informally, as private exchanges of ideas outside the framework of the negotiations (Susser 16 July 2001; Kershner 16 July 2001; *al-Sharq al-Awsat* 6 July 2000). In his book *A Place for All*, Ben-Ami set out a proposal for a solution in Jerusalem. It combined a functional arrangement with a territorial arrangement. The capital of Palestine would be established in the external suburbs of East Jerusalem, for example in Abu Dis. In the inner circle, the zone annexed by Israel, the Palestinians would be given maximal autonomy and the existing de facto state of affairs would be institutionalized, while preserving overarching Israeli sovereignty. Ben-Ami also proposed that the Temple Mount and the Church of the Holy Sepulcher be given extraterritorial status (Ben-Ami 1998: 116–29). At the time the book was published, Ben-Ami did not dare propose a far-reaching change in Israeli sovereignty over East Jerusalem. It seems that this was his position at the Stockholm talks as well.

In these talks and after them, it became clear to Israel that the Palestinians were willing to recognize the annexation of the Jewish neighborhoods that had been built after 1967 in East Jerusalem, including the Jewish Quarter in the Old City and the Western Wall, but no more than that (Shavit 14 September 2001).

Despite Ben-Ami's long-standing interest and experience in foreign affairs, he was at first blocked from participating in the negotiations by Barak and Foreign Minister David Levy. When he did succeed in becoming involved—over Levy's objections—he did not dare deviate much from the Barak model (Sher 2001: 83), either in substance or in work methods. Later on this came to mean centralization, a meticulous insistence on secrecy, compartmentalization, and absolute fidelity. Gilad Sher, a Barak loyalist who had played a central role in formulating the Sharm al-Sheikh declaration, participated in order to prevent Ben-Ami from deviating from the prime minister's guidelines. Ben-Ami practiced neither personal nor multichannel diplomacy, although these may in fact have been called for.

Barak's and Ben-Ami's approach held that most of East Jerusalem must remain under Israeli sovereignty. The official Palestinian position, on the other hand, held that all of East Jerusalem must serve as the capital of Palestine, under full Palestinian sovereignty (al-Sharq al-Awsat 11 April, 6 July, 2000). Prime Minister Barak was not willing to go any further than engaging in preliminary and nonbinding exchanges and scouting out positions on Jerusalem (Sher 2001: 88). The Stockholm talks had addressed all the issues under dispute that would later be tabled at Camp David, not just Jerusalem.

Both Ben-Ami and Abu 'Ala were of the opinion that the Stockholm channel should be pursued further, in order to complete preparation of a nonpaper draft for a framework for the final status agreement. Both of them, however, participated in the Camp David talks, and Ben-Ami was an enthusiastic supporter of convening the summit (Susser 16 July 2001). Ben-Ami accepted Barak's strategy that Israel should proceed in a different way than it had with the PLO in 1993.

The Israeli Preparations

In contrast to the behind-the-scenes activity during the Oslo negotiations in 1993, the framework for the permanent status agreement was not prepared before the leaders met personally. Barak wanted to place the issue of Jerusalem on the negotiating table only at a summit meeting with Clinton and Arafat, at which time the end of the conflict would be discussed and he would personally steer the Israeli delegation.

Barak publicly undertook to bring the principles of the final status agreement before the Israeli public in a referendum or election. Barak believed that his voting public would accept Israeli concessions only in return for an end to the Israeli-Palestinian conflict. The Israelis wanted to take advantage of Clinton's last months in the White House because of the American president's commitment to the peace process and his familiarity with the issues, as well as his deep friendship with Israel. The hope was that Clinton's personal involvement would lead to success. The Palestinians were also interested in discussing a permanent status agreement and an end to the conflict, as they had lost confidence in interim arrangements and in Israel's willingness to implement them. In addition, the Palestinians demanded that no subject related to the permanent status agreement, including Jerusalem, be deferred or removed from the agenda (*al-Sharq al-Awsat* 6 July 2000; *al-Ayyam* 11 April 2000). Arafat wanted to exploit Barak's craving for an end to the conflict to gain maximum concessions in the Palestinians' favor. Moreover, he no longer trusted Israel not to try to improve its position on the ground. In Palestinian eyes, deferring the issue of Jerusalem and drawing a permanent border between the city and the Palestinian state to be established at the first stage would not freeze the existing situation. In their opinion, in such a case Israel could, as it had in the past, exploit its physical control to unilaterally establish facts on the ground, in order to influence the final shape of the permanent status agreement. Therefore, the Palestinian Authority leadership demanded that Israel discuss all the issues at once. News of the Stockholm talks was leaked to the press in mid-May, apparently by officials like Abu Mazen who were upset about not having been included in them. Abu Mazen had, after all, initiated this channel. He argued that Abu ʿAla had made unnecessary concessions to Israel in the Stockholm talks. As a result, Abu ʿAla reversed himself on a number of positions he had taken in Stockholm (Beilin 2001: 116; Kaspit, 17 September 2001).

It was not this revelation, however, that diverted attention to Camp

David. The strategy of convening a summit was not a default plan but rather Barak's calculated preference. Barak had told Oded Eran that the Stockholm talks should be halted because they were causing more damage than benefit (Akiva Eldar, "Didn't See, Didn't Hear," *Ha'aretz* 17 September 2001). In June, Barak told Clinton and U.S. Secretary of State Madeline Albright that the Palestinians had not budged an inch in Stockholm, while his own team had reached the limit of the compromises it could make. There was no way to proceed except to call a summit, he maintained (Agha and Malley 2001).

But there were also other voices. Some members of the political leadership on both sides felt that it would be best to make do with an interim agreement or with an arrangement that excluded Jerusalem. On the Israeli side, this approach was advocated by cabinet ministers Haim Ramon, Shimon Peres, and Yossi Sarid, who claimed that the Jerusalem question would be difficult to solve and that discussing it would bring the entire track to a dead end.

However, Yossi Beilin and Shlomo Ben-Ami supported reaching a permanent agreement on all issues. First of all, on the basis of ongoing contacts with Palestinian personalities and ministers through informal channels, they felt that this was not only inevitable but also possible. Second, their familiarity with the subject of Jerusalem had taught them that it would not be possible to reach agreement on the issue of borders without deciding where Palestine ends and Jerusalem begins. The issue of Jerusalem's borders had been on the agenda since the beginning of the negotiations, and dealing with the future of the city could not be deferred. Third, for the Palestinians to concede on Jerusalem, the Israelis would in return have to concede on settlements or borders. Signing a permanent agreement on these two issues, without Jerusalem, would leave Israel without bargaining chips when the time came to negotiate over the city. Finally, excluding Jerusalem from a permanent status agreement would leave the city as an arena for competition and undermine the agreements already reached on the other issues.

During the period that Barak was concentrating on the Syrian track, he supported, with regard to the Palestinians, the position championed by Peres, Ramon, and Sarid. He had only limited familiarity with the question of Jerusalem. Since Jerusalem is a civilian and not a military issue, it was not one of the subjects that had come over his desk during his army career. But once he turned his attention to the subject and began studying it, Barak accepted the approach of Beilin and Ben-Ami. This led to his choice, for both political and personal reasons (and behind Foreign Minister Levy's back), of Ben-Ami to conduct the secret negotiations that were to lead to the Camp David summit.

A careful reading of Gilad Sher's book (2001) (for example, of pages 100 and 102–4) reveals that its author tried, throughout the negotiations, to promote ideas that all had one common denominator: the achievement of something less than a permanent settlement. He sought to postpone the permanent settlement as a whole; to delay the achievement of a detailed agreement, as opposed to an agreement on principles; and to put off certain issues in the permanent settlement, such as Jerusalem and the refugee problem, or to set aside agreeing on parts of these last two issues. In this Sher was faithfully representing Barak, and some of his recommendations were examined during the negotiations as second choices, with the approval of the Israeli prime minister.

There were also Palestinian political leaders who called for deferring the subject of Jerusalem. This group included, as far as we know, Abu Mazen and expert advisers such as Khalil Shikaki. At the end of 1999, Abu Mazen estimated that the gaps between the two sides were unbridgeable. He and the Palestinian experts believed that the Palestinians should sign an interim agreement on Jerusalem, and, until conclusion of the permanent status agreement, the Palestinians should strengthen the Palestinian identity of East Jerusalem in general, and the Old City in particular. This group proposed a plan of action that included the establishment of a Palestinian university within the territory of Israeli Jerusalem and increasing the pace of Palestinian construction in the heart of the city and in the northern zone connecting Jerusalem with Ramallah. In their opinion, Israel would not agree of its own free will to compromise on Jerusalem and must therefore be forced to do so. The existing situation in Jerusalem did not give Israel any incentive to compromise, these advisers said, because the Palestinians were in an inferior position in the city (*Kol HaIr* 18 February 2000; Beilin 2001: 89, 101, 124–27). They believed that time was not exclusively on the side of the stronger party, that is, Israel. Given time, the Palestinians could change reality in East Jerusalem, the only way to obtain an agreement that would satisfy Palestinian demands.

At the end of 1999 and the beginning of 2000, members of the Palestinian leadership demanded that Israel prepare an alternative program in case a permanent settlement, or a framework agreement for the permanent settlement, was not achieved. From his contacts with Barak, Abu Mazen reached the conclusion that this was a real possibility. Sa'eb Erekat, the negotiator for the implementation of the Wye agreements, which the Barak government had delayed, felt the same. They proposed that Israel implement existing agreements before the parties addressed the permanent settlement. Their intention was to strengthen Palestinian trust in Barak by ensuring that there would be some sort of achievement, and to signal to the Palestinian public that the change in government in Israel had indeed produced a change in Israeli attitudes. In particular, they wanted Israel to carry out the second and third withdrawals agreed on at the Wye Plantation and to release Palestinian security detainees and not just prisoners held on criminal charges. The release of criminal detainees by the Netanyahu government had been perceived by the Palestinians as a deception, and the Palestinian negotiators were sharply criticized within their own camp because of this. Their opponents charged that they had been foolish not to notice this loophole in the agreement (Beilin 2001: 94–95). Barak refused, however, to give up his territorial cards. At the same time, his position on the permanent settlement was relatively hawkish, relative to the position he adopted later on. The Barak government expressed its willingness to release Palestinian prisoners who had been accused of murdering alleged Palestinian collaborators with Israel, but not prisoners who stood accused of murdering Israelis.

On 3 July 2000, Barak rejected a proposal by Yossi Beilin and the ECF to postpone the deadline for concluding a final status agreement by a year, while in the meantime reaching an agreement on a Palestinian state comprising Zones A and B (together about 42 percent of the West Bank). A multinational force would be deployed in Palestine, settlement activity would be frozen, and Israeli-Palestinian committees would be established to jointly administer daily life in the Arab neighborhoods of East Jerusalem. An agreement on principles would be reached on a special regime for the holy basin (the Old City and the nearby holy sites). The full solution of the Jerusalem problem and of the problem of the 1948 refugees would be achieved within a year allotted to detailed negotiations (Beilin 2001: 126–27; Kaspit 17 September 2001). In other words, instead of reaching an agreement on principles on all the issues and then working out a detailed permanent settlement, they proposed reaching a permanent agreement on some subjects and then progressing to the rest of the issues on a tight and binding timetable. Both Barak and Arafat rejected this approach for the reasons noted above.

Israel's preparations for negotiations were made in the shadow of the public and political taboo on talking about border adjustments in Jerusalem. "United Jerusalem, Israel's eternal capital" was a national mantra as well as an election slogan, one that Barak himself continued to use once he was in office. Politicians did not willingly give it up, even though the city's reality contradicted it. The possibility of dividing Jerusalem had been a Damoclean sword threatening Israeli politicians since the 1996 elections, when the slogan "Peres will divide Jerusalem" contributed greatly to Netanyahu's victory. Israeli preparations for the conference were influenced by this, as well as by the hawkish parties in the coalition who opposed any change in the existing state of affairs. The upshot was that no member of Oded Eran's negotiating team was officially and publicly given the Jerusalem portfolio, the job of coordinating the staff work and conducting the negotiations on the city's future.

In contrast, within the Palestinian team headed by Yassir 'Abd Rabbu, this assignment was given to Faisal Husseini, who held the Jerusalem portfolio in the PLO Executive Committee. Husseini appointed a team of Orient House people to do the staff work necessary for the negotiations on Jerusalem. The team was headed by Manuel Hassassian, rector of Bethlehem University. In parallel, Samih al-'Abed, deputy minister for planning at the Ministry of Planning and International Cooperation, coordinated the staff work on all aspects of the permanent status agreement. He joined the delegation headed by Yassir 'Abd Rabbu and later participated in the Camp David and Taba talks as well.

The "peace directorate" created in the Israeli prime minister's office to coordinate staff work in preparation for and during the talks on the permanent status agreement did not include experts on Jerusalem. Although the vast majority of its members were government or defense officials, Prime Minister Barak feared that if staff work was done on Jerusalem, news of this would be leaked. Nor did he permit the planning division of the IDF general staff to deal with the subject of Jerusalem, for the same reason. The IDF dealt with Jerusalem only through issues touching on the West Bank, such as roads and settlements. (The army was not in any case equipped to deal with a manifestly civilian subject such as Jerusalem.) A handful of discussions were held among the senior members of Oded Eran's peace directorate, as well as between them and Barak. These discussions were of limited benefit, and the Israeli team was forced to rely on work done by nongovernmental organizations such as the Jerusalem Institute for Israel Studies and the ECF.

Members of the ECF sent Barak the Beilin–Abu Mazen paper and additional documents formulated on the basis of the foundation's accumulated knowledge. They opened a direct channel, mainly with Gilad Sher (Sher 2001: 62), while the Jerusalem Institute maintained its contacts with Oden Eran. The Jerusalem Institute and the foundation had for years been working in depth on the subject of Jerusalem. The institute had built up a pool of reliable information and a database, and both institutions had written a series of research papers, developed alternative possible solutions, and written policy papers and position papers. They had also conducted professional contacts on the subject of Jerusalem with their Palestinian counterparts, using an informal channel of communication. The members of the Jerusalem Institute's think tank, which began working in 1994, met and presented their papers to each successive Israeli prime minister as well as senior policymakers from both the coalition and the opposition. "The staff [of the Jerusalem Institute] presented its work, received and implemented reactions and thus influenced the consciousness of the senior people during their work, but was also influenced and changed by its own work plan" (Think Tank 2000: 1). All of the politicians with whom members of the Jerusalem Institute's think tank met noted the importance of the institute's work and emphasized the importance of keeping it confidential.

After Oded Eran was appointed as the head of Israel's peace directorate, the Jerusalem Institute offered to give the directorate access to all of the think tank's material, as well as the professional assistance of several of its members. Eran received the green light from Barak, and in November–December 1999 a small working group on the subject of Jerusalem, headed by Reuven Merhav of the Jerusalem Institute, began meeting. The group also included Israel Kimhi, Ruth Lapidoth, and Maya Choshen of the Jerusalem Institute, and Yisrael Hasson, Pinchas Midan, and Gidi Greenstein of the peace directorate.

Following extensive discussions, the team submitted its recommended ground rules for Israeli negotiations on Jerusalem. At first the recommendations were discussed at a meeting with Prime Minister Barak, Foreign Minister Levy, and their senior aides, and afterward in a restricted forum with Barak and his aides. This was the first time that Barak understood that it was vital to redraw the city's boundaries, especially because of demographic facts, and to consider Jerusalem from the metropolitan point of view. But the team's existence was leaked, and it halted its work in December 1999.

On the basis of these discussions, Barak permitted Oded Eran to float some "private" ideas in background, not-for-attribution conversations with Israeli journalists. One of these ideas was to hand the Arab neighborhoods in northeastern Jerusalem over to Palestinian administration. As I will clarify later, this idea was not in the least private. Floating it was meant to test what the public's reaction would be.

In May 2000, the Jerusalem Institute published its paper *Peace Arrangements in Jerusalem,* which summarized the work of the institute's think tank since its creation in 1994 (Think Tank 2000). The team presented three principal and several secondary alternative solutions for Jerusalem as a physically undivided city, without fully endorsing any one of them. The first alternative described a situation wherein the municipal area of Jerusalem would remain under Israeli sovereignty. The borders between Israel and the Palestinian Authority would be open, and freedom of worship would continue to be observed in the holy places while preserving the status quo. This option would for the most part perpetuate the present situation and is unacceptable to the Arab side and to the international community.

The second alternative would also leave Jerusalem under Israeli sovereignty but would, in Israel's interest, allow for limited exchanges of territory at the edges of the city with areas in the West Bank. Under this alternative, the Palestinians would enjoy functional autonomy under Israeli sovereignty. The Israeli municipality of Jerusalem would retain overriding authority over all the city's neighborhoods. In addition, services and networks for coordination and cooperation would be developed in the metropolitan area. This alternative does not dismiss outright the possibility that the Palestinians would be given a symbolic focus of sovereignty within the city, such as turning Orient House into the official Palestinian Authority legation in Jerusalem. The Temple Mount would be under supreme Israeli sovereignty and under Palestinian/Islamic/Jordanian administration. A similar status would be given to the Church of the Holy Sepulcher and/or the Christian Quarter. It would be possible under this alternative to grant special status within the walls or to the entire basin of the Old City. Many intermediate types of arrangements are possible under this alternative, which is dynamic and could be implemented gradually until overall permanent status agreement is formulated. However, it does not deviate from its own basic parameters, which would leave the eastern city under supreme Israeli sovereignty.

The third option is the most dramatic and radical of those proposed by the Jerusalem Institute. This option would divide the city into two capitals, with Palestinian sovereignty in its eastern part. This alternative would also leave the city open, without physical barriers, and would preserve continuity among its Israeli neighborhoods and among its Palestinian neighborhoods. A supramunicipality could also be established for the two separate municipalities. This alternative seeks to create a situation completely different from the existing one and proposes that this be decided in advance. Because of the great difference between the existing situation and that described by this alternative, and because a decision on the change would have to be taken all at once, this third alternative seemed to the members of the Jerusalem Institute to be unacceptable to official Israel.

In general, each of the alternatives assumes a different picture of sovereignty, and the Jerusalem Institute examined the advantages and disadvantages of each from Israel's point of view. The first and third alternatives are static and would bring about a final arrangement all at once. The second alternative is, in contrast, dynamic and would allow for a gradual transition from one situation to another. Therefore, this alternative may serve as the basis for an outline of an interim arrangement or a gradual transition to a permanent arrangement (Think Tank 2000: 3–4). It should be emphasized that in contrast to the Beilin–Abu Mazen proposal, the Jerusalem Institute's paper was not formulated in cooperation with the Palestinians but is rather an Israeli policy paper written with the Israeli interest in mind. Unsurprisingly, therefore, the paper served the Israeli negotiating team at Camp David as a basis for its work. Moreover, the similarity between President Clinton's proposals (see Appendix C) and the Beilin–Abu Mazen paper shows that the latter was a milestone for the American government as it sought a compromise between the two sides.

Publication of the Jerusalem Institute think tank's paper in June 2000 placed the subject of Jerusalem on the public agenda and it received extensive media coverage. The issue became a legitimate subject for discussion. Consequently, the Office of the Prime Minister asked Reuven Merhav to provide several supplements to the team's work, which he prepared together with Israel Kimhi. They provided the Israeli establishment with a database on the demographics and geography of Jerusalem in general and of the Old City in particular, and pointed out Israel's basic alternatives. Later, in July, Merhav was summoned to the Camp David summit to assist the Israeli team. All the basic data and background facts upon which the think tank's report was based were provided to the prime minister's office and served as a basis for the discussions of the senior staff at Camp David.

Documents published so far (see ch. 2) indicate that the substance of the ideas brought by Israel to Camp David was more or less that of the second alternative proposed by the Jerusalem Institute. The city's administration would be reorganized in the framework of quarters and a supramunicipality that would be headed by a representative of the Jewish majority. The supramunicipality would supervise the submunicipalities and the services provided jointly to Jews and Arabs and would set overall policy. Israel's sovereign area in Jerusalem would be redefined, and a territorial exchange would take place in the city. Ma'aleh Adumim and Givat Ze'ev would be annexed by Israel in return for the transfer to the new state of Palestine of neighborhoods on the outskirts of Jerusalem such as Kufr 'Aqeb, 'Arab Al-Shawawrah, Sur Baher, the Sho'afat refugee camp, and the neighborhoods of Sho'afat and Bait Hanina. In other words, Greater Jerusalem would not be as envisioned by prime ministers in the past, that is, the area within a radius of twenty kilometers from the city center, but rather an area in which two municipal and political bodies would coexist. The Old City and the inner circle of Arab neighborhoods would remain in Israel's hands in exchange for the areas mentioned above; this would create a demographic balance of 83 percent Jews and 17 percent Arabs. Should Israel remove from its sovereign area part of the inner circle of Arab neighborhoods such as Shaykh Jarah and leave the Old City and its surrounding area under Israeli sovereignty but under a special administration, the demographic ratio would be 88 percent Jews to 12 percent Arabs.

Arabs living within the special administrative area or the area remaining under Israeli sovereignty would not belong to the Israeli system for the purposes of their civil status and political obligations and citizenship. They would be citizens of Palestine, like the residents of al-Quds, Palestinian Jerusalem. They would be entitled to vote for and be elected to Palestinian institutions at both the municipal and national levels. Palestinian citizens in this area would enjoy autonomy in the administration of their quarters, but for administrative and functional purposes Israel would have supreme powers that would limit Palestinian authority. Israel would retain overall responsibility for security. In most areas of life the administrative bodies of the Palestinian quarters would be subject to the Palestinian municipality, which would oversee their activity. Neighborhood administrative powers in the Palestinian quarters would include collecting taxes, setting budgets, and running a court for local matters. They would also include the power to make decisions concerning planning and construction at the neighborhood level, but this would be subject to the Jewish municipality's veto power and to security powers within the neighborhood in a framework similar to the Civil Guard. The police force in the Palestinian areas would be made up of Arabs from East Jerusalem, who would cooperate with the Palestinian police. This means that the supra-neighborhood framework, the Palestinian municipality, would be remote, and each neighborhood would be connected to it separately. The Palestinian neighborhoods would be connected to the state from the administrative point of view through the municipality, as well as through each individual resident's civil status and political affiliation.

The Israelis also came up with the idea of including the Old City in the structure of neighborhood administrations proposed for Israeli Jerusalem. The Old City would be divided administratively. The administration of the Jewish and Armenian Quarters would be combined with the administration of the Jewish city center, and that of the Christian and Muslim Quarters with the Shaykh Jarah administration.

A completely different option for the Old City would preserve the area's unique character as an undivided whole and would grant special status, under Israeli sovereignty, to the holy basin and to the Old City at its center. The holy basin's administrative body would be composed of representatives of the relevant religions, residents, and states (Israel, Palestine, and the Arab and Islamic states). In the framework of this special status, places holy to more than one religion, such as the Temple Mount, would be jointly administered in religious matters. Security on the Temple Mount would be the responsibility of the Palestinian police or the Waqf, the Muslim religious administration. Outside its defined area there would be a joint Palestinian-Israeli patrol, and overall security in the holy basin would be Israel's responsibility. Jews would be ensured free access to the Temple Mount, and the Palestinians would be able to fly their flag there. In this indirect way, the representatives of different states could be involved on the day-to-day level without undermining Israeli sovereignty (*Ha'aretz* 18 May, 11 July 2000; Shragai 13 June 2000).

The third option regarding the Old City was developed by intellectuals and professionals working separately within the frameworks of the Jerusalem Institute and the ECF, who passed their ideas on to decision makers in Israel. Rather than Israeli superiority, they supported placing the holy basin under joint Israeli-Palestinian sovereignty and administration. The joint administration characterizing the regime in the holy basin would include a joint police force with limited powers. The area would be administered in coordination with the municipalities of Jerusalem and al-Quds, particularly in the fields of education, planning, and construction. The joint administrative committee for the area would provide some services, while others, mainly those dependent on physical infrastructure (water, electricity, communications, sanitation), would be provided by independent contractors. In order to preserve the character of the existing quarters and neighborhoods, a complicated system would be set up for acquiring land in and for moving into the holy basin. Finally, which criminal justice system would apply to a particular individual would depend on that individual's nationality—Israeli citizens would be subject to Israeli law and Palestinian citizens to Palestinian law. This concept of a special regime seeks to create a high level of differentiation between the holy basin and its surrounding area. The special arrangement would apply to most areas of life as well as to the operative code by which the area would be administered. Its complex structure would require close cooperation between the two sides, large quantities of good will, and mutual confidence both on the part of the local decision makers and on the part of the resident population and recipients of the services provided under the arrangement. These do not exist in Jerusalem at the present time; therefore, this option is inapplicable. Israel's leaders, however, could not accept this last alternative for a different reason: it reduced the scope of Israeli sovereignty.

These ideas percolated slowly into the consciousness of Barak and the members of his delegation. The partial and interrupted preparations, the tardiness in addressing the question of Jerusalem, and the fear of the taboo against the city's partition delayed the metamorphosis of the Israeli approach. According to the testimony of Sher and Ben-Ami, it was only on 17 July, in the midst of the Camp David summit, that what they call the conceptual breakthrough took place. It was only then that Barak told the members of the delegation that he believed that the demographic reality required Israel to concede the East Jerusalem neighborhoods it had annexed in 1967. Two days previously Barak had been unable to explicitly declare this belief to his colleagues. Barak summed up the discussion of the negotiations in general and the Jerusalem issue in particular with the words, "We have internal red lines, real ones, that everyone senses in the basic way of describing the state's vital interests" (Sher 2001: 165, 175; Shavit 14 September 2001).

The Palestinian Preparations

The Palestinians also commenced preparations for the permanent settlement. At the twenty-first convention of the Palestinian National Council, held in Gaza in April 1996, it was decided to establish a Jerusalem and Building of the Homeland Committee, with the goal of influencing the positions to be taken by Arafat in the negotiations over Jerusalem in the permanent status talks. The committee was headed by Faisal Husseini, whose presence was clearly felt in its decisions. The committee expressed the positions and concerns of Orient House and the political establishment in Jerusalem. The concluding report laid out the dangers to the Palestinian identity of East Jerusalem that would result from "the lack of a national Palestinian strategy for coping with the measures being taken by

Israel" (*al-Quds* 26 April 1996). The committee demanded that the Palestinians "prepare with precision their negotiating file on Jerusalem and decide what their red lines are on the subject. This requires enlisting all Palestinian potential, talent, and expertise, as well as the assistance of friends, in order to reinforce the position of the Palestinian negotiator" (*al-Quds* 26 April 1996). The committee's statement and its lines of action matched the plans that had previously been prepared by the Orient House staff (*Ha'aretz* 28 June 1996).

On the parliamentary level, the Palestinian Authority Legislative Council decided in mid-May 1996 that its permanent seat would be in Jerusalem and that, until the permanent seat could be established, the council would migrate between Gaza, Ramallah, and al-Bireh. This was a symbolic decision to which an organizational decision was appended. The council established a committee for Jerusalem affairs to track the permanent status talks, oversee the activities of the Jerusalem affairs ministry, and take part in determining "a comprehensive national strategy on Jerusalem that will take into consideration the city's needs and reinforce the steadfastness of its inhabitants" (*al-Quds* 17 May 1996; Ahmad 1997). This definition of roles and powers was supported by a majority in the Legislative Council, winning out over a formulation proposed by one of the Jerusalem representatives, Khatim 'Eid, who demanded that the statement of appointment declare explicitly that Jerusalem is an inseparable part of the territories occupied in 1967.

This was not Khatim 'Eid's only hawkish position. He also maintained that when the Jerusalem question was placed on the negotiating table, Israel would demand that the permanent agreement guarantee Israeli sovereignty over East Jerusalem. The Palestinian response, he insisted, must be to state the Palestinian claims to property that Palestinians left behind them in West Jerusalem in 1948. This position did not, however, win broad support (*Ha'aretz* 17 May 1996). The high level of activity of the Legislative Council members from Jerusalem with regard to their electoral district, and their stand against the national leadership, led Palestinian public opinion to identify the Legislative Council as an institution that was fighting for Jerusalem. According to a Center for Palestine Research and Studies (CPRS) survey conducted in September and October 1996, Jerusalem was the issue on which the Legislative Council received the highest marks. Nationally, among Palestinians in the West Bank and Gaza Strip, 70.8 percent of those surveyed claimed that the council's accomplishments in this area were "good" or "very good," which was 10.9 percent higher than the marks it received on its handling of the settlement issue. The council received high marks from the residents of Jerusalem as well, even if considerably lower than its rating on the national level—58.2 percent.

On the whole, two approaches could be discerned within the Palestinian establishment. The first was that of the Jerusalem delegation to the Palestinian Legislative Council and of the local political establishment centered on Orient House—in particular, Khatim 'Eid, Hanan Ashrawi, and Faisal Husseini. They sought to limit the distinction between Jerusalem and the rest of the 1967 territories to a single principle: preventing the physical division of the city by a wall like the one that divided it between 1948 and 1967. The border should be the one that preceded the 1967 war, and Palestinian political sovereignty over East Jerusalem should, they felt, be complete.

Knowing that Israel would demand that its annexation of East Jerusalem be recognized and grounded in the permanent settlement, Faisal Husseini remarked that the Palestinians would counter with a demand that Palestinian property in West Jerusalem be returned to them. Husseini stated that the permanent status talks would discuss West as well as East Jerusalem; according to him, 70 percent of the land in West Jerusalem was Palestinian property (al-Ayyam 27 September 1999). In keeping with this, two Palestinian institutions, the Institute for Land and Water Research and Legal Services and the Association for the Protection of Human Rights, began collecting material for a database that would serve as the basis for claims to ownership of this property (Ha'aretz 8, 19 February 1996, 22 September 1997, 24 September 1998).

These moves should be viewed as aimed at providing a card to play and not as a new Palestinian strategy for taking over large parts of West Jerusalem. Israel will in the end concede all or most of its claims in East Jerusalem, and the Palestinians will do the same with their claims in the west side of the city. If the area subject to negotiation is just East Jerusalem, the compromise lines will pass through the Arab part of the city and the Palestinians' gains in Jerusalem will be negligible. With this in mind, Husseini invoked Israel's classic, almost mythic, claim that Jerusalem is and must forever be a single and indivisible city. If the principle is that sovereignty over the city cannot be divided, then the two sides of the city must be discussed together. If Israel should refuse to do so, the Palestinians would be able to argue that Jerusalem is not one city but two and that sovereignty should be divided according to the 1967 lines (al-Ayyam 27 September 1999; al-Quds 14 May 1996; Husseini 1996: 203–8; 'Abdul Hadi 2000: 213–22; Musallam 1996: 121–26).

The major Palestinian national institutions in Gaza advocated the second approach. In his speech at the opening ceremony of the talks, Abu Mazen explicitly stated that the Palestinian capital was East Jerusalem alone. "We are eager to live in peace in the framework of an independent Palestinian state whose capital is East Jerusalem, and whose borders are secure and recognized, the June 4, 1967, borders" (al-Quds 6 May 1996). Arafat also stated more than once that "the Jerusalem that we are speaking of is East Jerusalem (al-Quds al-Sharqiyya), the capital of the Palestinian state" (al-Ayyam 6 December 1998, 2 November 1999; Ha'aretz 30 November 1998). In their opinion, Jerusalem is one of several issues to be resolved in the permanent status negotiations. It is not an issue that stands above all other issues; it is of equal importance and can therefore be discussed in the framework of a deal with Israel over a set of issues. It was this approach that in fact served as the basis of what is called the Beilin–Abu Mazen document (Beilin 1997: 167–70).

The opening of negotiations on the permanent settlement, in May 1996, sharpened the differences that had been evident earlier between the national Palestinian leadership, which was negotiating with Israel, and the local Jerusalem leadership. The opposition was led by Khatim 'Eid, a member of the Jerusalem delegation in the Palestinian Legislative Council. He was the moving force behind a leaflet published on 15 May 1996 that stated that "Arab Jerusalem is shrinking. . . . Jerusalem will not return to our hands by negotiation alone" (Yerushalayim 10 May 1996). The Palestinians had to take action, such as finding housing solutions within the Old City; renovating its dilapidated homes; setting a rent ceiling for the city; imposing rules on homeowners who preferred to rent their property to diplomats, foreign journalists, and UN representatives for high prices; and organizing mass demonstrations and strikes. 'Eid was also behind the protest activity organized in March 1998 by the Fatah's Jerusalem branch against Israel's policy in Jerusalem. Under the direction of the local Fatah, a commercial and school strike was organized, but Arafat clipped 'Eid's wings and did not permit the protest he organized.

In protest, 'Eid resigned his chairmanship of the Jerusalem committee in the Legislative Council (Kol HaIr 6, 27 March 1998) and stated that "the Palestinian Authority has conceded Jerusalem" (Kol HaIr 27 March 1998). "It looks to me as if they prefer a Palestinian state without Jerusalem to the opposite," he added (Cohen 29 April 1998). The elections to the Fatah leadership in Jerusalem, conducted on 16 November 1998, honed its activist profile. Sixty-two candidates competed for seventeen seats and fought for the support of some 2,000 voters who gathered for the election.

Those elected were young, largely between the ages of twenty-five and thirty-five, former Intifada and field activists with hawkish views (*Kol Ha'Ir* 20 November 1998). These positions were what led Arafat to declare in his speech to the assembly that if the way of peace did not lead to the realization of the Palestinian right to a state with Jerusalem as its capital, "our rifles are ready, and we are prepared to use them against all who might try to prevent us from praying in Jerusalem" (*Ha'aretz* 16 November 1998).

A countervailing statement was not long in coming and was made in Stockholm at an event marking the tenth anniversary of the PLO's recognition of Israel and condemnation of terror. In his speech, Arafat set out the guiding principles for a permanent settlement; with regard to Jerusalem he stated that the city should remain open "to all its inhabitants without prejudice. The city must remain physically undivided by roadblocks and fortifications. There is no solution to the Jerusalem question unless the interests of all sides are taken into account, together with standing firm on halting the Judaization of Jerusalem and the preservation of the rights of all communities and of adherents of all the monotheistic faiths equally" (*al-Ayyam* 6 December 1998).

The Palestinian staff conducted its work on two levels. At the local level in Jerusalem, Orient House coordinated the work of three teams of experts—in the Maps and Survey Department, headed by Khalil al-Tafugji; in the International Affairs Department, headed by Sharif Husseini; and at the International Peace and Cooperation Center (IPCC) under the direction of Rami Nasrallah, who worked at first within the framework of the Arab Studies Society in Orient House. The IPCC split off from Orient House in November 1997 and became an independent organization working on issues connected to Jerusalem, with the assistance of Dutch experts. These Palestinian departments have been in contact with their Israeli counterparts since 1996 and together with them organized seminars on municipal subjects. Such informal channels greatly helped the Palestinians to exchange information on Jerusalem, study the city's problems and Israel's positions, and locate areas of agreement and disagreement. The Orient House also engaged architects and city planners from abroad in order to fill in what was missing from the knowledge of local professionals. On the basis of the infrastructure prepared at Orient House, and because he held the Jerusalem portfolio on the PLO Executive Committee, Faisal Husseini was included in the Palestinian delegation to the permanent status negotiations headed by Yassir 'Abd Rabbu (December 1999). However, the local leadership was not, to its regret, invited to participate in the delegation that negotiated with Israel in Stockholm (April 2000) and at Camp David (July 2000).

At the national level, the staff work was coordinated by the PLO's Negotiation Affairs Department, headed by Abu Mazen, the secretary-general of the organization's executive committee. With financing from the British Foreign Office, this department began working with the Adam Smith Institute on all of the permanent status issues, including Jerusalem, in the summer of 1999. The institute employed a local staff in Ramallah and a team of experts in the United Kingdom. On the basis of material and data gathered by the staff in Ramallah, the British and local experts prepared position papers and alternative options. This work was coordinated by Yezid Sayigh of Cambridge University, who had previously served as adviser to the Palestinian delegation to the Madrid Conference (19 March 2000). So far as we know, this team's work was never completed; none of its members was included in the Palestinian delegation to Camp David. In fact, until the Taba talks of January 2001, none of Jerusalem's Palestinian experts, nor any of the experts working as part of the Palestinian national establishment, were closely involved in the negotiations. In Sayigh's opinion, Arafat's priorities are faulty and he blocks every possibility of thinking out the issues in an organized way for the purpose of political planning and the formation of a strategy. These fundamental flaws in the Palestinian leader's work habits showed themselves in the Palestinian side's defective preparation on the issue of Jerusalem. Arafat invested a great deal of superfluous effort in constraining Faisal Husseini by hemming in the local establishment that Husseini had set up and headed in Jerusalem. Arafat worked hard to identify himself as the defender of the Islamic holy city and to deny any other leader legitimacy in this role. Sayigh believes that Arafat should have put his effort into mobilizing Jerusalem's Arab inhabitants to conduct a nonviolent struggle, or civil disobedience, against the continued Israeli efforts at annexation (Sayigh 2001: 47).

Most of the members of the Palestinian delegation to the permanent status talks at and prior to the Camp David summit belonged to the national establishment. The delegation's tone was set by the PLO people who had returned from Tunis. The locals, who were left outside the picture, suspected that the negotiators were too eager to reach agreement with Israel in order to buttress their standing at the pinnacle of Palestinian power and to continue ruling by half-democratic means ('Abdul Hadi 2000). Criticism of the Palestinian establishment and ruling elite for undemocratic behavior and personal corruption found new expression as criticism of the lack of adequate representation of the various strata of

Palestinian society in the delegations to the negotiations. The population resented the composition of the delegation to the Camp David talks, mainly because West Bank and Gaza Strip residents were underrepresented, no experts familiar with the Jerusalem problem were included, and Faisal Husseini, who held the Jerusalem portfolio on the PLO Executive Committee, was excluded. This criticism was not expressed directly to Arafat but rather contributed to the tying of his hands politically. Those persons and organizations that were not represented in the delegation to Camp David organized demonstrations and wrote articles in the local press during the conference, supporting an uncompromising political line. Palestinian negotiators were congratulated each day in the press for "standing up to Israeli-American pressure," and when Arafat returned from Camp David without an agreement, he was given a victor's welcome.

2

The Official Talks and Their Crises

The Camp David Summit

Jerusalem was the focal point of the second Camp David summit (11–24 July 2000). This attempt to tackle the Jerusalem issue head-on was an approach diametrically opposed to that of the first Camp David summit of 6–18 September 1978 (Klein 2001: 90–94), when a decision was made to defer talks on Jerusalem to the end of the negotiating process. That strategy had been advocated by President Jimmy Carter. According to the Carter model, the Jerusalem problem would not be addressed until the end of the negotiating process, the fear being that the two sides' polarized positions on the city's future would ensure that any negotiations would end as soon as they began. Postponement of negotiations of Jerusalem would, it was thought, help lead to a solution. Once agreements were reached on all the other questions in dispute, the two sides would be forced to compromise on Jerusalem because failure to do so would threaten the agreements already reached on other issues. The assumption underlying this approach was that there was no a priori possibility for compromise on Jerusalem itself—it was inevitably a site of polarization and contention. Only an external threat could overcome, from top to bottom, the difficulties presented by the conflicted city. Carter's model was first adopted by President Sadat and afterward by Prime Minister Begin. Yet it turned out to be effective and useful for only a short time. It helped achieve peace between Israel and Egypt, as long as the Palestinians were outside the negotiating picture. But as soon as Israel and Egypt began talking about the autonomy plan for the Arab inhabitants of the West Bank and the Gaza Strip, profound differences emerged on the link that the Arab inhabitants of Jerusalem would have to the autonomous Palestinian entity. Both sides realized then that the Jerusalem problem could not be ignored.

The Israelis and Egyptians then faced the choice of abandoning the goal of an agreement on an autonomy plan and making do with a peace treaty between the two countries, or endangering the bilateral peace because of a dispute over territory that Egypt itself had no claims on. It was only natural that Egypt would prefer its own direct interests to risking the gains it had made. Both countries preferred to settle for the agreement they had reached between them. This bilateral peace proved to be stable even without a solution to the Jerusalem issue. The Egypt-Israel peace treaty made it through some difficult moments, first and foremost during Israel's war in Lebanon, which broke out in 1982, and then during the first Intifada of 1987–93.

The downside of the Carter model was that when Jerusalem was put on the negotiating table, all the problems it presented would have to be faced at once. Carter understood that this price would have to be paid for putting off discussion of Jerusalem, but he assumed that vital external factors would force a solution.

Events have proven that the assumptions of the Camp David model of 1978 were not realistic. In the end, discussion of Jerusalem was not put off to the end of the process, and compromises were not made all at once but rather little by little, as the Jerusalem issue was divided up into its constituent problems. The need to do this was so great that in the debate within Israel, even before bargaining with the Palestinians began, the Israeli government faced the necessity of addressing one of the many aspects of the Jerusalem problem. In May 1989, when Israel presented its program for elections in the West Bank and Gaza Strip, the question arose of how the inhabitants of East Jerusalem would vote, if at all. The Likud and the Labor Parties differed on this, leading to the dissolution of the national unity government in March 1990.

Although it was not planned that way, Jerusalem ended up being the central issue from quite an early stage of the second Camp David summit, dwarfing all other permanent status issues. Of the subjects comprising the Jerusalem problem, the question of sovereignty over the Temple Mount/al-Haram al-Sharif, the Old City, and its adjacent neighborhoods became the main sources of contention, preventing any progress on other subjects.

The first Camp David summit led to an Egypt-Israel peace treaty. The second Camp David summit did not produce an agreement. However, as I will show below, it would be incorrect to say that nothing at all happened at the conference and that it was a total failure. Its participants set for themselves a series of ambitious goals, including the conclusion of a permanent agreement on all subjects and the elimination of the Israeli-Palestinian, and perhaps even the entire Israeli-Arab, conflict. The delegations' leaders believed themselves to be at a historic crossroads. During the conference, Ehud Barak often compared himself to David Ben-Gurion, Israel's founding prime minister, and to Winston Churchill. He believed he faced a historic decision that would establish the permanent borders of the State of Israel, while ceding Israel's claim to parts of its historical homeland and to the settlements that had been built in those territories. President Clinton was about to complete his term of office and wanted to end it with a historic achievement. And Yasir Arafat, the eldest among them, found himself on the verge of achieving the Palestinian national movement's central goal: the establishment of a Palestinian state with East Jerusalem as its capital. He was steeped in historical consciousness and saw himself on a par with Caliph 'Omar Ibn al-Khattab, who conquered Jerusalem in 638, and with Salah al-Din, who liberated it from Crusader occupation in 1187 (Haniyya 2000). Each of these three leaders believed that an agreement over Jerusalem would be their crowning achievement. As a result, expectations ran high. The profusion of target dates set and missed for the conclusion of the permanent status agreement only raised expectations even further.

The second Camp David summit turned, very soon after it convened, into a conference on one main subject: Jerusalem. Barak and Arafat each came to the summit suspecting that his opposite number would not be willing to make the necessary concessions. "The Palestinian perspective was that Oslo was a compromise and that it was the last compromise. We were not aware of this. We all thought that somewhere down the road there would be another compromise which would then be final" (Ben-Ami quoted in *Jerusalem Report*; Susser 16 July 2001). Barak remarked many times before and during the conference that he was going to Camp David to determine whether Arafat was ready to make hard decisions—that is, concessions. Arafat, for his part, claimed that the Israelis were not ready to make the concessions he considered necessary to meet his minimal conditions on Jerusalem. Yet neither side deferred discussing the issue. Barak wanted to arrive at a full permanent status agreement and to receive, in exchange for his concessions, a Palestinian declaration that the conflict between the two peoples had come to an end. This could not be achieved without placing Jerusalem on the conference agenda. Neither did Arafat agree to defer discussion of Jerusalem. On the eve of the summit, at a meeting between Arafat and Ben-Ami, the latter proposed postponing discussion on Jerusalem for two years. Arafat replied that he refused to defer the subject for even two hours (Haniyya 2000).

Nonetheless, the Palestinians wanted to put off the summit itself from July to November, after the U.S. presidential elections. This was in order to increase President Clinton's effectiveness and free him from the constraints of the Jewish vote. They also requested additional time to organize themselves internally, suspecting that immediate talks on a general framework agreement would trap them, as the Oslo agreement had. In other words, they feared that detailed negotiations would go on for a long time and in the meantime Israel would create new "facts on the ground" in its favor. In the end, the Palestinians agreed to come to the summit in July in order not to hurt President Clinton and so that they would not be accused of obstructing the diplomatic process. Furthermore, Clinton extracted a commitment from Barak that there would be an Israeli withdrawal if the summit failed. He also told Arafat, in June, that in such a case Clinton would advocate that the withdrawal be a substantial one. On the eve of the summit, Clinton assured Arafat that he would not be blamed if the summit did not succeed (Agha and Malley 2001). In parallel, the Palestinian leadership proposed that a series of summit conferences be held, of which the July meeting at Camp David would be but the first. These conferences would culminate, after the U.S. elections, in the signing of a framework for the permanent status agreement (Haniyya 2000; Horowitz 2001; Abu Mazen to *al-Ayyam*, 28–29 July 2001).

The Palestinian suggestions that the summit be postponed were interpreted in Israel as being part of a game to demonstrate that the Palestinians were being brought to Camp David against their will (Sher 2001: 142). The suggestions for a delay were not seen as meaning that the Palestinians really needed more time to prepare themselves.

As Akram Haniyya testified, the Palestinian delegation expected Israel to concede on the conflict's core issues—Jerusalem and the refugees, both of them historically and symbolically charged subjects. The Palestinians expected to receive these concessions in order to justify the concessions that they were willing to make on settlements and security. But the Israeli delegation was not willing to go that far.

A Stormy Debate: Borders, Sovereignty, Settlements, Security, and Refugees

Israel was willing to make what it saw as concessions on sovereignty (the establishment of a Palestinian state) and borders (a Palestinian state that would cover some 87 percent of the area of the West Bank and the entire Gaza Strip and annexation by Israel of 13 percent of the West Bank) and was also willing to consider territorial exchange (the transfer of Israeli territory adjoining the Gaza Strip, equivalent to about 1.5 percent of the West Bank and Gaza Strip, to the sovereign area of the new state of Palestine; in other words, the ratio between the area that Israel would annex and the area that it would hand over would be 10:1). The territory annexed by Israel would be of much higher quality than the sandy tract of the Negev that Israel would hand over to the Palestinians. It should be emphasized that the principle of territorial exchange was not acceptable to the Israeli delegation. It was an American idea and Clinton pressed Barak to accept it, even if only on a miniscule scale. During the summit the Palestinians presented President Clinton with a map that included consent to Israel's annexation of 2.5 percent of the West Bank, comprising the following blocks of settlements: Gush Etzion (south of Jerusalem), Gush Modi'in near Latrun (west of Jerusalem), Ariel, Givat Ze'ev (north of Jerusalem), and Ma'aleh Adumim (east of Jerusalem). The map also marked the areas of sovereign Israeli territory that the Palestinians demanded in exchange (Kershner 16 July 2001; Sher 2001: 202). The Israelis and Americans had a hard time taking notice of and engaging this proposal during the Camp David summit, and they have had a hard time remembering it since then (Agha and Malley 2001; Dennis Ross, *Ma'ariv* 17 September 2001; Shavit 14 September 2001; Morris 13 June 2002). Neither did the Israelis engage the 4 percent annexation proposal raised by Abu 'Ala in the talks held prior to the summit. Instead, they preferred to repeat to the Americans the unofficial proposal made by Muhammad Dahlan about the annexation of 7.5 percent (Sher 2001: 212), apparently because this was close to the lower limit of 8–10 percent that Ben-Ami had cited, at his own discretion, in Stockholm and at Camp David.

The Israeli delegation also took note of the proposal that Arafat made for a short period at the height of the Camp David summit. On July 16 Arafat agreed, in Clinton's presence, to give up 8–10 percent of the West Bank's territory while leaving it to President Clinton to determine the size of the territory that the Palestinian state would receive from Israel in exchange, as well as the quality of that territory. With regard to Jerusalem, however, Arafat stood his ground. Only the Western Wall, the Jewish Quarter, and the Jewish neighborhoods built by Israel in East Jerusalem after the annexation would be under Israeli sovereignty, he said. Arafat demanded Palestinian sovereignty over all the Arab neighborhoods and the Temple Mount.

A short time later Arafat backtracked on his willingness to give up such a large amount of West Bank territory. Arafat's proposal may have been a

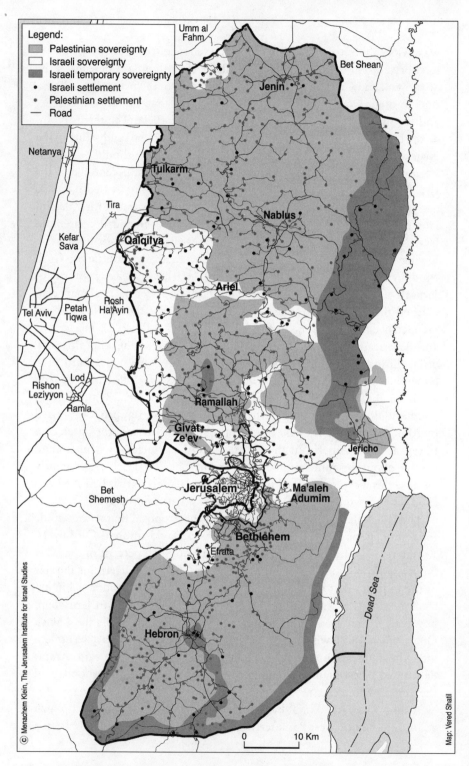

Map 2. Extrapolation of the Israeli map, January–July 2000

tactical move meant to signal to President Clinton that his intentions were sincere, or he may have wanted to test Israel's willingness to exchange settlements in the West Bank for the Arab neighborhoods in East Jerusalem. In any case, Israel interpreted it to mean that Arafat was in principle willing, under American and Israeli pressure, to give up 9 percent of the West Bank. In this light, Israel agreed unofficially to step down from the 12 percent annexation it had officially proposed in the Stockholm talks. Barak had repeated this demand at his meeting with Abu Mazen on 11 June 2000, and the demand was made a third time at the beginning of the Camp David summit. The Israelis were now willing to accept the percentages proposed by Arafat, with a small bargaining margin (Kaspit 17 September 2001; Shavit 14 September 2001; Sher 2001: 171–75). Ben-Ami's private willingness at Stockholm to go down to an 8 percent annexation reinforced the position of the members of the Israeli delegation. Israel's representatives were disappointed by Arafat's rejection of their proposal and from his retraction of what he had said to President Clinton. The Palestinian position, as it became etched in their own memory, was accession to Israel's annexation of 1.8 percent of the West Bank, the precise built-up land of the settlements, not including East Jerusalem. In exchange, the Palestinians demanded territory of the same size and quality, adjacent to the West Bank (Sher 2001).

According to the Palestinian Authority, some 120,000 Palestinians lived in the areas Israel was demanding to annex. Furthermore, it claimed, if Israel annexed these territories, the Palestinian state would be divided into three parts, each surrounded by areas under Israeli control. The state would not be viable and its parts would not be territorially contiguous. According to the Palestinian sources, at one stage a Palestinian negotiator proposed that Israel annex 4 percent of the West Bank and in return hand over the equivalent of 2 percent to the Palestinians as compensation. The proposal caused a fierce argument between two of the Palestinian negotiators, including an exchange of blows (Baskin 2001).

Israel also saw itself as willing to concede on settlements: it was willing to dismantle more than 40 settlements containing some 40,000 settlers, concentrating some 80 percent of the settlers residing in some 140 settlements into three blocks: Gush Ariel, Gush Etzion, and Ma'aleh Adumim–Givat Ze'ev. Finally, Israel sought to leave some of its Jordan Valley settlements and military bases in place, on an area equal to some 10 percent of the West Bank, by leasing the land for twelve to thirty years. Israel would keep three early warning stations that now operate, according to the Palestinians, on Mount Eval, Mount Ba'al Hatzor, and Mount Scopus, six army bases along the Jordan River and the northern shore of the Dead Sea, and security access to the settlements and army bases that would remain in Palestinian sovereign territory. Israel also demanded permanent control and the stationing of 800 troops within the area of Palestinian sovereignty, over 15 percent of the zone along the Jordan River and the shores of the Dead Sea, a presence at international border crossings, and control of the Palestinian airspace, which would legally be under Palestinian sovereignty (Horowitz 2001; Hassasian 2001; Sher 2001: 164, 209, 223, 226; Shavit 14 September 2001).

Israel was not willing to admit any responsibility for the creation of the refugee problem in 1948, refused to recognize the principle of the right of the 1948 Palestinian refugees to return, and categorically rejected UN resolution 194. Israel also rejected the Palestinian proposal of establishing a mechanism that would channel the refugees toward more attractive possibilities than return to Israel once the principle of the right of return was accepted. According to the Palestinian offer, the return of Palestinian refugees from Lebanon would serve as a pilot program for examining how the system would work and where the refugees would prefer to realize their right. Israel expressed a willingness to absorb a maximum of 2,000 refugees per year over a period of five to six years. This meant a total of 10,000–12,000 refugees, all in the framework of family reunification and as a humanitarian gesture only.

Israel did not agree to the Palestinian demand that Israel alone compensate the 1948 refugees, out of its own funds, for the property they had lost and for the great suffering they had undergone. Israel agreed only to participate in the establishment of an international fund that would raise the money for compensation. Furthermore, Israel claimed that compensation should also be paid to the Jews who left their homes in Arab countries as a result of the 1948 war and that Israel would thus share the compensation funds with those Jews. Israel proposed dismantling UNWRA within a ten-year period and establishing in its place a new body that would oversee the rehabilitation and resettlement of the refugees (Sher 2001: 199, 213–14, 216; Abu Mazen to *al-Ayyam* 29 July 2001). The gap between the positions of the two sides was so great that, for all practical purposes, no negotiations on the 1948 refugee issue took place at Camp David. At most of the encounters where the subject was raised, there were only exchanges of accusations and myths and unproductive arguments (Sher 2001: 216; Haniyya 2000). Real negotiations on the refugees took place only at Taba, where the two sides picked up where they had left off in the Stockholm channel (see the section on the Taba talks, p. 111).

Thus, Israel demanded that the Palestinians concede on Jerusalem and the refugee issue while settling for much less than all of the 1967 territories.

In the Eye of the Storm: Jerusalem

The fierce debate that took place at the second Camp David summit related to the issues of the refugees and Jerusalem, mostly the latter. All three cities that constitute the city of Jerusalem—the urban city, the political city, and the holy city—received extensive attention at the conference. Israel did not propose only one kind of arrangement for East Jerusalem. According to the Israeli proposal, the circle of external neighborhoods such as Sho'afat, Bait Hanina, and Sur Baher, containing some 130,000 Palestinians, would be transferred to Palestinian sovereignty as part of the municipality of al-Quds, which would also include such Jerusalem suburbs as Abu Dis and al-'Azariya. In return, Israel would annex settlements close to Jerusalem—Ma'aleh Adumim, Givat Ze'ev, and Gush Etzion—and connect them to Israel proper with a wide corridor that would be under Israeli sovereignty. The internal circle of neighborhoods (such as Silwan, Ras-al-Amud, al-Tur, Shaykh Jarah, and Saladin Street) would remain under Israeli sovereignty. These neighborhoods would enjoy municipal autonomy in the framework of neighborhood administrations or quarters. These Jerusalem neighborhoods would be under Palestinian civilian and police authority, while overall responsibility for security and supreme sovereignty would remain with Israel. In other words, in terms of sovereignty the existing situation would remain basically unchanged. In light of that fact, the Palestinians saw the Israeli proposals concerning the interior neighborhoods as giving them a status similar to that of Zone B under the interim agreements. According to Israel's proposal, buildings in Arab neighborhoods inhabited by Jews and under Jewish ownership would remain under Israeli sovereignty (Sher 2001: 228).

Israel put forward three proposals regarding the Temple Mount, the Old City, and the holy basin—that is, the historical and religious heart of Jerusalem that includes, besides the walled area of the Old City, Mount Zion and the nearby Christian cemetery, the archeological park along the Old City's southern wall and in the City of David, the Muslim cemetery along the eastern wall, and the Jewish cemetery and the churches on the Mount of Olives.

The first proposal provided for supreme Israeli sovereignty that would be largely formal, with the Palestinians receiving extensive functional sovereignty. The Palestinians remaining under Israeli sovereignty would enjoy full municipal-neighborhood powers, including planning and construction up to a specified height, and neighborhood policing. From these points of view the Old City would have the status of a neighborhood in the inner circle. The Waqf of the new state of Palestine would administer the sites holy to Islam, and an access road would be built from the Palestinian city to al-Haram al-Sharif/the Temple Mount through the Muslim Quarter in the Old City. Palestine, not Israel, would have sovereignty over the road. There would be no barriers or checkpoints on the road, and thus all would be ensured access to the Muslim holy places, as demanded by the Palestinian delegation. In other words, Israel offered the Palestinians sovereignty over defined areas of the Muslim Quarter. Israel also offered Arafat the establishment of a presidential area in the Muslim Quarter, which would be included in the corridor under Palestinian sovereignty. In this way, this part of the Muslim Quarter would be set apart from the other parts of the Old City and the circle of interior Jerusalem neighborhoods.

The second proposal was to leave the question of sovereignty over the Temple Mount undecided, whether for a defined period of time or indefinitely. In the rest of the Old City and the holy basin, the solution would take the form described above.

The third proposal was to leave sovereignty over the Temple Mount in Israel's hands but to give Arafat a kind of sovereignty similar to religious custody ("sovereign custody") and to consider him the guardian or "servant" of the Islamic holy places in Jerusalem, as the kings of Saudi Arabia are termed with regard to the sacred Islamic sites in Mecca and Medina. Custody would be granted not by Israel but by the members of the UN Security Council together with Morocco as representative of the Organization of the Islamic Conference. This sovereign custody would translate in practical terms into official Palestinian administration of the site and agreement that the Palestinians could fly their flag there. This proposal also included an Israeli undertaking to ensure free access to the Temple Mount to Muslims in general and to Arafat in particular. According to this proposal, the solution for the remaining areas would be in accordance with the first proposal.

In return for the concessions Israel was prepared to make in connection with the Old City and the Temple Mount, it demanded that the Palestinians set aside a defined place on the Temple Mount for public Jewish worship. In addition, Israel wanted to enjoy residual sovereignty over the Temple Mount, which would be expressed as a limit on Palestinian subterranean works and excavations at the site (*Ha'aretz* 23 July 2000; Haniyya 2000; Abu Mazen 2000, in *al-Quds* and at www.pna.org; Erekat 2000; Shikaki 2000; Shavit 14 September 2001; Sher 2001: 163–64, 173, 186, 203, 205, 212, 218, 230).

Toward the end of the conference, Israel demonstrated a willingness in principle to accept an American compromise proposal, on condition that the Palestinians also agree to it. In contrast to the Israeli proposals, whose territorial logic was horizontal, the Americans suggested a vertical division on the Temple Mount. They proposed granting the Palestinians supreme sovereignty over the zone and the buildings on the surface of the Mount, while Israel would be sovereign beneath the surface and at the Western Wall and adjoining plaza, which are located at a lower level than the Islamic holy sites. This proposal was rejected by the Palestinians, who demanded full sovereignty over the subterranean area of the Temple Mount as well (ibid.). The advantage of the American proposal was that it contained a clear division of ownership and authority over the various parts of the area. Its shortcoming was that to religious believers in each of the two constituencies, cutting a holy place into slices of sovereignty contradicts the concept of wholeness and unity that is synonymous with holiness and the One God who is at the same time whole and holy. The same qualities attributed to God are attributed to God's dwelling place, God's earthly home. Therefore, from a religious perspective it would be difficult to accept this approach.

Moreover, the Palestinians have a deep-seated, mythical fear that the Jews and Israelis intend to literally undermine the Islamic holy places. As far back as the mid-1920s, the Palestinian national movement claimed that Zionism's ultimate goal was to build the Third Temple. The Jewish attempt to undermine the status quo that existed at that time in the Western Wall area led to the 1929 riots (Porath 1974: 248–73). Attempts in 1981 by the Western Wall rabbi, Rabbi Yehuda Getz, and Ashkenazi chief rabbi Shlomo Goren to discover the exact location of the Holy of Holies and to dig a tunnel between the Western Wall and the Temple Mount led to violent confrontations. In similar circumstances and based on the same fear, violent confrontations broke out between Israeli forces and Palestinian mobs in July 1988 and again in September 1996 (Klein 2001: 273–78). The strengthening of the fundamentalist streams of Judaism and Christianity toward the end of the twentieth century further fueled Palestinian fears of Jewish-Christian collusion to reestablish the Jewish Temple on the ruins of the Islamic holy sites (Gorenberg 2000).

The Israelis proposed, through the United States, a different approach, which would preserve the Temple Mount area or alternatively the entire holy basin as one sovereign unit. Sovereignty, according to this proposal, would remain with Israel, while most operational powers would be in Palestinian hands. This may be seen as a kind of special arrangement or regime; similar proposals would later be put forward after the conclusion of the Camp David summit. However, the Palestinians did not agree and continued to demand full territorial sovereignty. Toward the end of the conference, the Americans also proposed dividing the Old City. The Muslim and Christian Quarters would be under full Palestinian sovereignty and administered by the municipality of al-Quds. Sovereignty over the Armenian and Jewish Quarters would be in Israeli hands, and they would be administered by the Jerusalem municipality (*Ha'aretz* 28 July 2000; *al-Quds* and *al-Ayyam* 21 July 2000; Haniyya 2000; *Kol al-Arab* 8 August 2000; Shikaki 2000; Sher 2001: 187–88).

The American formula linked sovereignty in the Old City to sovereignty in the interior neighborhoods. One possibility was to fully divide sovereignty between Israel and Palestine, as outlined above (the 2:2 formula). In that case, however, the Palestinians would receive fewer autonomous powers in the inner circle of Palestinian neighborhoods. Alternatively, they would receive full sovereignty in the inner neighborhoods and less than that in their two quarters of the Old City. As for the holy places, the Americans proposed preserving formal Israeli sovereignty but granting the Palestinians all actual administrative powers (*Ha'aretz* 21, 24, 26, 27, 28 July 2000). The Americans rejected the Palestinian demands, and as a general rule their position was closer to that of the Israelis than to that of the Palestinians in all matters concerning the dispute over the future of the historical and religious heart of Jerusalem.

It should be noted that the Americans laid the foundation at Camp David for a new international consensus, to replace the former consensus as expressed in UN Security Council resolution 242. According to the Arab and international interpretation of resolution 242, East Jerusalem is occupied territory and should be separated from West Jerusalem along the prewar line. This was the official Palestinian position, brought to the conference by the Palestinian delegation. Over the years, the Palestinian position has been based on the "international legitimacy" expressed by UN resolutions, especially resolution 242. At Camp David an attempt was made to create a new informal international consensus whereby resolution 242 would not apply to Jerusalem. Jerusalem's permanent border would not be along the 4 June 1967 lines. The Palestinians had hoped that the Americans would support their position on this issue, but they were disappointed. However, they could claim that the Americans had accepted the resolution 242 standard with regard to the rest of the West Bank territories conquered by Israel in 1967.

The Americans put pressure on Israel to agree to the principle of territorial exchange, and on the Palestinians to agree to the annexation to Israel of three principal settlement blocks, two of which are located in the Jerusalem metropolitan area. This could be seen as an application of resolution 242 to the West Bank and Gaza Strip because, in return for the territory of the three settlement blocks to be annexed by Israel, Palestine would receive territory that had been under Israeli sovereignty before 1967. The magnitude of territorial compensation for the settlement blocks to be annexed was a subject for separate negotiations, but the principle was established. The West Bank and Gaza Strip are one unit, and Israel must compensate the Palestinians out of its own sovereign territory for any diminution of their area. At the same time, the Palestinian state would cover only the 1967 territories.

The Palestinians demanded that the built-up areas of Jerusalem's Jewish neighborhoods (some 26 square kilometers) be counted as territory for which they would receive territorial compensation in a ratio of 1:1. Israel rejected this demand, considering these areas to be urban neighborhoods and not settlements. The Americans did not support the Palestinian position, even though the traditional American position since 1967 had been, as stated by Ambassador Charles W. Yost in a July 1969 speech at the United Nations, that "the part of Jerusalem that came under the control of Israel in the June war, like other areas occupied by Israel, is occupied territory" (Moore 1974: 993–94; and see Klein 2001: 93). This means that the dividing line in Jerusalem would pass through East Jerusalem and not between East and West Jerusalem. In addition, the territorial exchange would take place only within the territories conquered in 1967. Arafat reconciled himself to the necessity of recognizing the Jewish neighborhoods in East Jerusalem as part of Israel. He was deeply disappointed, however, by the Israeli and American position and their demand that Israel be given powers and status in the Arab Quarter of the Old City, the Temple Mount, and the neighborhoods adjoining these.

The Palestinians agreed in principle to Israel's proposal to "exchange neighborhoods" and that it annex Gush Etzion, Ma'aleh Adumim, and

Givat Ze'ev. But they rejected the Israeli proposals concerning the interior neighborhoods of East Jerusalem, including the Old City. The Palestinian delegation insisted on the grant of full sovereignty in these areas to the Palestinians and was shocked to hear Israel's demand for sovereignty over the Temple Mount. The combination of Israel's demand for sovereignty over the Temple Mount and its demand that an area for Jewish collective worship be set aside there was unacceptable to the Palestinian delegation. A more complicated version of the Israeli proposal was put forward, to the effect that Morocco as representative of the Islamic states would construct a building that would have the status of a diplomatic legation, part of which would serve as a synagogue. The Palestinians rejected this proposal as well. Members of the Palestinian delegation asked why a secular government would give so much weight to the position of religious and nationalist extremists and why Israel would court the danger of turning the national conflict into a religious one as well. According to the Palestinians, the subject had never before been raised in their contacts with Israeli individuals and institutions. They found it difficult to accept the claim presented by the Israeli negotiators that secular Jews also feel a connection, mainly historical, to the Temple Mount. If the site is so holy, asked the Palestinians, why is entry forbidden by Jewish law, and why did Moshe Dayan prohibit Jews from conducting organized prayer there in 1967?

The Palestinians further asked why the secular representatives of the Israeli government described the site as the location of the Temple and demanded the right to worship there. And although it was not explicitly stated, it may be that the Palestinians harbored the fear that permitting Jewish worship on the Temple Mount would lead to an Israeli demand that construction of the Jewish Temple be permitted as well, in the name of freedom of religion. The Palestinians found support for their fear in the reasoning employed by Minister Ben-Ami in favor of Israeli sovereignty over the entire Temple Mount or over its subterranean portion: the presence of the ruins of the Jewish Temple in the depths of the earth. They disputed the very determination that the Jewish Temple had stood there and claimed that it had never been archeologically proven (Haniyya 2000). "They claim that two thousand years ago they had a holy place there. I doubt this fact," said Abu Mazen after the Camp David summit (*Kol al-Arab* 8 August 2000). The Israeli delegation perceived the Palestinian response as derogatory and arrogant and an indication of Palestinian unwillingness to recognize a Jewish connection to the site (Shavit 14 September 2001).

Publicly and officially, the Palestinian position was that the Jewish Quarter and the Western Wall would be under autonomous Israeli administration but not under Israeli sovereignty, as all of East Jerusalem that was conquered in 1967 must return to its Palestinian owners (Abu Mazen 2000). But the Israelis understood at Camp David and even earlier that Arafat would agree to a division of sovereignty in the Old City according to a formula of 3:1. The Palestinian delegation demanded full Palestinian sovereignty over all the Arab neighborhoods in the eastern city. This would leave the Western Wall and the Jewish Quarter, as well as the new Jewish neighborhoods in East Jerusalem, under Israeli sovereignty (*Ha'aretz* 26 July 2000; Shikaki 2000). In other words, the Palestinians unofficially gave up on the application of their interpretation of the UN Security Council resolution 242 to East Jerusalem, which would mean dividing the eastern city from its western part along the 4 June 1967 lines. They accepted the principle that the dividing line would run through the eastern city between the Jewish and Arab neighborhoods. They did not, however, agree to any other compromise, particularly in the Arab neighborhoods in the heart of the city—the Old City and adjacent neighborhoods. The Palestinians claimed that, to them, Jerusalem is the Old City and the adjacent Arab neighborhoods, the city as it had been defined by the Jordanian authorities. Consequently, their sovereignty over that area must equal their full sovereignty over the suburbs of the eastern city (Abu Dis). Abu Dis is in no way a substitute for the Old City, they argued (Haniyya 2000).

The Israelis' impression was that there were differences of opinion within the Palestinian delegation. Muhammad Dahlan (head of the preventive security force in the Gaza Strip), Muhammad Rashid (Arafat's economic adviser and confidant in diplomatic matters), and Hassan 'Asfour (the minister responsible for nongovernmental organizations)—the "young leadership" of the Gaza Strip—believed that the Palestinians should further soften their position. They were sometimes joined by Sa'eb Erekat, minister of local government and municipal affairs, and Akram Haniyya, editor of the semiofficial daily *al-Ayyam*. However, the older and more senior Abu Mazen (secretary-general of the PLO Executive Committee) and Abu 'Ala (chairman of the Palestinian Authority's Legislative Council) insisted that the Palestinians not make any concessions beyond what their delegation had already conceded (Benziman 23 March 2001; Sher 2001: 186).

When the conference reached a dead end, there was discussion of the possibility of deferring decision on either the entire Jerusalem question or only the issue of sovereignty over the three disputed areas, for a greater or lesser amount of time. In the meantime, the Arab neighborhoods would enjoy the special autonomous status proposed by Israel. That way, neither side would formally concede its demand for sovereignty in the disputed area. Barak was willing to discuss this idea, even though it did not fulfill his goal of signing of a agreement ending the conflict as a whole and of resolving the dispute over sovereignty on the Temple Mount. At least those disagreements would not prevent an agreement from being signed on the rest of the permanent status issues. Arafat, however, rejected this proposal as well (*Ha'aretz* 21 July 2000).

During the summit, Arafat demanded sovereignty over the churches in the Christian Quarter. He was careful to emphasize that the question of East Jerusalem was not only an Islamic issue but a Christian one as well, just as it was not only a Palestinian but also a Muslim issue. Christians make up some 3 percent of the Palestinian population and some 8 percent of Jerusalem's inhabitants. Christian leaders were alarmed by the idea of Palestinian sovereignty over the Christian holy sites and by the American compromise proposal distinguishing between sovereignty over the Armenian Quarter, which would remain with Israel, and sovereignty over the Christian Quarter, which would be in Palestinian hands. The heads of the Latin Catholic, Greek Orthodox, and Armenian Orthodox Churches wrote to Clinton, Barak, and Arafat to express their opposition to the two Christian quarters being placed under different sovereign regimes. They also demanded international guarantees ensuring that believers of all three faiths would enjoy freedom of access to their religious institutions as well as freedom of worship; they sought to go to Camp David in order to make their voices heard there (*Ha'aretz* 23, 25 July 2000). This unusual step revealed a lack of confidence in both the Israeli and the Palestinian authorities. Although most Christian Arabs are Palestinian by nationality, they did not receive significant support from the Palestinian authorities in dealing with the pressures of radical Islam in Jerusalem. Therefore, the heads of the Christian communities sought to ensure through international guarantees that their religious rights would be respected. In principle, the international guarantees were not meant to guarantee the rights of Christians only. However, the fact that Islamic and Jewish rights were supposed to be protected by the two governments respectively placed Christian rights at a disadvantage. This invited the idea of creating an international framework that would ensure their protection.

A basic agreement had already been signed, in February 2000, between the PLO and the Holy See in its capacity as the sovereign authority of the

Roman Catholic Church. In the preamble to the agreement both sides called for granting Jerusalem a special status and for securing it with international guarantees. This special status was meant to ensure freedom of worship and conscience for all, as well as equality before Palestinian law for the three monotheistic religions, their institutions, and their communities of believers. It was also intended to protect the special identity and holy character of the city, its universal significance and cultural and religious heritage, and its holy places, as well as freedom of access to and worship at those sites. Finally, the status quo was to be preserved in those holy places to which the status quo applied (notably, the Church of the Holy Sepulcher).

The agreement set out the PLO's commitment to preserve freedom of worship and of conscience. The PLO also promised to anchor in legislation the principle of the equality of persons and the human and civil rights of all the citizens of Palestine and to prevent discrimination against individuals or groups on the basis of their membership in any religious community, or of their faith or form of worship. The PLO further undertook to grant autonomy in practice to the institutions of the Roman Catholic Church. The PLO recognized the authority of the Roman Catholic Church to operate its religious, welfare, charitable, educational, and cultural institutions as it saw fit. The PLO also recognized the right of Church institutions to autonomously determine their own internal procedures as well as to enjoy fiscal autonomy (*al-Quds* 16 February 2000; www.pna.net/ events 16 February 2000). The agreement assumed that the PLO would be sovereign in East Jerusalem, including the Old City. In return for this support of its demand, the PLO undertook to grant autonomy to the Roman Catholic Church in all of the areas of its activity and to establish freedom of worship and conscience by law in Palestine. However, this agreement did not satisfy the representatives of the Latin Catholic, Greek Orthodox, and Armenian Orthodox Churches, and they demanded that their rights be anchored in an international document such as that discussed at Camp David.

After the Camp David summit, the Holy See announced in Rome that it supported the establishment of an international mechanism for supervising the Christian holy places in the holy basin, without internationalizing the city as it had previously wanted (the Corpus Spiritus separation mandated in the UN partition plan of 1947). "Only a special status and international guarantees can protect the holiest parts of the Holy City and ensure freedom of religion and of belief to all believers in the Zone and in the entire world, who look to Jerusalem as to the hub of peace and of coexistence" (*Ha'aretz* 24 July, 16 August 2000). The patriarchs' letter and the pope's words prodded Arafat to include Christian representatives in the official delegations that accompanied him, immediately following Camp David, to the meeting of the Arab League and to the special session of the Jerusalem Committee of the Conference of Islamic States. In this way Arafat hoped to allay Christian fears, to minimize the damage caused by the letter sent by the patriarchs to Camp David, and to cultivate the image of an enlightened leader.

The summary published at the conclusion of the Camp David conference emphasized first of all that both sides agreed that the negotiations' aim was to put an end to decades of conflict and to reach a final and fair peace agreement. Second, both sides undertook to continue their efforts to reach an agreement on all of the permanent status issues as quickly as possible. Third, they agreed that the only way to attain such an agreement was through negotiations based on UN Security Council resolutions 242 and 338 (www.yale.edu/lawweb/avalon/mideast/mid028.htm). The last item is important, as prior to and during the conference, the Palestinians demanded that Israel recognize these resolutions as the basis for the talks and implement them as they had been implemented in the Israel-Egypt and Israel-Jordan peace agreements. Israel refused, however, claiming that the Palestinians were not a relevant party to those resolutions because they did not have a state entity either when the resolutions were adopted or at present. The Palestinians saw the Israeli position as provocative arrogance and denial of one of the basic principles of the Israeli-Palestinian peace process to which Israel had committed itself in the Oslo accords.

The summary also states that both sides understand the importance of refraining from unilateral actions that would influence the results of the negotiations and that the dispute between them is to be solved only through negotiations and good will (*Ha'aretz* 26 July 2000). Israel interpreted this as a Palestinian undertaking to refrain from unilaterally declaring a Palestinian state, and the Palestinians interpreted it as an Israeli undertaking to refrain from expanding settlements and from taking unilateral actions in Jerusalem.

With regard to the remaining unresolved questions on sovereignty in Jerusalem, the Palestinians perceived Israel's discourse at Camp David as hegemonic. Israel's proposals were based on the preservation of its superior legal and symbolic position on the Temple Mount, the Old City, and the adjacent neighborhoods. These proposals granted Israel sovereignty over the territory, which would contain enclaves of Palestinian personal and institutional identity. Israel proposed to the Palestinians a hierarchy of sovereign status and powers and the establishment of a special regime on the Temple Mount. The Israeli proposal would have upgraded the status of Palestinians living under Israeli supreme sovereignty. They would go from being East Jerusalemites holding Jordanian passports and the right to vote for the Palestinian Authority's national political institutions to being full citizens of the new state of Palestine living in Jerusalem. In addition, the political status of the Palestinian institutions ("Orient House plus," as the Israeli delegation put it) would be formalized, but the territory and overall administration would be under Israeli sovereignty.

The Palestinian discourse, on the other hand, was perceived by the Israelis as exclusivist. Arafat wanted exclusive and full sovereignty over these areas, except for the Jewish Quarter and the Western Wall. The Palestinians saw the Israeli discourse as perpetuating the situation created by the Oslo accords. Israel could rid itself of having to rule over the Palestinian population of East Jerusalem and at the same time keep its sovereignty over the area. The fear was also expressed among the Palestinians that Israel would use its sovereignty to create a situation whereby Palestinians living in Israeli territory would be pushed out of the city (Haniyya 2000). They feared that the Palestinian identity of people living in the area would contradict Israel's supreme sovereignty there. The Palestinians refused to accept a situation in which they would enjoy many but not all municipal powers and would cede political sovereignty over the historical and religious heart of Jerusalem. It should be emphasized that the Palestinians accompanied their exclusivist stance with a denial of any Jewish historical or religious connection to the Temple Mount. This negatively impinged on the atmosphere at the talks, as well as the willingness of the Israeli delegation to listen to the Palestinians' claims. Once the dispute became public, the Palestinian rejection of the Jewish people's historical and religious connection to the Temple Mount enraged the Israeli public, which felt hurt, threatened, and rejected. The atmosphere was further inflamed by the publicity in Israel surrounding excavations and works performed by the Muslims beneath the Temple Mount, which crudely damaged Jewish archeological remnants.

The Public Discourse

The Camp David summit broke three Israeli taboos. The first was against any negotiation of Jerusalem's borders. The second was against conceding Israeli sovereignty anywhere or in any form. The third was against challenging the assumption of a national consensus against dividing Jerusalem. Growing out of a small-scale public discussion begun earlier, the public debate in Israel on the fate of Jerusalem intensified during the conference. The discussion centered on questions that only a handful of people had ever asked publicly: What is Jewish Jerusalem? What is the fundamental Israeli interest in Jerusalem? Is Jerusalem really united? Furthermore, these questions received answers that would have been unthinkable in the past. Only weeks earlier such questions had been proscribed and anyone who asked them was denounced.

The public discourse that commenced once the taboos were broken was at base traditionally Zionist. It centered around one of the primary doctrines of Zionism—the vital need to obtain and maintain a massive Jewish majority in Israel as a whole and in all its parts, including Jerusalem. In this case, the demographic issue was the necessity of preserving the Jewish-Zionist character of Israel's capital. The public was now open, as it had not been previously, to learning about how life was really lived in Jerusalem and to contemplating Jerusalem as it really was rather than how they imagined it to be.

The Jerusalem Institute for Israel Studies publications and conferences in 1999–2000 made an important contribution to freeing the public from the myth of united Jerusalem. As a result, many Israelis became willing to apply to the capital the same demographic criteria that had long been applied to the West Bank and Gaza Strip. The institute worked to demystify the land held by Israel in Jerusalem and to introduce new concepts into the public discourse. The most important of these were new concepts of sovereignty that could serve as alternatives to the conventional concept. One of these, for example, was the concept of functional sovereignty developed by Ruth Lapidoth. The institute also proposed alternatives for redrawing the city's boundaries, published some forty background papers, organized dozens of public conferences, and promoted its messages through the local and foreign media.

Ironically, the Israeli right wing and the political parties that represent it made a considerable contribution to opening up the Jerusalem issue. When right-wing leaders issued warnings of the growing Palestinian presence in Jerusalem and accused the dovish Israeli government of doing nothing to halt it, the Israeli "person in the street" learned that a third of Jerusalem's inhabitants were Palestinians and that Jerusalem's Palestinian community had developed its own local institutions and a vibrant community in the eastern city. The existence of this discussion pleased the delegation at Camp David. They were encouraged by the fact that ideas for dividing control in East Jerusalem had been broached without the sky falling in. Many Israelis began to support the delegation's position that redrawing the lines of Israeli sovereignty in Jerusalem was in Israel's interest. Indications of this could be seen in a public opinion poll commissioned by the Peace Now movement, according to which the proposal on Jerusalem put forward by Barak and his delegation was supported by 73 percent of Barak voters and 43 percent of the general public. Furthermore, 47 percent of Barak voters and 27 percent of the general public supported dividing sovereignty in Jerusalem in a manner similar to the formula proposed by Arafat, with the Jewish neighborhoods to Israel and the Arab neighborhoods to the Palestinians (*Ha'aretz* 12 September 2000).

The understandings reached at the conference broke a Palestinian taboo as well. This taboo held that nothing short of a full Israeli withdrawal to the pre-1967-war lines was acceptable and that unilateral Israeli policies based on force were always to be rejected. Palestinian adherence to UN resolution 242, which was based on the principle that territory is not to be acquired by war, would have required the Palestinian leadership to demand that the Jewish neighborhoods in East Jerusalem come under Palestinian sovereignty and that settlements in the West Bank, such as Ma'aleh Adumim and Givat Ze'ev, be evacuated. The Palestinian delegation broke this taboo during the Camp David talks but not in the public discourse that developed during and after Camp David. Several of the conference's participants were among the spokesmen in the post–Camp David Palestinian public discourse.

Yet the new flexibility in Israeli public opinion did not include most of the religious and ultraorthodox public. On the contrary, their position became more radical, and they put pressure from below on their spiritual and political leaders (Shilhav 2001: 34–35; Yuchtman-Ya'ar and Hermann 2000: 48–50). According to a public opinion poll commissioned by Peace Now (*Ha'aretz* 12 September 2000), there was a clear correlation between a person's level of religious observance and his or her position on the Jerusalem question. As the level of religious observance rose, so support for any compromise in Jerusalem declined. An inverse correlation was also found between the change in the public consensus and the change in the religious public's position. As the general consensus on Jerusalem changed, so the position in religious circles, particularly with regard to the Old City and the Temple Mount, became more radical. This was expressed in the growing support for the radicals' demand to change the status quo on the Temple Mount. The pressures reached as far as the Chief Rabbinical Council, the highest forum in the state-sponsored rabbinate. In 1967, immediately after the Six Day War, that body had ruled that Jews were prohibited from entering the Temple Mount; in August 2000, its members conducted a discussion on whether and where to erect a synagogue on the Temple Mount. The subject was tabled by the chief rabbi of Haifa, Rabbi Shear Yashuv Hacohen. The council decided to form a committee "to examine all the ways of realizing our rights and our sovereignty on the Temple Mount," including the right to erect a synagogue and the grant of permission for Jews to enter defined places within the area (*Ha'aretz* 8 August 2000). An organization called Temple Seekers presented the Chief Rabbinical Council with possible locations for erecting a synagogue within or adjoining the area—on the roof of the Golden Gate, over the Western Wall, or over the southern wall, locations at which the synagogue would overlook the Temple Mount without entering its sanctified air or ground space (*Ha'aretz* 10 August 2000).

Even before these events, the Chief Rabbinical Council had come out against a letter written by the Sephardi chief rabbi, Eliahu Bakshi-Doron, in which Bakshi-Doron expressed the hope that the dispute over the Temple Mount would be resolved "through honest negotiations based on mutual understanding and respect, justice and equality, and the recognition for the need to preserve the rights of every individual as a human being and every people as a people." He also wrote that "we must preserve and respect the current status and sanctity of the holy Temple Mount, which is known to others as the area of the al-Aqsa Mosque. We must be wary of every change in its status for it could desecrate the sanctity of the place and lead to the kind of bloodshed that is opposed by every religion and civilized society" (*Ha'aretz* 28, 29 June 2000). His letter raised a storm in the national-religious public and among the radicals, and there were those who called for establishing an alternative center of Jewish religious legal authority. As a result of this storm, Rabbi Bakshi-Doron explained that what he meant was that the present situation, in which sovereignty was in Israeli hands and actual administration in the hands of the Palestinian Waqf, should be preserved, and that he was concentrating on calming Palestinian fears of being ejected from the site. He wanted to prevent Jews from entering the site and also to prevent bloodshed (Kra 2 July 2000). The public pressure caused the Chief Rabbinical Council to reconsider the status quo on the Temple Mount in July 2000, and it decided to continue to prohibit Jews from entering the Temple Mount. At the same time, it came out against the excavations and construction work that the Palestinians were performing at the site (*Ha'aretz* 30 June, 4 July 2000). Only a month later, as noted above, the Chief Rabbinate decided to examine all possible ways of realizing Jewish rights and sovereignty on the

Mount. Due to differences of opinion on the subject (*Ha'aretz* 5 January 2001), the rabbinical committee has not, as of the present time (January 2002), made any decision.

The grassroots pressures and the continuing negotiations on the Temple Mount at the end of 2000 and the beginning of 2001 led a group of Knesset members from the National Religious Party to make a formal request to the two chief rabbis that they issue a special temporary dispensation to the prohibition against entering the Temple Mount so that Jews could go there to reclaim it. They claimed that the Israeli government was considering ceding sovereignty over the Temple Mount because of the Jewish legal prohibition on entering the site. The rest of the world had misunderstood the rabbinic proscription against entering the Temple Mount and had assumed that it meant that Israel could cede the site. Both chief rabbis rejected, first of all, the idea of canceling such a strict religious prohibition for political reasons. Second, they rejected the request to permit entry into the entire Temple Mount zone and not only the marginal area where, according to some rabbis, Jews may enter because it is outside the perimeters of the holy temple area. The rabbinate refused to cancel the religious prohibition, even as a temporary ruling. In parallel, it placed religious restraints on Ehud Barak's freedom to maneuver politically. The Chief Rabbinical Council ruled, "There is an absolute prohibition according to Jewish law on transferring to foreigners, indirectly or directly, any sovereignty or ownership on the Temple Mount. The very discussion of such [a step] constitutes the desecration of God's Name. . . . We remind the prime minister once again that he undertook not to cede the holy places of Israel and there is no place holier to the people of Israel than the Temple Mount" (*Ha'aretz* 5 January 2001).

Knesset member Sharon's visit to the Temple Mount; the negotiations, both before and after the visit, over who would receive sovereignty over the site; and the Intifada that broke out the day after the visit led to a change in the status quo on the visit of non-Muslims to the Temple Mount. Jews and members of the Temple Mount movements were brought in in small groups and accompanied by policemen. Those who declared in advance that they intended to pray on the Temple Mount were kept from entering, and those who prayed were escorted out by the Israeli police. Supervision of the entry to the al-Aqsa Mosque and to the Dome of the Rock had since 1967 been exclusively in the hands of the Waqf, and the Israel police did not intervene in its decisions (*Ha'aretz* 10 September 2000). In any case, the majority of Jewish Temple Mount activists refrained, for religious reasons, from approaching the Muslim places of worship. The Temple Mount has been closed to non-Muslims since September 2000. In May 2001, hawkish ministers Uzi Landau (internal security) and Limor Livnat (education) called on Prime Minister Sharon to use force to open the site to all. Police commanders took the opposite view and recommended restraint in the use of force so as to avoid sparking a confrontation over such a sensitive subject. Sharon, now prime minister, accepted their recommendation in 2001. He also decided to pressure the Waqf indirectly to reopen the Temple Mount, by imposing new restrictions on Muslim access to the site for Friday prayers (*Ha'aretz* 30 July 2001). However, this decision was not implemented.

Sharon's decision was not well received among the radical groups. The Committee of Settlement Rabbis called on Israeli rabbis to instruct their congregants to go up to the Temple Mount in order to prevent the Muslims from taking complete control of the site. In the long run, they said, this would also keep the government from giving foreigners sovereignty over the Temple Mount. In their estimation, the Jewish public was indifferent to the fate of the Temple Mount because it had not been made a focus of national-religious sentiment. This they sought to change by encouraging large numbers of religious Jews to visit the place (*Ha'aretz* 20 July 2001). The Temple Mount Faithful announced that they would conduct, on the Tisha B'Av fast in July 2001, a cornerstone-laying ceremony for the Third Temple next to the Mount's Mughrabi Gate. They also declared that they would try to insinuate some of their members into the Temple Mount by dressing them as Arabs.

Rumors began circulating in East Jerusalem connecting these two plans, claiming that the cornerstone would be laid on the Temple Mount under police protection. The Arab-Muslim leadership in East Jerusalem and among Israel's Arab citizens called on their own publics to come to defend al-Haram al-Sharif. It is not clear whether the rumor was spread deliberately in order to mobilize the Palestinian public to action in the framework of the Intifada, or whether it expressed an authentic fear. In any case, the call spread quickly. In an attempt to calm tempers, the Israel Police issued a clarification, stating that the ceremony would be conducted outside the walls and on a very small scale. The police also cooperated with members of the Palestinian security forces and with Arab members of the Knesset in preserving public order on the Temple Mount. Remembering that seventeen Palestinians had been killed in similar circumstances in 1990 at the height of the first Intifada, the police wanted to prevent violence. The measures taken in 2001 did not prevent Arabs from throwing stones down on Jews praying at the Western Wall and policemen who were guarding them, but in the resulting altercations no one was killed. Nineteen policemen and twenty Palestinians were injured, however (*Ha'aretz* 30 July 2001). Reacting to the call issued by the settlement rabbis and to the Temple Mount Faithful's actions, Israel's chief rabbi, Eliahu Bakshi-Doron, issued an announcement addressed to the country's rabbis that emphasized that "only God will instruct the rabbis of Israel how to renew the Temple ritual. We believe that the Third Temple will be built by God himself. . . . In no case can an individual or group be allowed to take matters into their own hands and to perform an act like laying a cornerstone for the Third Temple." Rabbi Bakshi-Doron stressed that this was not just his personal opinion. His pronouncement, he said, expressed the consensus of "all rabbis all over the world who are faithful to the Torah and the law we have received from generations past." He signed his declaration in the name of the Israeli chief rabbinate (document in possession of the author).

Rabbi Bakshi-Doron's declaration made it clear that there are profound disagreements between the chief rabbi and the settlement rabbis. The latter are an important group of rabbis who back the institution of the chief rabbinate and the chief rabbis themselves. It was exceptional for them to come out against an official and traditional (since 1967) position held by the chief rabbinate. When they focus their gaze on the Temple Mount, and radical movements and personalities call for the use of force to maintain the right of Jews to enter the Temple Mount, they are expressing profound concern about changes that have taken place in the position of the public at large and of the Israeli leadership on the Temple Mount and Jerusalem. Their demands were not meant to reflect a dominant mood but rather to change it.

The Palestinian delegation was no less pleased with the discussions taking place within its constituency (Haniyya 2000). There was, however, a big difference. While the Israeli nonreligious public discourse was dovish and moving in the direction of compromise, the Palestinian public discourse was hawkish and uniform. In fact, the Palestinian public discourse reflected changes that had taken place in public opinion. The Palestinian public no longer believed that Israel wished to achieve an agreement and respect its previous obligations. A new Palestinian political opposition had also come into being. In light of events at Camp David, the Palestinian leadership made no effort to change the public discourse. On the contrary, the leadership encouraged the new thinking and hoped to benefit from it.

The Palestinian public demanded that the Palestinian delegation make no concessions on Jerusalem and that it adhere to the concept of international legitimacy. This meant implementation of the principle of dividing sovereignty in Jerusalem along the 4 June 1967 lines, in the context of a solution based not on the current balance of power and Israeli superiority but rather on justice and "international legitimacy." Rather than concede on the demand for Palestinian sovereignty over the Jewish neighborhoods in former Jordanian territory, articles in the Palestinian dailies proposed that Israelis who were so inclined could remain in the neighborhoods and accept Palestinian citizenship. Their neighborhoods would, however, also be open to Palestinian habitation.

In addition, during the Camp David summit, in July 2000, the Palestinian Legislative Council passed a law declaring that any interpretation or agreement that attempted to diminish or deny Palestinian rights in Jerusalem would be considered null and void. The council also added paragraphs to the Local Institutions Law providing for Jerusalem to be the capital of the state of Palestine and the seat of all three branches of the Palestinian government, executive, legislative, and judicial. The law also declares that Palestine is sovereign over all the holy places in Jerusalem and responsible for ensuring freedom of religion in those places. The Palestinian legislation came as a response to the Knesset's enactment in 1980 of the "Basic Law: Jerusalem," which defined Jerusalem as Israel's capital, and the amendment to that law passed in 2000. The Israeli amendment provides that "No power that concerns the area of Jerusalem and that is granted according to law to the State of Israel or to the Municipality of Jerusalem, is to be transferred to a foreign entity of a political governmental character or to any other similar foreign entity, whether permanently or for a limited period of time" unless such transfer has been approved by a majority of sixty-one Knesset members (*Ha'aretz* 27, 28 November 2000). The legislative initiatives in the Knesset in 1980 and twenty years later originated with the hawkish opposition, which wanted to tie the government's hands in negotiations, in 1980 in the negotiations with the Egyptians and in 2000 with the Palestinians. The same was true of the Palestinians, who wanted to rein in Arafat. Hawks on both sides wanted to constrain their negotiators and keep them from making concessions that were too generous.

Prominent among those hawks on the Palestinian side were the members of the local Jerusalem establishment centered at Orient House (Hass 25 July 2000). At the beginning of July and in early August, the Jerusalem Palestinian leadership staged the signing of documents called the Covenant of Jerusalem (*'Ahad al-Quds*). These are documents in which the heads of Palestinian institutions in Jerusalem express their adherence to the principle of Palestinian sovereignty in the city.

The first such document was composed in reaction to talks between the representatives of Israel and the PLO in preparation for the Camp David summit. The document's authors sensed that the Palestinian negotiators might go too far in their concessions and that they needed to be restrained. Written in flowery language, it mainly constitutes a vow in Allah's name to continue to carry the banner of the Palestinian and Arab connection to Jerusalem and a pledge to continue working toward the elimination of the Israeli occupation in East Jerusalem. The Palestinian document's starting point is completely religious: Jerusalem's holiness to Muslims, their religious and historical right to the city, and their commitment to grant religious recognition to the Jews, in keeping with an earlier Muslim covenant on Jerusalem known in English as the Covenant of ʿOmar. (Research indicates that the source of the covenant is Umayyad caliph ʿOmar Ibn ʿAbed al-ʾAziz, who was caliph from 717 to 720. But Muslim tradition attributes the covenant to the second caliph, ʿOmar Ibn al-Khattab, who conquered Jerusalem in 638. The Covenant of ʿOmar granted Christians and Jews a protected but inferior status in the framework of the Islamic caliphate.) The new Palestinian document emphasizes that Jerusalem is Arab, Palestinian, Islamic, and Christian, the eternal capital of the state of Palestine. Its signatories must protect the Arab, Muslim, and Christian character of Jerusalem and fight against the distortion of the truth as well as the physical Judaization in which Israel is engaging in the city. They must oppose the occupation in every possible way and cultivate internal unity. In short, no Palestinian right in Jerusalem is to be ceded.

The document was signed by religious figures, foremost among them Shaykh ʿAkramah Sabri, head of the Supreme Muslim Council; Faisal Husseini, who held the Jerusalem portfolio on the PLO Executive Committee; Jamal Othman Nasser, governor of the Jerusalem district; and members of the Legislative Council from the Jerusalem district (al-Quds 8 June 2000). After the Camp David summit and the renewal of the permanent status talks, Orient House organized an additional show of loyalty to Jerusalem at the end of August 2000, centered on a second text, also called the Covenant of Jerusalem. This document stated that Jerusalem is an Arab, Palestinian, Islamic, and Christian city, the eternal capital and heart of hearts of the state of Palestine, but it ignored the Jewish religious connection to Jerusalem. Sovereignty over Jerusalem is a national right that is not to be ceded, and without recognition of this right there will be no peace. This document demanded that the Palestinian authorities strengthen the Arab and Palestinian identity of Jerusalem by Palestinian action and by not recognizing Israel's actions in the eastern city as legitimate (*al-Quds* and *al-Ayyam* 1 August 2000; *al-Ayyam* 30 August 2000).

The radical discourse also encompassed Arab countries that were American allies—Jordan, Egypt, and Saudi Arabia. Their leaders categorically refused the requests of several Palestinian leaders that the public be prepared for concessions to Israel. Their pressure on Arafat to compromise was restricted to telephone calls; in public they promised to stand behind him no matter what he did, while enthusiastically defending his position on the Islamic holy sites in Jerusalem (Beilin 2001).

In Abeyance: Post–Camp David Talks

After his failure to reach an agreement with Israel at Camp David, Arafat hoped he would be able to achieve his objectives by putting into operation a de facto Palestinian state. He embarked on this strategy on 13 September 2000, seven years after the signing of the Israeli-Palestinian Declaration of Principles and two years after the two sides were to have reached a permanent settlement. Such a state did not require a euphonious declaration of independence but rather an internationally recognized and active political apparatus that could counterbalance the political power of a strong, U.S.-supported Israel. To achieve this, he set off from Camp David for a long series of visits to other countries. His hopes were dashed. The leaders of the world's most influential nations made it clear that they would not support the unilateral Palestinian declaration of independence and unilateral operation of a Palestinian state. Arafat, as a consequence, realized that the only way for him to get a state was by reaching an agreement with Israel first, only after which an internationally recognized state would follow. Israel's concessions at Camp David and the subsequent dramatic change in Israeli public opinion about Jerusalem had led to a sharp change in the international diplomatic climate—it now favored Israel. Clinton had constructed a new, if still informal, international consensus on the Israel-Palestine conflict (*Ha'aretz* 25 September 2000), summed up in his statement at the end of the conference that Israel had gone a longer way toward an agreement than had the Palestinians. However, the Palestinian leadership's political crisis did not lead it to soften its position. Moreover, from the Palestinian point of view the Camp David dialogue had not yet reached its end. Arafat claimed, rather, that Camp David had been a "pre-summit." The true summit conference would be convened in the future

(Haniyya 2000). From within the Palestinian community there was strong pressure on Arafat and the rest of the leadership to pursue an aggressive line with Israel and not to give in to international demands for flexibility.

Between the time of the Camp David summit and the Taba talks in January 2001, thirty-eight meetings took place between the two sides, all aimed at achieving a breakthrough. Most of Israel's positions remained as they had been at Camp David; on some issues it became less flexible. Israel demanded that the Sho'afat refugee camp and the village of al-Za'im, suburbs of East Jerusalem, be moved to create a broad contiguous area of Israeli sovereignty that would include Ma'aleh Adumim and the road to the Dead Sea. Nor did Israel want to evacuate its settlements within the city of Hebron or adjacent Kiryat Arba. Israel also demanded the annexation of two small settlements in the northern Gaza Strip, on the border with Israel. Finally, it also demanded a declaration of the end of the conflict between the two peoples upon the signing of the declaration of principles for the permanent status agreement, even before the signing of the detailed agreement and before its full implementation (Sher 2001: 253, 257–58). Here Barak was demonstrating his, and Israel's, political and psychological need to achieve a quick end to the historic conflict. For their part, the Palestinians feared a trap. They were suspicious because of the failure of several Israeli governments to implement a number of parts of the Oslo agreements.

It should be noted that Israel's representatives, led by Barak, had concluded from the Palestinian position at Camp David that Israel had no partner for reaching an agreement. But the United States consistently sought to mitigate this extreme conclusion (Sher 2001: 231, 249). The Americans' measure of the Palestinians' room for maneuverability was apparently made on the basis of an aggregation of Dahlan's position, according to which the Palestinian Authority would agree to a 7 percent annexation by Israel in exchange for Israel's ceding an area equivalent to 2 percent adjacent to the Gaza Strip, together with Abu 'Ala's position, which allowed for restricted Israeli air force use of West Bank airspace. Israel would not be able to leave ground forces on the Jordan River in routine periods but could deploy its forces there in an emergency. The American view of the refugee issue was that there was no escaping mention of the right of return in the final agreement but that its actual implementation could be restricted. In any case, the Americans made clear to Israel that they opposed the Israeli demand of a Jerusalem–Dead Sea corridor, nor would they support an annexation of 10.5 percent of the West Bank to Israel because that meant turning 60,000 Palestinians into permanent residents of Israel. The Americans offered to supply Israel with a map in which 80 percent of the settlers would be annexed on only 5 percent of the West Bank's land, with only 4,000 Palestinians becoming residents of Israel (Sher 2001: 278, 285).

The critical issue that prevented agreement at Camp David and thereafter was the Temple Mount. The American approach remained as it had been: dividing the disputed areas into "slices" of sovereignty. At a certain stage, the Americans proposed dividing the Temple Mount into four areas of sovereignty: the main buildings, that is, the al-Aqsa Mosque and Dome of the Rock; the plaza area; the external wall including the Western Wall; and the subterranean spaces. The two sides would have a different mix of powers over each of these areas, according to the American proposal. This form of partnership and division was supposed to satisfy the demand for a Jewish connection to the Temple Mount as well as the demand for a Muslim connection to the Western Wall, and vice versa, and to divide powers and sovereignty between the two sides (*Ha'aretz* 30 August 2000). But Arafat rejected the proposal.

In parallel, Egypt and the United States worked to create a comfortable atmosphere for continuing the talks behind the scenes. The United States saw to the cancellation of a meeting in Tehran of the Conference of Islamic States plenum, which had been requested by Arafat. Instead, the organization's Jerusalem Committee met in Morocco. The United States made sure that the concluding statement of that meeting would be tepid and would not tie Arafat's hands. However, Arafat tied his own hands when he repeated, in his speech at that forum, the position he had expressed at Camp David. The United States also arranged summit meetings between Clinton and Arafat and between Clinton and Barak, at an unusual international forum: the Millennium Conference held in New York on 6 September, with more than 100 heads of state participating. In his speech before the leaders of the world, President Clinton emphasized the importance of peace between Israel and the Palestinians. At that point, had Arafat accepted even one of the compromise proposals raised since the conclusion of the Camp David summit, all the world's leaders would have cheered him. After praising Barak for the flexibility he demonstrated at Camp David, they would have commended Arafat's contribution to peace. But he did not avail himself of the opportunity.

After the Camp David summit, another Jerusalem Institute fellow and I drafted a document that was presented to Prime Minister Barak on 6 August. We suggested several possible solutions to the problem of sovereignty. It was obvious that the Palestinians rejected out of hand full Israeli territorial sovereignty; nor would they accept a grant of functional sovereignty while Israel preserved a hegemonic status. Therefore, we proposed that the sides agree to joint sovereignty or to defer deciding the issue of sovereignty on the Temple Mount for an agreed period of time. Another idea was that the Temple Mount might be declared a sovereignty-free area or a site of divine sovereignty. Should neither of these proposals be acceptable, the paper suggested, the agreement could declare that the parties had not agreed on the question of supreme sovereignty, but for the purpose of everyday life they had agreed to a division of administrative and judicial powers (*Jerusalem Post* 28 September 2000; *Ma'ariv* 28 August 2000; *Ha'aretz* 20 August, 1 September 2000; Sher 2001: 246).

Israel then proposed that the entire Old City be placed under a special regime. Instead of dividing sovereignty, the two sides would divide powers and authorities between them, while agreeing to defer the issue of whose sovereignty—including the possibility of divine sovereignty—should apply to the site. These proposals created an egalitarian discourse in that they placed both sides on an equal footing, as opposed to Israel's proposals at Camp David emphasizing its own superiority. The proposals were passed on to Egypt and the United States, who checked with Arafat as to whether he would be willing to accept them (*Ha'aretz* 1 September 2000). Arafat rejected outright any form of joint sovereignty over the Temple Mount. He also rejected the Israeli proposal to defer the sovereignty issue while freezing the existing situation on the Temple Mount and the Old City and declaring the conflict ended, even though the two sides would still have conflicting claims. Arafat continued to demand full Palestinian sovereignty over the site (*Ha'aretz* 30 August 2000).

After the Camp David summit, President Clinton contacted King Abdallah of Jordan and President Hosni Mubarak of Egypt and asked them to help persuade Arafat to compromise on Jerusalem. Egypt was piqued at not being updated in real time about events at Camp David and about having been scolded by the White House for not acting as America expected it to act, but it took up the challenge. Together with the Americans and Palestinians, Egypt studied the concepts of joint sovereignty, absence of sovereignty, and divine sovereignty that were suggested to it by the United States. Egypt made clear to Israel from the start that Israeli sovereignty was not an option. After examining them, Egypt announced that it rejected these alternative concepts (Sher 2001: 250, 253, 257). It seems that the rejection was due not just to Israel's position on the Temple Mount and the holy basin but rather to Israel's positions on the entire range of issues in dispute. Israel suggested that the Temple Mount be left without sovereignty, while each side would ask the UN to recognize its claim to sovereignty. The UN would also recognize the division of sovereign powers between the two sides, as set out in an agreement signed by them. The Israeli proposal was based on an approach developed by academic experts who had met with Barak and on the working papers produced by the ECF and the Jerusalem Institute concerning the special regime in the holy basin. The official Israeli proposal included a restriction on placing national symbols such as flags anywhere other than at the entry point to the holy basin; a prohibition against locating government institutions in the holy basin, with the exception of religious-management bodies; administration of the holy basin by a joint committee; and location of national institutions at an equal distance from the holy basin (a direct line drawn from the Temple Mount to the Knesset building is the same length as a line drawn from the Temple Mount to the building designated for the Palestinian parliament in Abu Dis). Security and public order would be administered jointly. Muslims and Arabs would enter the holy basin at points different from those used by Israeli citizens. Within the holy basin there would be freedom of movement with the exception of restrictions that would apply to the Temple Mount—the entry of Jews to the Temple Mount would be coordinated with the Palestinian Waqf. Jurisdiction would be linked to the individual, with Israelis subject to Israeli law and Palestinians subject to Palestinian law.

To these egalitarian principles Israel added, however, a few proposals in the same spirit as those it, and President Clinton, had offered at Camp David. Residual rights in the Jewish and Armenian Quarters would be in Israeli hands, and in the Muslim and Christian Quarters in Palestinian hands. On the Temple Mount Israel wanted to receive powers and standing equal to that of Palestine, including freedom of worship for Jews, a prohibition against excavations or construction by both the Waqf and Israel, and a statement that Palestinian custodianship applied to the al-Aqsa Mosque and the Dome of the Rock and Jewish custodianship on the Temple Mount (Sher 2001: 248). This approach, which granted Israel powers and status on the Temple Mount, had been opposed by the Palestinian side at Camp David. The Palestinians had also then rejected the 2:2 compromise that Clinton had suggested for the Old City, which Israel's current proposal resembled. Instead, the Palestinians proposed to transfer to Israel about half of the Armenian Quarter, that part of it bordering the Jewish Quarter (Sher 2001: 257). Israel rejected this proposal, as it rejected the suggestion by Egyptian foreign minister Amr Musa that the

Temple Mount be placed under UN custodianship, without Israel's having any powers there (Sher 2001: 277).

Israel, for its part, rejected explicit Egyptian proposals that would have created a package deal including the Western Wall. For example, one proposal combined custodial sovereignty with residual sovereignty. The Palestinians would have custodial sovereignty over the Temple Mount and residual sovereignty over the Western Wall, whereas Israel would have residual sovereignty over the Temple Mount and custodial sovereignty over the Western Wall (*Ha'aretz* 1 September 2000). Accepting this proposal would have given the Palestinians a foothold in an area that among Jews had always been identified exclusively with Judaism, even though Islam, for its own reasons, also considers the site sacred. As an alternative, Israel proposed returning to the idea raised by President Clinton at Camp David. That is, both sides would agree to give sovereignty over the Temple Mount to a third party, the permanent members of the UN Security Council. The United States proposed adding to this international entity one or more representatives of the Islamic states. This representative would entrust Arafat with administrative and judicial authority at the Temple Mount and would appoint him as guardian of the sacred site. The agreement would set out which governmental powers would be granted to the Palestinians and the nature of the residual powers that Israel would enjoy on the Temple Mount (*Jerusalem Post* 28 September 2000; *al-Ayyam* 18 September 2000; *Ha'aretz* 12, 13, 22, 26 September 2000). As at Camp David, Arafat rejected this proposal and demanded exclusive Palestinian sovereignty.

In an attempt to reach a compromise between the egalitarian model favored by Israel and the United States and Arafat's exclusivist model, there was discussion of combining horizontal and vertical divisions of the site. The al-Aqsa Mosque and Dome of the Rock would be under Islamic sovereignty and the surrounding plaza under that of the Security Council, either alone or with representatives of the Conference of Islamic States. An alternative idea was also raised whereby the plaza would be under Islamic sovereignty, the half-meter of ground just under the surface would be under Security Council sovereignty, and the rest of the subterranean area would be under Israeli sovereignty (Eldar 27 September 2000).

Toward the end of the Millennium Conference, on 6 September 2000, Arafat rejected the idea of divine sovereignty. Divine sovereignty applies everywhere, even to the White House, he said to President Clinton. Arafat did not consider the idea of divine sovereignty as setting al-Haram al-

Sharif/the Temple Mount apart and as expressing its unique sanctity, but rather as the opposite—an idea meant to blur the site's special character. In Arafat's view, the religious element of al-Haram al-Sharif must be linked with Palestinian national identity and authority; only this would provide it with a special identity. It is not religion in and of itself that sets the site apart, but rather its connection to the Palestinian national entity. He proposed, alternatively, giving the site an Islamic and Palestinian-national identity. Israel would transfer sovereignty over al-Haram al-Sharif to Islam, through the Jerusalem Committee of the Conference of Islamic States. Egypt, Saudi Arabia, and Morocco would negotiate with Israel on behalf of the committee. The committee would grant the Palestinians sovereign jurisdiction and other powers, but the Western Wall would remain under Israeli sovereignty (al-Quds 12 September 2000).

Israel rejected this proposal outright in September. However, in December 2000, under pressure from the Intifada and with President Clinton's ideas appearing on the horizon, Israel tried to resurrect Arafat's proposal and combine it with the Israeli proposal at Camp David. Foreign Minister Shlomo Ben-Ami tried to push this idea at a Paris meeting with the foreign minister of Qatar (Ma'ariv and Ha'aretz 13 December 2000). It should be emphasized that there is a legal problem with granting sovereignty to an organization that is not a sovereign state and has no binding international status, such as the Conference of Islamic States. Moreover, such an arrangement could cause practical problems for Israel, were it to become involved in a dispute with Palestine concerning the site. Palestine would direct Israel to the Conference of Islamic States, and Israel could thus find itself without recourse to a responsible and authoritative body. From this point of view, the simplest solution would be to place the Temple Mount/ al-Haram al-Sharif under Palestinian or Israeli sovereignty. In the latter case, a problem could arise for Israel because it would bear, as the sovereign, responsibility for the site, yet the site would be administered by another entity outside its sovereignty (the Palestinian Islamic Waqf). But the symbolic value of sovereignty over the Temple Mount was stronger than any logic.

In sum, after the Camp David summit Israel sought to understand, first, whether the Palestinians' main aim was to prevent Israel from being the sole and supreme sovereign, or whether the Palestinian demand for full territorial sovereignty, according to the conservative definition of the term, was an ultimatum. Second, Israel wanted to know whether Arafat required an Arab and international safety net in order to make concessions on the Temple Mount and in the Old City. By the end of September it became clear to Israel that the Palestinian demand was in fact an ultimatum. The Palestinians insisted on possessing full sovereignty, according to the conservative nineteenth- and early-twentieth-century definitions of the term. At most, Arafat was willing to commit himself not to conduct excavations beneath the Temple Mount plaza under his sovereignty (al-Quds 12 September 2000). Barak was also willing to give a similar undertaking in the event that Arafat accepted the proposal whereby the subterranean zone beneath the Temple Mount plaza would be under Israeli sovereignty. Arafat's motivation was not negative, that is, to negate Israeli sovereignty, but rather positive—to attain Palestinian sovereignty over the site, either exclusively or through Islamic sovereignty.

High Flame: The Outbreak of the al-Aqsa Intifada

The talks did not end in agreement, and violent confrontations broke out as a result of a series of factors that were individually minor, spontaneously occurring together. Each of these factors fueled the others and contributed to the escalation of the violence. The al-Aqsa Intifada was thus not inevitable. It was a possibility that in a specific set of circumstances became reality. Palestinian popular discontent, the failure of the Camp David summit, the Palestinian public discourse, and the pressures exerted by some organizations to allow them to use force during the period of diplomatic talks all prepared the ground for the outbreak of violence. All these were in place before opposition leader Ariel Sharon visited the Temple Mount. These mounting pressures were given a powerful impetus at the end of September and beginning of October 2000: the large number of Palestinians killed and severely wounded by Israeli fire in response to the violent outbreak of the al-Aqsa Intifada. According to Palestinian Red Crescent data, on 29 September seven Palestinians were killed and 300 wounded; details on the nature of the wounds are unavailable. On 30 September, 13 Palestinians were killed and 104 wounded by live fire, and another 464 were wounded by rubber-coated steel bullets. On 1 October, the day that followed, 10 Palestinians were killed and 103 wounded by live fire, and another 314 were wounded by rubber-coated bullets. On 2 October the trend continued—9 Palestinians were killed and 114 wounded by live fire, and 230 were wounded by rubber-coated bullets. On 3 October, the number of Palestinians killed declined to 8, while 51 were wounded by live fire and 205 by rubber-coated bullets. In total, 20 Palestinians were killed in the last two days of September, 121 in October, and 123 in November (www.prc.org), whereas 4 Israelis were killed by Palestinian fire during the first five days of the Intifada. In September one Israeli was killed, 10 in October, and 22 in November. By 8 November, a full 284 Israeli citizens and military personnel had been wounded (www.mfa.gov.il).

Sharon visited the Temple Mount on 28 September 2000, with the permission of the Israeli government and despite requests by Arafat, Sa'eb Erekat, and Faisal Husseini that he not do so (Erekat 2000: 24; Stuart Macleod 26 February 2000; Husseini to Akiva Eldar, *Ha'aretz* 30 October 2000). The permit was issued for fear that prohibiting the visit would strengthen the opposition's criticism of the government, which, according to the opposition, was prepared to concede Israeli sovereignty on the Temple Mount (Mitchell Report, *Ha'aretz* 6 May 2001). It would seem that Israel's helmsmen were unaware of the fact that the visit took place ten days after the official Palestinian memorial day for the Palestinians massacred at the Sabra and Shatilla refugee camps in Beirut during the war with Israel in September 1982, when Sharon was defense minister and the Christian Phalangists who committed the massacre were Israel's allies in the war.

Because of warnings of possible Palestinian protest, about 1,000 security personnel accompanied Sharon, and force was employed against Palestinian demonstrators protesting the visit. At that time, there were about 2,000 worshipers on the Temple Mount. Faisal Husseini, who led the protesters against Sharon's visit, assumed that the protest had passed its peak and left for abroad at its conclusion. The result was that the political leader who could have calmed the atmosphere on the Temple Mount plaza was not present the next day, Friday, 29 September, which was also the eve of the two-day Jewish New Year holiday. Demonstrations continued on the al-Aqsa plaza over this long weekend. About 50,000 worshipers attended the prayers, during which Palestinian youths threw stones at police present at the Western Wall plaza. One of the first stones wounded the Jerusalem district police commander, who was evacuated to the hospital. In response, the police stormed the Temple Mount. Their entry was accompanied by the use of massive force, which caused four deaths and wounded more than 200 Palestinians at the site. Two Palestinians were killed in the Old City, and another near the al-Maqasid hospital on the Mount of Olives. In the confrontations that occurred that day all over East Jerusalem, more than seventy Israeli policemen were injured (B'tselem December 2000: 43).

The events on the Temple Mount were broadcast over the Palestinian Authority's official radio station, which was transmitting the Friday prayer service live, as it always did. The Palestinian radio's description of the confrontations gave the impression that the Palestinians were fighting to defend the Temple Mount against a brutal enemy that was spilling the blood of innocent Muslim worshipers. A few hours later, the protest spread from the Temple Mount plaza all over the West Bank and Gaza Strip. In the Palestinian consciousness, the events on al-Haram al-Sharif invoked memories of past Israeli aggressions. The fact that Sharon was involved further heightened the sense of emergency. Palestinians perceived Sharon's visit to al-Haram al-Sharif as part of a conspiracy between Sharon and Barak aimed at dictating a settlement in Israel's favor on the Temple Mount, along the lines Israel had presented at Camp David.

The Israeli army's reaction was based on the lessons it had learned from the Western Wall tunnel incident of 1996, when sixteen IDF soldiers were killed. Israeli snipers were deployed to maximize damage to the Palestinians. The large number of Palestinian wounded in turn sparked confrontations with Israeli soldiers and settlers in the West Bank and Gaza Strip.

Al-Aqsa was the center point of the 2000 Intifada and gave it its name. But defending al-Aqsa was only the original goal. Afterward, independence became another goal of the fighting, giving the conflict an alternative name: al-Istiqlal Intifada. The appearance of Sharon, whom the Palestinians regarded as a symbol of Israeli aggression against Palestinians, on al-Haram al-Sharif, their most holy site in Palestine, was especially galling to the Palestinians and symbolized the fact that Israel and the Palestinians both claimed sovereignty there. This contributed to the outbreak of the Intifada but neither prepared the way for it nor caused it. The immediate reason why this local protest turned into a mass uprising was the large number of Palestinians injured during the initial four or five days, at first on the Temple Mount and afterward in the West Bank and Gaza Strip. The fact that Palestinian Israelis were also killed at the same time, some on the Temple Mount and some near their cities within Israel, helped turn a local incident into a national Intifada. Agitation, protest, frustration, and disappointment all sought a symbol and a goal, and they found it in the image of al-Aqsa. The Palestinian sacrifice, together with the Palestinian national struggle, was glorified with the crown of al-Aqsa. The nemesis was Sharon, a Satanic figure who personified Israel's aspirations and policy on the West Bank and Gaza Strip.

The al-Aqsa Intifada turned the Oslo accords into history. Oslo was the name both of a specific agreement and of a system in which negotiations were to be conducted in an atmosphere of mutual trust while the situation on the ground was frozen. It was based on a concept of continuous diplomatic progress toward a permanent agreement. The Intifada put an end to this. As public opinion polls and the mass participation in the funerals of the Palestinian casualties showed, the Palestinian public accepted conflict as reality and united around an ethos of sacrifice and resistance to Israel's presence and actions. In the Palestinian consciousness, the Oslo accords are perceived as a failure and an act of Israeli duplicity. As far as the Palestinians are concerned, the Oslo accords can no longer serve as a legitimate framework for the establishment of the Palestinian state (Bir Zeit University, Development Studies Surveys 2000, 2001).

Israeli society has also united around its casualties. Palestinian terrorism during the Intifada, including attacks on Israeli citizens living within the Green Line, has caused public support for the peace process to plummet. The Israeli public at large sees the Palestinian as a threatening figure who does not want to reach an agreement of peace and compromise. The Oslo index published by the Tami Steinmetz Center for Peace Research at Tel Aviv University measures the level of public support for the peace process. This index reveals that in September 2001 the level of public support stood at 29.8 percent, as opposed to 50 percent in January 2000. From the creation of the first Oslo agreement in 1993, such a low level of support for the Israeli-Palestinian peace process had never been measured in Israel (www.tau.ac.il/peace).

President Clinton's Bridging Ideas: The Right Start toward the End

After efforts to end the Intifada failed, American mediation efforts focused on President Clinton's ideas for a framework for the Israeli-Palestinian permanent status agreement. Once the U.S. government saw that the two sides were unable to reach a compromise on their own, Clinton decided to present to the parties a compromise proposal which he developed following the conclusion of the Camp David summit. Two weeks before leaving the White House, on 23 December 2000, Clinton presented his ideas to the Israeli and PLO delegations.

For the first time since the permanent status talks began, the American government put forth a compromise proposal of its own devising. Instead of acting as a go-between, President Clinton made use of his presidential authority to propose ideas from which the permanent status agreement could be fashioned. His proposal was based on his own experience and on that of the American agencies that had participated in mediating between Israel and the Palestinians. Before it reached its final form, there were preliminary contacts with both sides in order to receive their reactions.

Clinton's personal prestige and presidential stature rode on these proposals.

Clinton addressed the issues that remained open after Camp David had ended. His ideas were not meant to replace the understandings reached at the conference but rather to suggest compromises on the subjects still in dispute. The fundamental assumption of the Clinton proposals, as of the Camp David summit, was that the goal was to reach an agreement that would end the Israeli-Palestinian conflict. A sovereign and viable Palestinian state would be established, which would be recognized by the international community, with Jerusalem as its capital.

Clinton took a demographic-territorial approach to Jerusalem and the other permanent status issues. First, sovereignty and powers in the common historic homeland of the two peoples would be divided between them according to their main population concentration. Israel would withdraw from approximately 94–96 percent of the West Bank. It would territorially compensate the Palestinians out of its own sovereign territory, in an amount of 1–3 percent of the area of the West Bank and Gaza Strip. In return, it would annex the settlement blocks that comprised the remaining 5 percent of the West Bank and Gaza Strip. This principle would also be applied in Jerusalem (to be discussed). On the security question, Clinton proposed an international presence that could be withdrawn only by mutual consent. This force would monitor the Jordan Valley border and the implementation of the agreement by both sides. Under the aegis of these forces, Israel would retain a military presence in fixed locations in the Jordan Valley for thirty-six months. However, Israel would have a right to deploy its forces in certain areas in the Jordan Valley using defined routes in a case of imminent and demonstrable threat to Israel's national security of a military nature. A special agreement would cover the use of Palestinian airspace, taking into account Israeli training and operational requirements, and requiring Palestinian consent.

According to Clinton, the solution would "have to be consistent with the two-state approach" in which "the state of Palestine [is] the homeland of the Palestinian people and the state of Israel [is] the homeland of the Jewish people. . . . The Palestinian state should be the focal point for Palestinians who choose to return to the area without ruling out that Israel will accept some of these refugees" (app. C). Clinton asked both sides to find a formulation that "will make clear that there is no specific right of return to Israel itself but that does not negate the aspiration of the Palestinian people to return to the area." Such a formulation could be either to recognize the right of the refugees to return to historic Palestine or to their homeland. A subsequent agreement would define the implementation of this general right (serving also as the implementation of resolution 194) according to one of five options, one of which would be "admission to Israel." Israel would have the right to indicate in the agreement that "some of the refugees would be absorbed into Israel consistent with Israel's sovereign decision."

In Jerusalem, as on the West Bank, a minimum of territory would be annexed to Israel, a minimal number of Palestinians would be affected, and territorial contiguity would be preserved between Palestinian areas. Therefore, Clinton's proposal contained, right at the beginning of the paragraph on Jerusalem, the following declaration: "The general principle is that Arab areas are Palestinian and Jewish ones are Israeli. This would apply to the Old City as well. I urge the two sides to work on maps to create maximum contiguity for both sides" (app. C).

Clinton did not suggest the manner in which the proposed territorial-demographic principle was to be implemented, leaving that to the sides themselves. But the high level of segregation between the Jewish and Arab populations in housing, political systems, services, and infrastructures enables us to conceive of a political and administrative separation between the two sides in Jerusalem. It is reasonable to assume that the implementation of the principle in Jerusalem would be different from its implementation in the rest of the country. Creating an open metropolitan zone containing two cities would require that the borderline between East and West Jerusalem differ from the border between the states of Israel and Palestine elsewhere. What was to be the nature of this intracity boundary, and how was the international border surrounding Jerusalem to look? These questions were left open for the sides to deal with in the framework of their continued contact.

It should be emphasized that President Clinton extended the application of the principle of separation to the Old City as well. He did not relate to the practical aspects of separation in that one-square-kilometer area but only to the principle. In other words, the Jewish Quarter would be connected to the Israeli municipality and the Arab Quarters (Muslim, Christian, and Armenian) to the Palestinian municipality and administration. This concept differs from that of the "sacred basin," in that the Old City would not be an independent unit. Administration would be based on national connection to a state rather than on religious affiliation. Clinton did not relate to such specific questions as the status of about 2,000 Jews living in Palestinian neighborhoods. He also did not say explicitly that the Jewish cemetery on the Mount of Olives would be under Israeli sovereignty. The Palestinians demanded that the site be placed under their sovereignty, together with all the other Jewish holy places and archeological sites in the sacred basin. However, said the Palestinians, Israel would administer these sites. On the basis of the criterion proposed by Clinton, Israel claimed that the places at issue were clearly Jewish and therefore must be under Israeli sovereignty. And this is certainly true of the Jewish cemetery on the Mount of Olives, which is an actively used sacred site.

"Regarding the Haram/Temple Mount I believe that the gaps are not related to practical administration but to the symbolic issues of sovereignty and to finding a way to accord respect to the religious beliefs of both sides" (app. C). In other words, in Clinton's opinion there was no dispute between the sides concerning administrative powers at the site and the regime that would prevail there in practice. All these would be Palestinian. The dispute focused first on sovereignty as a symbol and the symbols of sovereignty, and second on the manner in which each side would respect the other's religious belief regarding the Temple Mount.

> I know you have been discussing a number of formulations, and you can agree on one of these. I add to these two additional formulations guaranteeing Palestinian effective control over the Haram while respecting the conviction of the Jewish people. Regarding either one of these two formulations will be international monitoring to provide mutual confidence.
>
> 1. Palestinian sovereignty over the Haram and Israeli sovereignty over the Western Wall and the space sacred to Judaism of which it is a part (the Western Wall and the Holy of Holies of which it is a part). There will be a firm commitment by both not to excavate beneath the Haram or behind the Wall.
>
> 2. Palestinian sovereignty over the Haram and Israeli sovereignty over the Western Wall and shared functional sovereignty over the issue of excavation under the Haram and behind the Wall, as that mutual consent would be requested before any excavation can take place. (app. C)

The president chose his words carefully, using the names Temple Mount and "Haram" in a calculated manner, in accordance with the appropriate text and context. Substantively, the American president proposed that Palestine would be sovereign over the Temple Mount not only in practical terms but also legally and symbolically. In return, Palestine would honor the Jewish belief as to the Jewish connection to the site. The Jewish connection to the Temple Mount would not be expressed through symbols of sovereignty or by setting aside a place for Jewish worship at the edge of the area. Should the sides not be satisfied with a Palestinian declaration respecting the religious and historical Jewish connection to the Temple Mount, President Clinton offered two alternatives of his own.

It should be noted that the president believed that the two sides would be able to agree on one of the formulations. The negotiations about the framework for a permanent status agreement had been going on since the conclusion of the Camp David summit, and the expression "respecting the conviction" used by Clinton was taken from the vocabulary of expressions formulated during those negotiations. At first the Palestinians refused even to discuss the issue. Consistent with the Islamic worldview, the Palestinian negotiators denied the legitimacy of the Jewish narrative regarding the Temple Mount.

The Israeli position also played a part in this. Israel demanded that the opposite side recognize the Temple Mount's links to Jewish heritage and culture and that these links be translated into powers that would be given to Israel or denied the Palestinians, including the negation of their sovereignty at the site. In addition, Israel demanded sovereignty on the entire length of the Temple Mount's western retaining wall, not just on the Western Wall—that part of the retaining wall that is Judaism's holiest prayer site. Just before President Clinton put forth his ideas, Ben-Ami suggested to the Palestinians—without the knowledge of his delegation colleagues Gilad Sher and Yisrael Hasson—a formula that makes no mention of Israeli sovereignty on the site but rather refers to its sanctity to the Jewish people and its centrality in Jewish history. But the Israeli representative could not avoid translating this principle into an explicit Palestinian obligation not to excavate under the Temple Mount plaza, implicitly so as not to harm the remains of the Jewish Temple there. Furthermore, Ben-Ami also demanded that Jews be allowed to pray on the Temple Mount, in a specific place to be agreed upon (Sher 2001: 249, 338–42, 355–57).

However, the Palestinians' position softened during the course of the negotiations. Pressure from their American and European interlocutors, together with the education and liberal-Western orientation of most of the Palestinian negotiators, prevailed to some degree over their social and cultural connection to Islam. Their perspective became more balanced and a multicultural dimension came to the fore that differed from the monistic and one-dimensional conception of religious belief. Sa'eb Erekat declared on 5 September 2000 that as a Palestinian he did not demand that the Jews stop believing what they believe about the Temple Mount. But, he said, the Jews may not force the Palestinians to believe what the Jews believe in order to prove that the Palestinians sincerely intend to make peace with them (Erekat 2000). That is, Erekat proposed a mutual recognition in which each side would recognize the legitimacy of the other's narrative regarding the Temple Mount.

A similar formulation was proposed in November 2000 by a group of about 150 Palestinian intellectuals who addressed the Israeli public with an "urgent call" to reach a peace agreement on a different basis from that of the Oslo accords and the Camp David talks. The alternative principles they proposed included the following formulation: "Both sides must recognize the spiritual and historical affinities of each other to sites and locations within their own borders and they must affirm and guarantee the access and protection of the other people to these places within their own borders. But in neither case should the existence of such sites be used to advance extra-territorial claims to locations within each other's borders" (http://arabrights.org).

Just as he proposed drawing boundaries in the Old City, so Clinton proposed drawing boundaries on the Temple Mount/al-Haram al-Sharif. The division he proposed on the Temple Mount was, however, "softer" than in the other parts of the city. First, each side would recognize the other's beliefs about and connection to the site. Second, an international force would supervise the implementation of the agreement and would reinforce the confidence of the two sides in each other. Clinton's logic for the division allowed him to tie the Western Wall to the Temple Mount because they are connected in both religions. The sanctity of the Western Wall in Judaism derives from a belief in the divine presence that never departed from the Temple Mount and from the First and Second Temples that stood there. The source of the wall's sanctity in Islam is the al-Aqsa Mosque. But at the present time the Western Wall is the site of active Jewish worship, while the Muslims have no share in it as a place of worship; the opposite is true of the Temple Mount. This fact helped the president establish a link between the two sites and at the same time propose a way of dividing them.

The president proposed that if the parties could not agree on one of the formulations described above, then symbolic Israeli sovereignty could be recognized over the subterranean part of the Temple Mount in return for Israel's concession of its symbolic sovereignty above the surface. Israel would not, according to this alternative, be able to exercise its sovereignty over the subterranean part of the Temple Mount by performing excavations. The Palestinians would also not be permitted to infringe on Israel's sovereignty by excavating. In any event, Clinton's proposal made it necessary to answer two questions. First, what exactly is the Holy of Holies of which the Western Wall is a part, in Clinton's words? Second, does the subterranean expansion of the al-Aqsa Mosque now under way constitute a violation of this agreement?

The other possibility proposed by President Clinton was to divide between the two sides the single practical consequence of sovereignty over the subterranean section of the Temple Mount—the right to excavate. The agreement would state that the two sides are equally sovereign for this purpose, in the Palestinian case because of their sovereignty above ground, and in the Jewish and Israeli case because of their religious and historical connection to the site. Except on this point, Palestinian sovereignty over the Temple Mount would begin at the depths of the earth and stretch all the way to the heavens—as demanded by the Palestinian delegation. Palestinian sovereignty underground would, however, have no practical significance because there would be a mutual power of veto over excavations. In order for this option to be realized, a high level of confidence and communication must exist between the parties, from the leadership echelon to the professionals conducting the excavations. But since the events at the Western Wall tunnel in October 1996, fears and mutual accusations have multiplied on both sides. In both Israel's and the Palestinians' collective consciousness, archeological excavations are a symbol of Israeli sovereignty over, ownership of, and belonging to the site or, alternatively, of Palestinian rejection of these Israeli settlements through the creation of a Palestinian counterarchaeology. Israel and the Palestinians were not the only ones to use archeology to build a nation; Iraq, Egypt, Syria, and Lebanon also used the discipline for that purpose.

The political focus on the Temple Mount tied the archeological discourse more than ever to the dispute over sovereignty and over religious ownership of the site. The expansion or maintenance work performed by the Muslims was perceived as aiming to destroy Israeli sovereignty as well as the remnants of the ancient Jewish presence at the site. The Palestinians, for their part, perceived Israel's opening of the Western Wall tunnel in 1996 as aimed at destroying the foundations of the al-Aqsa Mosque and the Dome of the Rock (Klein 2001: 273–78). Ever since, both Jews and Muslims have been increasingly preoccupied with the Temple Mount (Gorenberg 2000). In 1996, the Palestinian Islamic Waqf and the Israeli Islamic Movement began constructing underground prayer halls in Solomon's Stables, a subterranean chamber underneath al-Aqsa. The maintenance and renovations this involved were performed there without first applying for and receiving a permit from the Israeli authorities and without coordination with Israel's archeologists. Prime Minister Netanyahu gave a retroactive permit for the work at Solomon's Stables and, in 1997, for the preparation of the subterranean area under the al-Aqsa Mosque (the ancient al-Aqsa) as an additional prayer area.

At the end of 1998 and the beginning of 1999, work was undertaken to prepare the chambers underneath the al-Aqsa Mosque for prayer services. The Israeli authorities were displeased, seeing this as a change in the status quo. In August 1999, the Islamic Movement in Israel worked together with the Waqf on the Temple Mount to break a large opening in the Temple Mount's southern retaining wall. There had originally been a small opening there, but it was now broadened into the size of a door, in order to allow entry of fresh air into the subterranean prayer chambers. The Barak government viewed this as a change in the status quo of the outer perimeter of the Temple Mount and an opening that could in the future turn into an additional entry gate to the Mount. The Waqf claimed that they had no such intention and that they had even put bars on the opening—to prevent, they said, Jewish extremists from getting into the prayer area. But the Barak government ordered the police to seal the breach. Barak's government was willing to accept measures taken within the compound, but not physical changes on the outside of the Mount. The opening was closed by the police. The Israeli action passed quietly because the Waqf and Islamic Movement in Israel had acted without coordination with the Palestinian Authority (*Ha'aretz* 10, 11 August 1999), and the Palestinian Authority had an interest in teaching them a lesson.

The Waqf and the Israeli Islamic Movement subsequently opened spacious entrances to the new prayer site at the end of 1999. This work was performed without archeological supervision on Israel's part. "The academic department of the Waqf is the only entity authorized to document the works . . . during the course of the work no Jewish findings were discovered. . . . I suggest that the Jews look elsewhere for the Temple," claimed Shaykh Najah Bakhirat of the Israeli Islamic Movement, which was involved in the works at the site (Regular, 30 June 2000). In practice, the Waqf extended the application of the permits it received from the Israel Police to prepare emergency exits for the underground mosques. Maintenance and development work on a smaller scale were performed in June 2000, on the eve of the Camp David summit, and in January 2000 as President Clinton's ideas were being discussed.

Israel's archeological supervision of the works on the Temple Mount had been more a dialogue between equals and coordination between professionals than supervision by a governmental authority of its citizens' activities. The Western Wall tunnel events stopped the official coordination between Israel's Antiquities Authority and Yusuf al-Natshe, who is responsible for antiquities on behalf of the Islamic Waqf. Since then archeologists have visited the Temple Mount to the same extent that other Israeli citizens and tourists have been permitted to enter the site. When the Barak government was formed in 1999 there was sporadic coordination, but this was suspended as a result of Knesset member Ariel Sharon's visit to the Temple Mount at the end of September 2000 and of the al-Aqsa Intifada. The Temple Mount has been closed to Jews ever since.

The dispute over the Waqf's work on the Temple Mount took place simultaneously on several planes. It was a dispute between religious personages who saw the site as a holy, living, and active place, and archeologists interested in antiquities and the past. It was also a dispute between Israeli authorities wishing to enforce the law and Israeli sovereignty over the site, and Palestinian Islamic bodies seeking to be fully independent as well as to preserve their autonomy while under Israeli rule and to challenge the legitimacy of the State of Israel. Finally, it was also an internal Israeli and internal Palestinian dispute, between radicals and moderates in each respective governing body.

The Islamic Waqf's work on the Temple Mount at the end of January 2000 led to an exchange of accusations within Israel, and pressure was put on the Barak government to halt the Palestinian work. The Jerusalem municipality and the Israel Antiquities Authority wanted to impose Israeli law on the Waqf. The political echelon, with the support of Israel's Supreme Court, refrained from doing so and sought a quiet way of concluding the matter without causing Palestinian riots. A group of Israeli archeologists and intellectuals calling themselves the Committee to Prevent the Destruction of Antiquities entered the fray during the second half of 2000, claiming that the excavations were extending to the depths of the mountain and were thus liable to damage the remains of the Jewish Temple if not performed under appropriate supervision. "Something terrible is happening on the Temple Mount . . . the damage caused to research into the past is enormous and irreversible," stated archeologist Eilat Mazar (Mazar 28 June 2000). The Israel Police stated, in contrast, that the work consisted of flooring and digging at a fairly shallow level in order to lay water and electrical pipes. The police provided photographs to back up their claim. In response, the committee claimed that the police were either lying or did not know how to distinguish between the two kinds of excavation and that only archeological supervision would prove who was right. The poet Haim Guri and the archeologist Amos Kluner visited the

Temple Mount on 24 January 2001, in coordination with the Waqf; their visit proved the police's claim to be true (*Ha'aretz* 23 January, 1 March, 15, 16 June 2001; Ben Dov 19 June 2001; Benziman 26 January 2001). The committee submitted a petition to the High Court of Justice in March 2001, claiming that the Israeli government had deliberately ignored crimes committed by the Waqf and publicly denied the facts known to it. While the police claimed that enforcing Israeli law on the site would constitute a significant security risk, the committee said that this was just a fig leaf the police were using to cover up the government's failure to act. The Waqf's aim was "to turn the entire area into an exclusively Muslim holy place and thus prevent any possible Jewish foothold within the area" (*Ha'aretz* 9 March 2001).

A government committee headed by Ami Glouska of the Ministry of Internal Security defined four goals of Israeli policy. The first was preserving the status quo and preventing any work that was not routine maintenance unless it was carried out under the supervision of the Israel Antiquities Authority. The second was the cessation of violations of agreements on the Temple Mount and prevention of Palestinian security force activity there. Third was the opening of the Temple Mount to visits by non-Muslims. The fourth was an end to anti-Israel incitement in the Friday sermons delivered in the al-Aqsa Mosque. The committee also recommended trying to restore to Jordan its status on the Temple Mount as a counterweight to the growing power of the Palestinian Authority. In order to achieve these four goals, the committee recommended the use of coercive and administrative measures. These might include placing sanctions on the leaders of the Israeli Islamic Movement, restricting Muslim entry to the Temple Mount, and preventing construction materials and mechanical equipment from entering the Temple Mount to be used for work in the subterranean chambers. The committee rejected the claim that work had been carried out in the subterranean chambers, but it found that work along the eastern retaining wall had caused serious archaeological damage (*Ha'aretz* 6 April 2001). Most of the committee's recommendations were accepted by Prime Minister Sharon, but Israel does not have the ability to enforce them fully.

Making the Temple Mount the focus of the Israeli-Palestinian dispute since Camp David has both widened and changed the status of the public discourse on the Temple Mount. What had previously been a discourse of radical elements in both the Israeli and Palestinian national systems turned into a discourse conducted by their national leaderships. The circle of participants in the discourse widened, and the discourse moved from the margins to the center. Denial by certain Palestinian elements of the Temple Mount's Jewish past on the one hand and Israel's demand for sovereignty, which was interpreted as a denial of an Islamic-Palestinian connection to the site, on the other hand fueled the dispute and strengthened the site's symbolic value. The Temple Mount had become a symbol of collective identity for most Israelis, and this directly contradicted its long-standing status as a symbol of Palestinian collective identity. As in the case of every frontier area, in Jerusalem as well a site located on the front lines has a high symbolic value (Klein 2001: 9–41).

Both sides accepted President Clinton's ideas in principle but added their own reservations (Eldar 15 February 2002). Israel was not willing to concede sovereignty over the Temple Mount and demanded assurances of territorial contiguity between its sovereign areas of the Mount of Olives, Mount Scopus, and the City of David and the Jewish Quarter of the Old City, as well as between the settlements planned for annexation (Ma'aleh Adumim, Givat Ze'ev, and Gush Etzion) and West Jerusalem (*Ha'aretz* 29 December 2000). Israel lost much of its trust in special arrangements at holy sites under Palestinian control and rule. This was so particularly because Joseph's Tomb in Nablus had already been destroyed at the beginning of the al-Aqsa Intifada by a Palestinian mob, and the ancient Jewish synagogue near Jericho had been set afire. Both of these sacred sites had been operated within Palestinian Authority areas in the framework of special arrangements. In addition, the proximity of Rachel's Tomb at the entrance to Bethlehem to IDF positions turned that site into an Israeli-Palestinian friction point. As a result, the IDF suspended Jewish visits to the location, even though Rachel's Tomb is under full Israeli sovereignty.

At the same time, one may not ignore the influence of electoral pressures on Barak not to agree to Palestinian sovereignty over the Jerusalem sites sacred to Judaism, in particular over the Temple Mount. The Israeli government accepted Clinton's proposal regarding sovereignty in the interior neighborhoods of East Jerusalem and in the Arab areas of the Old City but did not move from its position as to the Temple Mount. The Palestinians also accompanied their positive response in principle with reservations. They understood that Clinton's ideas provided for continued Israeli sovereignty not only over the large prayer area in front of the Western Wall but also the Western Wall tunnel, and they objected to this. They also feared that the Palestinian neighborhoods in Jerusalem would be cut off by roads connecting the Jewish neighborhoods to each other. Like the Israelis, they demanded uninterrupted contiguity among the Arab neighborhoods and between the Palestinian city and the rest of the West Bank.

The Palestinians suspected Israel's intentions and demanded that Israel provide them with a map precisely defining those holy sites and access roads over which Israel was demanding to preserve its sovereignty. Finally, the Palestinians wanted Clinton's ideas to explicitly include the principles of freedom of access to Jerusalem for all, freedom of access to holy places, and freedom of worship (www.pna.net/events). Altogether, the Palestinian reservations regarding Jerusalem were not as substantive as the Israeli reservations. Israel, after all, had more to lose, compared with its initial claims in Jerusalem. However, Israel's "yes" to Clinton's ideas when taken as a package was stronger and speedier than that of the Palestinians. As hesitant and reserved as the Palestinian "yes" was, though, it was the first official "yes" that had been given in relation to the permanent status agreement in general and Jerusalem in particular. This response may be seen as the continuation of the Palestinian delegation's proposal at Camp David to divide sovereignty in Jerusalem's Old City according to a 3:1 ratio.

The Taba Talks: Closing the Chapter with Progress

The negotiations over President Clinton's ideas were conducted intensively in Taba during the last week of January 2001, in the shadow of the Israeli prime ministerial elections scheduled for 6 February. Both sides arrived at Taba with little confidence in the other. Barak, for example, demanded that the end of the conflict and the cessation of demands be part of the framework agreement. But the Palestinian side, fed up with promises and with past experiences of such Israeli demands, was prepared to include this only if the agreement stated what demands they referred to. If not, then the end of the conflict and cessation of demands would take force only after full implementation of the agreement (Sher 2001: 258, 261, 273, 276, 283). Despite their mutual suspicion and disappointments with each other, their talks achieved some progress. At Taba, the Palestinians submitted for the first time a map in which they formally accepted annexation of the Jewish neighborhoods in East Jerusalem and of the Etzion and Ariel blocks of settlements.

Israel, for its part, gave up on leaving clusters of settlements as islands of Israeli sovereignty, as it had proposed at Camp David and after. At Taba, Israel proposed to annex only settlement blocks connected to Israel in sovereign territorial contiguity. Its map reduced the area to be annexed by Israel as compared with the map submitted by Israel at Camp David, and it did not include the roads from Ma'aleh Adumim north to Beit El

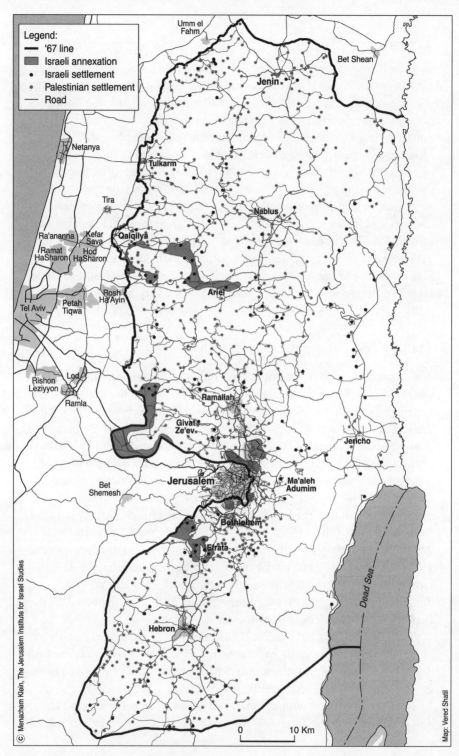

Legend:
— '67 line
▨ Israeli annexation
• Israeli settlement
• Palestinian settlement
— Road

Umm el Fahm

Bet Shean

Jenin

Netanya

Tulkarm

Tira

Nablus

Ra'ananna

Kefar Sava

Qalqilya

Ramat HaSharon

Hod HaSharon

Rosh Ha'Ayin

Ariel

Tel Aviv

Petah Tiqwa

Rishon Leziyyon

Lod

Ramla

Ramallah

Givat Ze'ev

Jericho

Bet Shemesh

Jerusalem

Ma'aleh Adumim

Bethlehem

Efrata

Dead Sea

Hebron

0   10 Km

© Menachem Klein, The Jerusalem Institute for Israel Studies

Map: Vered Shatil

Map 3. Palestinians' proposal in Taba

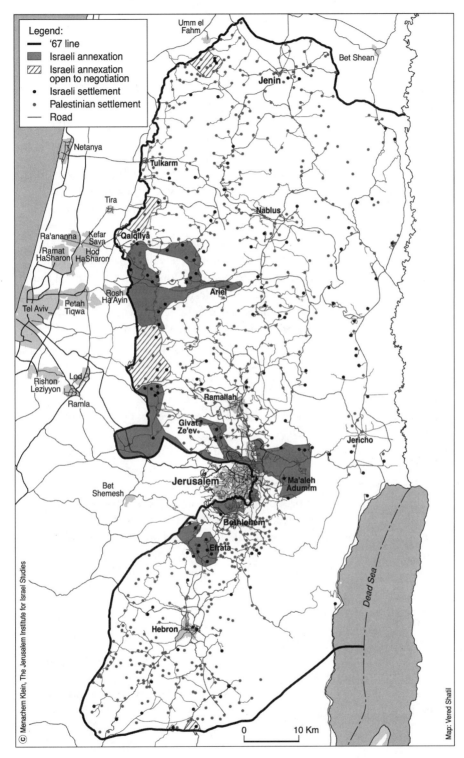

Legend:
—— '67 line
▨ Israeli annexation
▨ Israeli annexation open to negotiation
• Israeli settlement
• Palestinian settlement
—— Road

Umm el Fahm

Bet Shean

Jenin

Netanya

Tulkarm

Tira

Nablus

Ra'ananna
Kefar Sava
Qalqilya

Ramat HaSharon
Hod HaSharon

Rosh Ha'Ayin
Ariel

Tel Aviv
Petah Tiqwa

Rishon Leziyyon
Lod
Ramla

Ramallah

Givat Ze'ev

Jericho

Bet Shemesh

Jerusalem

Ma'aleh Adumim

Bethlehem

Efrata

Dead Sea

Hebron

0   10 Km

Map 4. Israelis' proposal in Taba

and Ofra, and east to Kalia and Almog on the shores of the Dead Sea. The debate was conducted over the settlement blocks' dimensions and the extent of their annexation to Israel. The Palestinians were willing to accept the annexation of a zone comprising 3.1 percent of the territory of the West Bank, saying that this represented almost twice the built-up area of the settlements. Acceptance of this meant the evacuation of about 130 settlements in which 100,000–120,000 people lived. The map submitted by Israel was drawn up according to the principle of an 8 percent annexation. But the Israeli delegates orally indicated where they would be willing to reduce this by 2 percent and thus arrive at the upper limit proposed by President Clinton. This would be on condition that the Palestinians added another 2 percent to their proposal, bringing it as well to 6 percent. Israel demanded to retain its ability to move freely into the Jordan Valley in times of emergency, to leave its army on the Jordan, and to control the airspace of the Palestinian state. The Palestinians rejected all these demands as well as the Israeli-suggested timetable for withdrawal of the operation of five army locations in the Jordan Valley and control of the Palestinian electromagnetic sphere. They were prepared to accept the deployment of an international force in which Israel would take part. The international force would be located in the Jordan Valley on their country's eastern border. On the issue of territorial exchange, Israel agreed to give up an area of its territory equivalent to 50 percent of the West Bank area that it would annex. The Palestinians, however, insisted on one-for-one size and value abutting the West Bank and Gaza Strip. According to the Israeli proposal, no Arab settlement would be annexed to Israel, and all would be physically connected to Palestine by a narrow passage or a bridge. The Palestinians proposed a similar arrangement for some of the Jewish settlements. Thus, according to Palestinian calculations, not only the area to be annexed to Israel would be reduced but also the number of Palestinians affected by the annexation—from some 30,000 under the Israeli proposal to 1,500 under the Palestinian proposal. The Palestinian side stated that Palestinian needs must take priority over settlements, and they rejected the Israeli demand of allowing further development of settlements (Shavit 14 September 2001; Beilin 2001: 215–16; Sher 2001: 371, 399, 405; Agha and Malley 13 June 2002; Eldar 15 February 2002).

The Palestinians objected to an Israeli proposal to annex, in the Ma'aleh Adumim area, a very extensive block of territory covering the area from the Kedar settlement to the south all the way to the Nofei Prat and Kfar Adumim settlements to the northeast of Mishor Adumim, and from there west to Jerusalem. According to the Palestinians, Israel's annexation of such a large area would allow the settlements to swell, at the expense of Palestinian Jerusalem's neighborhoods: 'Anata, 'Isawiyah, al-Za'im, al-'Azariya, and Hizme. A similar debate was conducted regarding Givat Ze'ev. Israel demanded not only to annex Givat Ze'ev and Giv'on but also the Beit Horon settlement northwest of Givat Ze'ev, and to connect them by a wide corridor to the Ramot neighborhood. The Palestinians claimed that this would come at the expense of the development of Sho'afat, Bait Iksa, and Bait Hanina. In response to the Israeli demand, the Palestinians withdrew their agreement to include Ma'aleh Adumim and Givat Ze'ev in the settlement blocks to be annexed by Israel, and they removed them from the Palestinian map. They made it clear, however, that they would return these blocks to the map when they received a fairer Israeli proposal. It should be emphasized that a similar dispute did not take place over the Gush Etzion and Ariel areas. There, the difference between the maps was not such as to cause the block's removal from the map the Palestinians submitted to Israel. The debate regarding the Gush Etzion and Ariel blocks was of more modest proportions, dealing with both the size of those blocks and the issue of connecting Jewish or Palestinian settlements where they bordered on one another's main roads (Shavit 2001; Beilin 2001: 215–16; Sher 2001: 371, 399, 405; Agha and Malley 13 June 2002; Eldar 15 February 2002).

In contrast to what took place at Camp David, at Taba there was no dispute over the internal circle of Arab neighborhoods or over the Jewish neighborhoods on former Jordanian territory. Both sides accepted President Clinton's ideas concerning these neighborhoods. Israel agreed to place the neighborhoods close to the Old City (such as Silwan, al-Tur, Ras al-'Amud, and Shaykh Jarah) under Palestinian sovereignty, and the Palestinians, for their part, reconfirmed that neighborhoods such as Gilo, East Talpiot, French Hill, and Ramot would be part of Israel. But the Palestinians did not include Har Homa/Jabel Abu Ghneim (a Jewish neighborhood in East Jerusalem that is now under construction) in their map, and they demanded sovereignty over all of Bait Safafa—both the formerly Jordanian and the Israeli parts. Bait Safafa was to have territorial contiguity with Bethlehem. The Gilo neighborhood would be connected to West Jerusalem through Ein Ya'el and, unlike on the Israeli map, would not include Har Gilo. Furthermore, the Palestinian agreement to the annexation of the group of Jewish neighborhoods from French Hill on the east to Ramot on the west should be noted, for these neighborhoods cut off the Palestinian north-south axis. The French Hill junction is where the two axes intersect, and a technical solution will need to be found enabling each side's traffic to flow along its natural route (ibid.).

As opposed to previous ideas (such as those proposed in the Beilin–Abu Mazen paper), both sides objected at Taba to the idea of a supramunicipality, instead discussing only the formation of a coordinating committee. This committee would deal with security, planning and construction, economics, and general coordination between the particular interests of each municipality. Moreover, the Palestinians opposed any administrative structure or special arrangement that could limit their independent activity in any way (ibid.).

Electoral considerations apparently forced Barak to take a hard line at Taba regarding ancient Jerusalem and the Temple Mount. He may have hoped that the possibility that Ariel Sharon would be elected would so intimidate the Palestinians that they would agree to the kind of arrangement they had rejected in the past. Furthermore, the Israeli participants felt that during the negotiations they had compromised again and again without receiving enough in exchange in the form of substantial Palestinian concessions on the territorial issue, the settlements, and Jerusalem and without receiving the Palestinian delegation's agreement that there were no more Palestinian demands. Every time the Israeli delegation felt that they had reached the last Palestinian demand, it turned out that it was but an opening for a new claim. The Israeli delegation felt that it was not facing a coherent team led by one leader. Each of the senior Palestinians pulled the cart in his own direction and wanted to attain Israeli concessions on the issue most important to him, at the expense of the subjects most important to his colleagues. In the Israeli view, the various preferences on the Palestinian side flowed to the lowest common denominator, without Arafat's imposing his own preferences from above (see chapter 3). This perspective also influenced Israel's position at the Taba talks.

According to Abu 'Ala (al-Ayyam 28 January 2001), Israel proposed at Taba, as it had at Camp David and thereafter, establishing a special regime in the sacred basin. The special regime would apply both to Israel and to Palestine. In this, according to the Palestinians, Israel went back on its agreement to the Clinton principles regarding a clear division of sovereignty in the Old City. Alternatively, Israel proposed dividing sovereignty in the sacred basin in accordance with its proposal at Camp David: Israeli sovereignty in the Jewish and Armenian Quarters, the Western Wall, and the Jewish-owned houses in Arab neighborhoods including Ras al-'Amud and Shaykh Jarah, which are outside the sacred basin. Israel also included

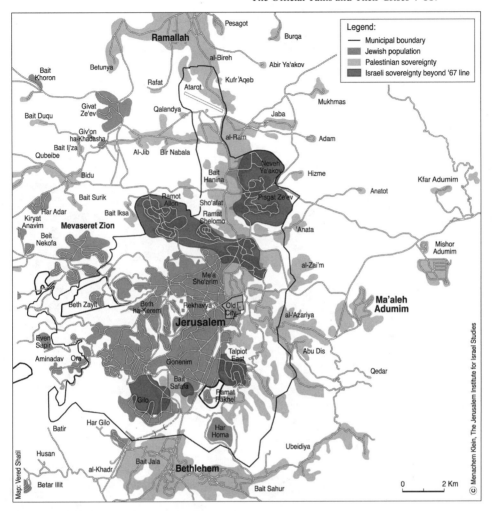

Map 5. Jerusalem area, from Palestinians' proposal in Taba

in the sacred basin the sacred sites next to the Old City over which it wished to remain sovereign: Mount Zion and the archeological park next to the southern wall, the City of David and the Ofel, Jehoshaphat Valley and the Jewish cemetery on the Mount of Olives, the churches at Gethsemane, and the Muslim cemetery along the eastern wall. At the end of the bargaining, Israel agreed to cede the Muslim cemetery and the Gethsemane churches but not the Jewish cemetery and the road leading there. The Palestinians objected to this, claiming that for them the road is a main street connecting East Jerusalem with Abu Dis and Ras al-'Amud.

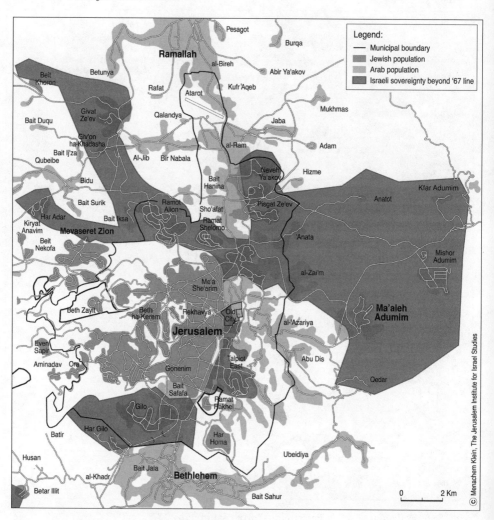

Map 6. Jerusalem area, from Israelis' proposal in Taba

The Israeli proposal would have given the Palestinians sovereignty over the Christian and Muslim Quarters, not including Jewish-owned houses there. According to Palestinian sources, in order to sweeten the pill Israel was willing to call the Israeli neighborhoods in East Jerusalem "settlements," on condition that the Palestinian accept its proposal. But the Palestinians did not wish to do so.

Another option put forth by the Israelis was to defer the decision on the sacred basin for three to five years, during which Israel and the Palestinians would jointly administer the basin. During this intermediate period, the existing situation would continue in the areas of sovereignty, law, and justice. This option would have given Israel time, and that was precisely what the Palestinians feared. Experience had taught the Palestinians that deferring decisions did them no good. The Oslo accords extended beyond the five years set for their expiration, without any clear indication as to when the permanent status negotiations would end. During that period the Israeli government had changed several times, but the Israeli attempts to alter the situation on the ground by creating unilateral facts went on. This concern also caused the Palestinians to object to an Israeli proposal to commit to ending the conflict immediately upon the signing of the agreement; the Palestinians were willing to do so only upon its full implementation.

A fourth option was to transfer sovereignty to an outside entity—the UN Security Council and representatives of the Jerusalem Committee of the Conference of Islamic States. This option also stipulated joint administration, since the third party would grant each side administrative powers in accordance with the principles established by President Clinton. Another proposal combined the last two options with regard to the Temple Mount/al-Haram al-Sharif. It stipulated that, for an agreed period, such as three years, al-Haram al-Sharif/the Temple Mount would be under international sovereignty of the five permanent UN Security Council members and a representative of the Jerusalem Committee of the Conference of Islamic States. The Palestinians would be the guardian/custodian of the Muslim shrine. At the end of that period either the parties would agree to a new solution or agree to extend the existing arrangements. In the absence of an agreement, the parties would go back to implementing the Clinton formulation (*Ma'ariv* 31 January 2001; *Ha'aretz* and *al-Ayyam* 28 January, 1 February 2001; Hassasian 2001; Abu Mazen to *al-Ayyam* 28, 29 July 2001; Sher 2001: 382–88; Eldar 15 February 2002).

Israel's proposals reminded the Palestinians of the proposals the Palestinians had rejected at Camp David. Thus, they pulled back as well and officially demanded sovereignty over the entire Old City. According to the Palestinian proposal, special arrangements would apply to the Jews living in the quarters under Palestinian sovereignty, with assurances that their daily life would not be negatively affected by Palestinian sovereignty. Special arrangements would also apply to the places sacred to Judaism in sovereign Palestinian areas (such as the Jewish cemetery on the Mount of Olives), which would be administered by Israel. Unofficially, the Palestinians were willing to recognize Israeli sovereignty in the Jewish Quarter and the adjacent houses occupied by Jews in the Armenian Quarter (Sher 2001: 410). According to the Palestinian proposal, Israel would be sovereign over the Wailing Wall (the area of Jewish worship, as distinguished from the Western Wall, which continues into the Muslim Quarter) but not over the Western Wall tunnel, which passes under the Muslim Quarter. A proposal was raised on the Palestinian side to accept territorial compensation out of the area of West Jerusalem according to a 1:1 ratio, in exchange for the annexation of the Jewish neighborhoods in the eastern city. A similar demand came up concerning the Palestinian property that remained in the area of West Jerusalem after the 1948 war. There were those on the Palestinian side who demanded that Israel establish arrangements for paying compensation for or making restitution of this Palestinian property.

For the first time ever, a discussion was held in Taba on the meaning of the term "open city" used by Israel with respect to Jerusalem since June 1967. Ever since June 1967, Israel has taken care to identify its rule in East Jerusalem with the concept of an open city accessible to members of all faiths—in contrast with the Jordanian government's prohibition between 1948 and 1967 on Israelis worshipping at the Western Wall, burying their dead on the Mount of Olives, and operating the university research facilities that remained in the Israeli enclave on Mount Scopus. In this way, Jordan violated the terms of the cease-fire agreement it had signed in 1949. At Taba, Israel proposed that there be a "soft" border between the two capitals mainly along Route 1, which runs north-south and separates East from West Jerusalem. This would enable a degree of control and supervision of passage from one city to the other. Traffic would be regulated at a number of transit points, and passage would be free only to the residents of Israeli or Palestinian Jerusalem. Residents of the two cities would be required to present a special certificate of residence in order to enjoy this right of free passage. All other entrants into West Jerusalem would need to go through passport control. These border arrangements would not, however, apply to the Old City or the sacred basin. That area would be open to all, and entrance into and exit from the area would be free. Special arrangements would be instituted to ensure that opening the area to all would not harm the daily life of its inhabitants. For example, steps taken to prevent terror in the open area would not disturb the inhabitants' normal course of life. These special arrangements, proposed Israel, would not replace either side's sovereignty over its part of the open city (Eldar 15 February 2002; Hassasian 2001).

The Palestinians were very surprised at the Israeli proposal, as they had internalized the Israeli claim that Jerusalem must be preserved as a completely free and open city. In contrast to the Israeli model of "soft" physical separation, the Palestinian delegation took the position that the entire area of Jerusalem and al-Quds must be open. They did not define the boundaries of the open area, where Jerusalem would end for them. They presented Israel with two alternatives. The first was to set up border control around both cities. These external control arrangements would be in the form of an international border for Israelis wishing to enter Palestine from the south, north, and east, and for Palestinians and other Arabs wishing to enter Israel from the west. Traffic between the two cities would be completely free. Traffic into each city would be free for the citizens of the relevant country and controlled for foreign citizens. Alternatively, the Palestinians proposed fixing a "hard" border between Jerusalem and al-Quds.

This was the first time an official Israeli-Palestinian discussion had been held on the meaning of the concept of an open city, and an attempt was made to examine how it could be implemented. In light of the present Intifada and in order to institute a border in Jerusalem that would be as similar as possible to the arrangements that would prevail along the border separating Israel from Palestine, Israel proposed creating three degrees of openness in Jerusalem. There would be total freedom within the sacred basin or the Old City. There would be minimal control for Jerusalemites holding a Jerusalem residence certificate who wished to pass between the two capital cities. And there would be maximal control for non-Jerusalemites wishing to cross the sovereign line separating the two cities and the two states in Jerusalem. In other words, Israel proposed a complex arrangement instituting a variable level of openness according to geographical and personal criteria. This was to arrive at a situation wherein, on the one hand, entry into West Jerusalem would be considered entry into Israel—though without limiting the freedom of movement currently enjoyed by the Arab Palestinian residents of East Jerusalem, which enables these residents to work in West Jerusalem or other parts of Israel and earn more than their brethren in the West Bank and Gaza Strip—and on the other hand the myth of a Jerusalem open to all would not be completely destroyed.

The Palestinians saw Israel's proposal as a hybrid whose implementation would complicate life in the city. The Palestinian spokesmen claimed that only complete freedom of movement, access, and internal passage between the two cities would ensure Jerusalem's development. A half-closed area that could be crossed only at certain points would harm the city's natural fabric of life as well as its development. As an alternative, the Palestinians proposed a simpler organizing principle: either completely dividing the city by a hard border or placing the international border around the two cities. According to the second option, which they clearly preferred, the control arrangements around the city would apply only to the "other"—Israelis entering Palestine and Palestinians or tourists entering Israel through Jerusalem. In any event, it should be noted, control points would create the symbols of separation between the two capitals and the other parts of each state. Moreover, the "other" citizen's passage from one capital to the other within Jerusalem would not be considered as a passage from one state—Israel or Palestine—to the other (Eldar 15 February 2002; Hassassian 2001).

The issue of sovereignty over the Temple Mount did not come up in the Taba talks, and each side held fast to its position. To this, and to Israel's unwillingness at Taba to unequivocally recognize direct Palestinian sovereignty over the sacred basin, the Palestinians added Barak's public commitment to preserve Israeli sovereignty over the Temple Mount and the other Jewish holy places in the Old City. "The Temple Mount is the cradle of Jewish history and there is no way that I will sign a document transferring sovereignty over the Temple Mount to the Palestinians. For Israel, this would be a betrayal of its Holy of Holies," wrote Barak to U.S. president George W. Bush (*Ha'aretz* 25 January 2001).

The Taba talks achieved great progress in the subcommittees that dealt with the issue of the 1948 refugees. In practical terms, this was the first time since the Stockholm talks that the two sides had conducted serious negotiations over this question. This was due in no small part to the fact that Yossi Beilin and Nabil Sha'ath, who bore no scars from Camp David and the subsequent talks, were placed at the head of this subcommittee.

It should be noted that the problem of the 1967 refugees had been solved in principle in the first Oslo agreement. They would be allowed to return to the West Bank and Gaza Strip, and a quadrilateral committee including Israel, the PLO, Jordan, and Egypt was set up to work out the way that this decision would be implemented. This committee's activity was frozen, and not only because of difficulties caused by Israel. The PLO/Palestinian Authority also had an interest in suspending these talks, since the Palestinians had limited absorption capacity in their territories and were already weighed down with infrastructure, social, economic, and welfare problems.

Many Israelis have trouble accepting the term "the right of return" and fear that accepting this Palestinian symbol will not end the conflict but rather entrench it. Instead of a permanent agreement that would bring to an end the case of the 1967 refugees, it would open up the case of the 1948 refugees, which was a shaping experience for both sides. Furthermore, acceptance of the term "right" would grant the right to demand the full realization of that right in the future. The Palestinian difficulty was different. For years the PLO had claimed that the Palestinian problem was not a refugee problem but rather a problem of self-determination and national liberation. The return was not perceived as the return of individuals but rather as a collective return (Klein 2001: 1–19). The establishment's return ethos was collective, while the memories of the refugees and their descendents were personal and concrete. So long as the moment of decision had not come, there was no contradiction between the two, and they could exist in parallel. Unrest in the refugee camps, the growth of a new opposition, and the fact that the Palestinian Authority neglected the rehabilitation of the refugee camps under its control created a problem for the Palestinian leadership. It had difficulty accepting the Israeli demand that it wash its hands of any right to return to Israel itself, and it sought to transfer at least part of the burden of deciding this to the individuals themselves. The leadership proposed a framework in which there would be various options. It would indicate its preference and try to channel individuals in that direction, but the decision would be that of every individual or family on its own.

The negotiators at Taba in January 2001 grappled with these problems on the basis of President Clinton's ideas and those produced in the Stockholm talks, via a series of solutions. However, no understanding was reached on responsibility for the refugees of 1948. The Palestinians demanded an Israeli recognition of Israel's moral and legal responsibility for displacing the civilian population during the 1948 war and preventing their return thereafter, as well as the acceptance of the right of each 1948 refugee and his descendants and spouse to return to his home in Israel according to UN General Assembly resolution 194. The right of return of each refugee should not expire, the Palestinians said, until he has exercised it according to the agreement without a time limit ("Palestinian Proposal on Palestinian Refugees" 2001; Eldar 15 February 2002).

In its private response to the Palestinian proposal, Israel used only once the term "the right of return," putting it in quotation marks and describing it as a Palestinian yearning. The Israeli paper did not include unqualified acceptance of resolution 194, which deals with the return of 1948 refugees to their homes on an individual and voluntary basis. Rather it related to the implementation of this resolution in a manner consistent with the existence of the State of Israel as the homeland of the Jewish people. The two Palestinian principles of the right of return and resolution 194 were put in the Israeli paper in connection with issues Israel had already accepted: the establishment of an independent Palestinian state and UN Security Council resolution 242. Israel suggested a joint narrative in which Israel was ready to accept a certain responsibility for the creation of the refugee problem and was prepared to express regret for it but was not willing to accept legal responsibility. Therefore, the two sides agreed that each side would retain the right to maintain its own narrative about the circumstances under which the problem of the 1948 refugees came into being. They also ratified their commitment to a solution based on two national ethnic states, so that the refugee problem would not upset Israel's existence as the state of the Jewish nation. Israel suggested a "return basket" that would include five options: rehabilitation and citizenship in the refugee's current location; absorption into the Palestinian state; settlement in territories that Israel would transfer into Palestinian sovereignty in the framework of territorial exchange; emigration to a country outside the region; and emigration to Israel. Preference in all the five options would be given to Palestinian refugees in Lebanon. The options would not have equal status. The incentives and financial aid would be used to encourage refugees to waive their right to return to Israel. Yet the Palestinian side stressed that the above must be subject to the individual free choice of the refugees and not prejudice their right to return to their homes (ibid.).

In keeping with President Clinton's ideas from December 2000, it was understood that Israel's immigration quotas would be low relative to the quotas for immigration to other destinations. No numbers were agreed upon, but unofficially Israel referred to 25,000 in the first three years of a 15-year absorption program and 40,000 in the first five years, while the Palestinian paper would enable all refugees residing in Lebanon to return, as well as an unfixed number from other countries (ibid.). Both sides concluded that Israel would also have the sovereign right to decide which refugees had the right to return to its territory and which did not, subject to criteria agreed on by both sides. Another agreement reached at Taba was that refugees would have to give up their refugee status and accept full and equal citizenship in their new place of residence. Their choice of residence would be their final location as a refugee. Israel stressed that in accepting this refugees would also give up all property claims against Israel. Refugees who did not give notice within five years of which option they preferred would lose their status and rights as a refugee. Both parties agreed that during this five-year period an international commission and international fund would be established as a mechanism for dealing with compensation. These would replace UNRWA (the United Nations Relief and Works Agency) in administering the rehabilitation of the refugees. The two international bodies would raise money for the rehabilitation of the refugees and would grant compensation for private real estate expropriated from the refugees. The question of public property remained in dispute, as did the level of compensation that Israel would grant. These issues were tabled for discussion in the talks on the detailed agreement. Israel would play a central role in raising financial resources for the new body's operations. The Taba talks established the procedure for submitting a claim for compensation. It was agreed that there would be two channels for such claims. There would be a fast track that would grant compensation on the basis of a general estimation of property, on the basis of criteria agreed on by Israel and the PLO. This estimate would be based on fixed and unitary measures for each refugee. The slow track, in contrast, would allow interested refugees to submit a detailed property claim against Israel. No understanding was reached on calculation of compensation for material losses, land and assets expropriated, and restitution of refugee property (ibid.; Eldar 31 May 2001; Beilin 2001: 204–8, 214–16).

The Taba talks did end without agreement, but it seems that there was a basic willingness on the part of both sides to regard President Clinton's ideas as an appropriate framework. Substantial progress was made on several issues. To members of both delegations, the possibility that an agreement could be drafted seemed greater than ever before. According to David Matz, the talks ended without an agreement first and foremost because the two leaders decided, each on his own, that reaching an agreement might well cause him more problems than ending the talks without an agreement. Operating under the pressure of Israeli prime ministerial elections, scheduled for 6 February, both Barak and Arafat, each for his own reasons, decided that they would suffer the least damage if they ended the negotiations. According to this analysis, Barak assumed that any agreement reached in Taba would include concessions that the Israeli people would reject by voting him out of office. Arafat, for his part, did not want to pay twice, first to Barak, whose chances of winning the elections were nil, and thereafter to Ariel Sharon (Matz 8 February 2002).

Moreover, a detailed examination of the Taba talks shows that a gap remained between Israeli and Palestinian positions on the symbolic issues of sovereignty over the Temple Mount/al-Haram al-Sharif and the right of 1948 refugees to return to Israel. Nor had an understanding been reached on the fate of the Old City of Jerusalem. Nevertheless, both sides' departure from the parameters proposed by the president took place in a game in which each threatened to break the framework proposed by Clinton on the issue most important to it, demanding of the other that it concede. The ability to get up and leave also plays a role in negotiations. This ability was utilized both by Israel and by the United States after Ariel Sharon was elected as Israel's prime minister and President Bush took office. This led the Israeli and American governments to declare that the Camp David understandings, President Clinton's ideas, and the Taba talks were not binding on the new governments of Israel and the United States because they had not been turned into official and binding documents. In contrast, the PLO demanded that the previous understandings, ideas, and talks continue to be seen as a frame of reference and that negotiations continue from the point at which they stopped at Taba (*Ha'aretz* 12 February 2001; *al-Ayyam* 8, 9 February 2001). This development sharply presents the following questions: why the talks ended as they did, and whether anything remains of them.

3

Jerusalem, a City without a Status Quo

No Status Quo on the Ground

The negotiations over a permanent settlement in Jerusalem, at Camp David and beyond, are another illustration of just how enmeshed Israel and the Palestinian Authority are. Any act of commission or omission by one side, even if motivated by internal political considerations, has a direct effect on the other side. The physical proximity of the Israelis and Palestinians rarely produces intimacy, either among the populations or the negotiators. On the contrary, estrangement and alienation frequently set the tone for relations between the two sides. Nor has proximity prevented misinterpretations and misunderstandings. Each side has routinely accused its proximate "other" of malicious intent and conspiracy.

No other people in the Arab world, and no other leadership, has such close and extensive ties and relations with Israel as do the Palestinian public and its leaders. This extensive and complex relationship developed, it should be kept in mind, in the absence of a permanent agreement. This makes Israeli-Palestinian relations quite unlike anything else in the region.

Prior to the peace agreement between the two countries, Israel's contacts with Jordan were limited to the royal house and the security establishment. Since the treaty was signed, contact between the Israeli and Jordanian peoples has been limited. The same is true of the relations between Israel and Egypt. Before President Sadat's trip to Jerusalem, only foreign emissaries and intelligence agents came and went between the two countries. While the Israel-Egypt peace treaty opened many possibilities, few have been realized. There is little mutual exposure between Israeli society and Jordanian or Egyptian society.

The situation is clearly different in the Palestinian case. Israel's direct (until 1995 and during the al-Aqsa Intifada) and remote (1995–2000) control over Palestinian life, the presence of many Palestinian workers in Israel, and Israeli settlements in the heart of populated Palestinian territory have generated close encounters between the two societies. Such contact may often have been benevolent, as in personal relations between a Jewish doctor and an Arab patient or between a compassionate Jewish employer and a Palestinian laborer or service provider. However, in many cases it was hurtful and painful to both peoples.

As long as all discussion of the future of Jerusalem was taboo, the city was perceived as a city characterized above all by a status quo. Breaking the taboo revealed that Jerusalem is a city without a status quo. It is not a static entity; its metropolitan boundaries have continued to change as diplomacy has proceeded. During the tenure of the Netanyahu government (1996–99), Palestinian-Israeli competition focused on the city itself; during the subsequent Barak government it moved outside the municipal boundaries to adjacent areas. Both sides have endeavored to build up and populate open areas to the north and northeast of the city proper.

The Barak government effectively froze a series of decisions the previous administration had made as part of a policy of creating a Jewish presence in Arab parts of the city. Netanyahu had sought to expand the number of Jewish settlers in the city's Arab neighborhoods and had promoted the plan to pave the eastern ring road—a project necessary to clear up Jerusalem's traffic jams but requiring the expropriation of approximately 650 dunams of land (*Ha'aretz* 15 March 2001) and the destruction of about 100 Arab homes. Netanyahu's government had also taken forceful measures against Palestinian institutions and agencies operating in East Jerusalem, moved to implement a plan to physically connect the eastern West Bank suburb of Ma'aleh Adumim with Jerusalem's Jewish neighborhoods (Plan 1E), and approved stage two of the plan to build the Har Homa neighborhood next to Bait Sahur and Bethlehem, a plan whose centerpiece was the construction of 2,832 housing units (*Ha'aretz* 16 March 2001; Klein 2001: 278–90). Barak either halted these plans or relegated them to a back burner. His government preferred to reach quiet understandings, for example with Faisal Husseini and the Waqf concerning the parameters of their activity, rather than cause conflict and react to the unilateral Palestinian actions in Jerusalem. Instead of competing with the Palestinians in Jerusalem (Klein 2001: 183–204, 247–93), the Barak government preferred to calm the city and compete with Palestinian actions in the metropolitan area of Jerusalem, beyond its municipal boundaries. This policy, together with the special political profile that distinguishes the residents of East Jerusalem from the other residents of the territories (Klein 2001: 205–46), meant that during 2001 the Intifada in its more violent expressions did not penetrate to the heart of the eastern city. Palestinian violence was expressed by shooting incidents only in the suburbs of Jerusalem, from Bait Jala into the Gilo neighborhood and from Kufr 'Aqeb toward Neveh Ya'akov, and by shooting at Israeli citizens in the Atarot industrial area and on the roads to Gush Etzion and Ma'aleh Adumim.

During the Intifada, streets and neighborhoods in the eastern city have been closed to Jewish-Israeli traffic by order of the Israeli police, for fear of loss of life. Furthermore, the number of Israeli tourists in the eastern city has plummeted. This is in sharp contrast with the year that preceded the Intifada, during which many Israelis returned to the markets and narrow streets of the Old City. The sale of apartments in Har Homa and in the new neighborhoods built in the settlements around Jerusalem almost ceased due to lack of demand. Only 750 out of the 2,400 apartments offered for sale in Har Homa were sold, all prior to the Intifada. During the first year of the Intifada not a single apartment in Efrat, the largest settlement in Gush Etzion, was sold, compared to 29 apartments sold during the preceding months of 2000. During the same period, the number of apartments sold in Ma'aleh Adumim declined from 75 to 44, and in Betar Illit from 352 to 33 (*Ha'aretz* 12 March 2001).

As was proven in Beirut and Belfast, in the reality of an ethnic-national conflict one may not disconnect a city from its surroundings. Conflict penetrates the capital, spreading from its periphery to its center (Klein 2001: 14–18). The Intifada reached Jerusalem during its second stage, when the IDF penetrated Zone A more deeply, more often, and for longer periods than ever before. Terrorist attacks were again hitting Israel proper. In 2001, Palestinian terrorist attacks killed 208 Israelis within the Green Line, among them 33 (16 percent) in Jerusalem; 1,600 were wounded, 513 (32 percent) of these in Jerusalem. Up to September 2002, 486 civilians had been killed within Israel proper, 85 of these in Jerusalem—more than any other place in the country. Some 21 percent of the total number of terrorist acts against targets within Israel in the period 2001–02 happened in Jerusalem (*Ha'aretz* 29 January, 2 June 2002; Nadav Shragai, "Blood Index," *Ha'aretz* 15 September 2002). Furthermore, the year 2002 saw the first terror cells made up of residents of East Jerusalem. They murdered 35 people and injured 210, most of them in West Jerusalem. Prior to this, Palestinian residents of East Jerusalem provided aid to terror squads that arrived from outside the city. One of the East Jerusalem cells planned a terrorist act of a type Israel has not yet experienced—fatally poisoning diners at a restaurant (*Ha'aretz* 10, 13 September 2002). Likewise, Israeli Jews also committed terrorist acts in and around Jerusalem. Jewish-Israeli terror organizations took responsibility for killing two Palestinian drivers in June and August 2001 near Ma'aleh Adumim, and for an explosion in the boys' school of the village of Sur Baher, in which seven children and a teacher were injured. In May 2002 the Israeli authorities rounded up a Jewish terror cell that planted a bomb in the girls' school in al-Tur.

In an attempt to achieve a drastic reduction in terrorist attacks in Jerusalem, the Israeli government approved, in January 2002, an "Envelop Jerusalem" plan that included the construction of a wall, or barrier fence, between annexed East Jerusalem and the West Bank, the establishment of roadblocks between East and West Jerusalem, and the installation of closed-circuit television cameras and sensors between East and West Jerusalem for the purpose of monitoring the movement of Arabs to the Jewish side of the city (*Ha'aretz* 29, 30 January, 5 February 2002).

The plan suffers from internal contradictions deriving, first, from the geographical/urban reality and, second, from the political views of those involved in its approval. The operational bodies—the army and the police—suggested segregating Jewish and Arab neighborhoods on an ethnic-national basis. The Jerusalem municipality sought a dividing line that would follow the municipal border with only minor changes, and Prime Minister Sharon wanted to include settlements close to the city within the fence. In practice, the plan contains elements of all three of these positions. This, together with the geographical-urban reality, makes it difficult to carry out the plan.

It is simply not possible to isolate entirely the section of Jerusalem that Israel annexed in June 1967 from the West Bank. The annexation line has been blurred. In many cases the city boundary runs down the middle of houses and Arab neighborhoods, and over the years villages that lie outside the municipal boundaries have become suburbs of East Jerusalem.

It is also difficult to erect a fence and rigid and workable dividing line between the Jewish and Arab neighborhoods of East Jerusalem. The seam between the Jewish and Arab neighborhoods in the capital is nearly twenty-one miles long. Furthermore, in northeast Jerusalem the Jewish neighborhoods, which are strung along an east-west axis of activity, cross a line of Palestinian neighborhoods whose axis is north-south. In addition to shattering the myth of Jerusalem as an open city without roadblocks by turning it into a kind of Belfast, the erection of roadblocks between East and West Jerusalem would interfere with the functioning of the city's economy and with tourism, transportation, and medical services.

At the direction of Prime Minister Sharon, the sections of the plan that mandated the establishment of a permanent fence and roadblocks between East and West Jerusalem were removed, and Ma'aleh Adumim, Givat Ze'ev, and Har Gilo, all of them outside the annexed part of Jerusalem, were included in the plan. According to the plan, the roadblocks adjacent to these settlements would be border crossings. Unlike the 200,000 Arabs who live in East Jerusalem, the 120,000 Arabs in those areas of the West Bank adjacent to Jerusalem who would find themselves within the "Jerusalem envelope" would not be annexed to Israel and would not be granted the status of permanent resident (*Ha'aretz,* 29, 30 January, 5 February 2002). In other words, Israel would have under its direct rule two groups of Arab-Palestinian populations with two different statuses. One, the residents of East Jerusalem, would be permanent residents but not citizens of Israel, while the second group of Palestinians would lack a formal status of any type. The demographic balance would be to Israel's disadvantage, since there would be some 320,000 Palestinians as against some 437,000 Jews, and there would be a border forty-three miles long. The population that would be added to Israel would be disconnected from its hinterland in the Palestinian territories and would not enjoy the legal rights enjoyed by the Arabs of East Jerusalem.

In fact, until October 2002 only part of the program was implemented. In a few places in Jerusalem's east and north, earthworks were erected, roads destroyed, ditches dug, and a fence or other barrier was installed in order to prevent the free movement of people and vehicles. A number of villages and suburbs that had been annexed to Israel in 1967, such as Ras Hamis and al-Shayakh and parts of Dahiat al-Barid, Bait Hanina, and Isawiyah, as well as the Kalamdia/Atarot airport, remained on the Palestinian side and were thus, for all intents and purposes, placed outside Israel's borders (*Ha'aretz* 6, 29 May 2002). The village of Abu Dis has been divided by a fence that was erected along the municipal border. Homes in the village of Kufr 'Aqeb lie outside the planned line of the fence, but their lands will be on the inside. Finally, in September 2002, the Israeli cabinet decided on a de facto annexation of Rachel's Tomb, which lies in Zone C on the outskirts of Bethlehem. The area around the tomb will be separated by a wall from the Palestinian territory around it, and the Palestinian access road to Bethlehem will be rerouted elsewhere (*Ha'aretz* 12 September 2002). (See map 1 on p. 18.)

In turn, East Jerusalem Palestinians have tended to detach themselves and their institutions from Israel. They have displayed a preference for a strategy of disconnection and separation from Israeli governing bodies rather than a model of joint institutions and special arrangements. There has been a sharp decline in the provision of municipal services by the Jerusalem municipality to the Arab neighborhoods; the disconnection first took effect in the peripheral neighborhoods of Kufr ʿAqeb and Semiramis in the north and in Bir ʿUna in the south, which sits on the municipal boundary with the Palestinian Authority, placing part of it under Israeli sovereignty and part of it in Palestinian territory.

In Kufr ʿAqeb, competition has developed over waste disposal. At the beginning of the Intifada, attacks on city sanitation workers prompted the Jerusalem municipality to halt its garbage collection in the nearby municipality of al-Bireh, which is under the control of the Palestinian Authority. Al-Bireh started collecting the garbage that had piled up. In reaction, at the beginning of 2001 the Jerusalem municipality hired a local contractor to collect garbage. However, the contractor is not under the supervision of the city's sanitation department, though he is paid indirectly by the community center of the East Jerusalem Bait Hanina neighborhood, which is connected to the Israeli Jerusalem municipality. Similarly, the Palestinian Ministry of Communications set up its own telephone network in Kufr ʿAqeb after employees of Bezek, the Israeli telephone company, refused to enter the neighborhood. The Palestinian Ministry of Infrastructure also repaved the neighborhood's main road, which the Jerusalem municipality had not done even prior to the Intifada (*Kol HaIr* 19 January, 6 April 2001). Furthermore, during the present Intifada IDF tanks fired on Palestinian houses in Kufr ʿAqeb, in Israeli territory. And when the IDF put the Ramallah area under siege in mid-March 2001, the Kufr ʿAqeb and Semiramis neighborhoods, both within Israeli Jerusalem's municipal boundaries, were included in the military action. The IDF treats any area north of the al-Ram junction bordering on the northernmost Jewish neighborhood as Zone B (ruled by the Palestinian Authority but with overriding Israeli security authority) even if legally it is located in Israel's territory (*Ha'aretz* 11 April 2001; *Kol HaIr* 16 March 2001).

Negotiation Dynamics

The negotiations over Jerusalem illustrate a familiar phenomenon in diplomacy: it is not only one's interlocutor who changes his positions during talks. So does the "I," the self who is negotiating. Part of the change results from outside pressure, and part from the knowledge gained and internalized during the dialogue. Every negotiation is an educational process, and this stands out particularly in connection with Jerusalem. Barak had almost no previous familiarity with the subject of Jerusalem. Naturally suspicious, centralized in his working style, and constrained by his multiparty coalition, Barak had to make a study of Jerusalem on the way to and during the Camp David summit. Furthermore, Jerusalem was not negotiable as far as Israeli public opinion was concerned, and Barak took no steps to expand the boundaries of the Israeli discourse to create legitimacy for such talks. To a great extent, Barak was held back by constraints that he had imposed on himself during his election campaign and thereafter as well, when he unambiguously undertook not to divide Jerusalem and not to transfer any of its territory to foreign sovereignty. The boundaries of public discourse determined how far Israel was prepared to go at Camp David. At most, Israel was willing to change the existing situation from de facto to de jure because public discussion revealed the limitations of Israeli rule in East Jerusalem.

It should be recalled that the public discourse in the pre-state Jewish community in Palestine, and subsequently in the State of Israel, was traditionally shaped in light of the contention that Israel is a small Jewish state surrounded by millions of hostile Arabs. The 1967 war changed the tone of the discourse but not its substance. The post-1967 discourse was directed principally by the demographic issue—whether Israel could continue to rule areas of the historic Land of Israel that are heavily populated by Arabs. Until mid-2000, however, Jerusalem lay outside these demographic considerations, and any discussion of it was off-limits. In fact, from the beginning of 1996 onward, Israel's right-wing parties gained considerable political capital by claiming that supporters of the Oslo process, the Labor-led governments of Rabin, Peres, and Barak chief among them, were endangering Israeli sovereignty over Jerusalem. This self-styled "national camp" defended the old principle of the inviolability of Jerusalem within the boundaries established by Israel at the end of June 1967. Yet, in doing so it inevitably focused attention on the short reach of Israeli authority in East Jerusalem and thus prepared the ground for the city's inclusion in the demographic discourse. The only explanation for Israel's powerlessness in East Jerusalem is, after all, the existence of a large and organized Palestinian population that may no longer be ignored.

At the same time, preservation of Israeli sovereignty over the historical and religious heart of Jerusalem has remained a significant concern for a large part of the Israeli public. It would be easier for Israel to propose separation from the Arab population there than to separate itself from the territory and from control over the territory on the supraneighborhood and symbolic levels. To supraneighborhood rule must be added the principle of responsibility for security. Powers and responsibility in the field of security are perceived by the Israeli establishment as expressions of sovereignty and control, and they have constituted a very important value in the Israeli national ethos ever since the establishment of the Haganah (1920) and Palmach (1945), the defense organizations of the Yishuv before the founding of the State of Israel. It should be emphasized that the Israeli idea of placing the historical and holy basin of Jerusalem under a special regime that would restrict or make Israeli rule there indirect was not perceived by Israel as being intended to increase Palestinian control and sovereignty. According to this concept, both sides were asked to place limitations on themselves in the holy basin. This approach was developed in Israel by intellectuals and professionals, and there was no real public discussion of it. There was even less within the Palestinian public.

Why Did It Happen? Faulty Explanations

What motivated Arafat and his negotiators to stubbornly refuse to cede full Palestinian sovereignty over the Temple Mount? I will present a number of explanations that have been offered, ones that have attracted a large number of adherents around the world and in Israel. In fact, some of the premises on which these explanations are based have become common wisdom.

One possible explanation is that the refusal was tactical—a way of gaining more in the general negotiations. Brinkmanship has long been a tactic of Arafat's, and it is reinforced by his explosive personality and unpredictable character. Outbursts and caprices may be part of his character (Rubinstein 2001: 123–26), or they may be a negotiating tactic that, perhaps, over time has been internalized to such an extent that it is no longer conscious. Either way, the weight of decision was thrown onto Arafat's shoulders at Camp David. His colleagues in the Palestinian leadership were just as happy not to have to share the responsibility for such an important decision. The heads of the important Arab states warned him privately that they would denounce him if he ceded al-Haram al-Sharif, and they supported him publicly in his steadfast opposition to Israeli sovereignty over the holy compound. The decision was placed in the hands of Arafat the leader and the man. This is a basically optimistic explanation, as it assumes that Arafat is guiding his people and its institutions toward an arrangement with Israel. If it is true, and if his brink-manship does not topple him into the abyss or lead to his loss of control over his people, it promises that a compromise arrangement will eventually be attained.

An opposite kind of personal explanation goes back to Arafat's formative years. Arafat is a believer who received a religious Qur'anic education. His interest in Islamic holy places is authentic and not tactical. Palestinian sovereignty over the Islamic holy places in Jerusalem, or at least Islamic sovereignty, is for him the politics of personal and public identity. This explanation is pessimistic and assumes that Arafat cannot cede his sovereignty with respect to the Temple Mount and the Old City. And he certainly cannot agree both to Israeli sovereignty and to the setting aside of a place for Jewish prayer on the Temple Mount, as Israel demanded at Camp David.

The third and fourth explanations strengthen this assumption and transfer it from the personal plane of the leader Arafat to the political and biographical portrait of the Palestinian leadership and to the starting point of the coming state of Palestine. The establishment of a Palestinian state and the end of the conflict with Israel also mean the end of the heroic and romantic era. It would mean a lessening of the inter-Arab and international standing of the leaders of the PLO, as well as a lessening of the status of the national movement that won, in the second half of the twentieth century, more international sympathy and support than any other. The drudgery of building a state that will be born with severe fundamental problems is not an attractive prospect. It could be that the prospect of such a sharp transition deterred Arafat and his colleagues, and the struggle for a Palestinian state is more attractive than its realization. If this explanation is correct, then the Palestinian leadership is interested in a process leading toward independence but not in independence itself. In other words, Arafat is a partner not to an agreement but to a struggle.

This thesis is, however, problematic for several reasons. First of all, with the right strategy the Palestinian state could continue the romantic era by claiming that Israel left it scorched earth and that it needs to construct its state from the bottom up. This argument could also help to raise moral, political, and financial support for the new state from the international community. Second, this thesis contradicts the expectations of the Palestinian public as well as the direction in which the Palestinian leadership has been moving since the mid-1970s, when it began making decisions that created fissures in the PLO coalition and in the consensual and representative politics that characterized it during its formative period. The armed struggle was weakened in favor of the political process and the Intifada. The Palestinian Covenant, the collective identity card of the national movement since 1968, also lost its validity at the end of the 1980s, and most of its clauses were finally officially nullified in 1996. The PLO no longer defined Palestinian identity as negation of the Israeli other but rather as the negation of some of Israel's characteristics and actions, primarily its desire to continue to rule over the Palestinians and conquer their land.

This change in Palestinian ideology caused a sharp internal debate because it contradicted the classical concept of the PLO. Hamas, with its Islamic Covenant, published in August 1988, took the PLO's place as the standard-bearer for the classic concept as expressed in the Palestinian National Covenant. The debate launched, in turn, a debate on the orientation of the national movement (Klein 1996; Hroub 2000). Since the PLO's founding in 1964, the national movement looked outward and considered the liberation of Palestine as the axis on which everything turned. The Intifada in 1987 and the establishment of the Palestinian Authority in 1994 forced the PLO to look inward as well, toward building institutions and providing services to the Palestinian population in the West Bank and the Gaza Strip. The PLO was forced to take this new direction before it attained its primary goal and before all of Palestine was liberated. The relationship between the two was the focal point of the internal debate between the organizations and people at the head of the PLO. This went beyond the debate that took place over the structure of the institutions of the Palestinian Authority, the division of its positions of power, and the division of functions and resources between the PLO and the newly established Palestinian Authority, to whom substantial international donations had been made (Klein 1997: 383–404). And there was more. In addition to key concepts such as "struggle," "sacrifice," "steadfastness," "liberation," and "self-definition," which characterized the PLO as a revolutionary liberation movement, new basic concepts were added to the discourse, such as "institution building," "democratic legitimization," "realism," and "responsibility," all of which characterize the nation-building stage (Schultz 1999: 160–63; Klein 31 July 1994). The internal debate was conducted not only over the fact of thinking in terms of these new concepts but also over their practical significance. A political leadership oriented to a struggle will not pay a high strategic price, in the form of the loss of its internal unity and the abandonment of its identity, just to make a tactical move. The willingness to make decisions even at the price of an internal split is a sign that the realization of the central goal of statehood is approaching.

A fourth explanation is based on the politics of status and on the political interests of Palestine. Weak states and new states insist on gaining or keeping full territorial sovereignty in the classic sense of this concept. The concepts of sovereignty that characterize the era of high tech, globalization, and the internet belong to rich and secure societies and long-established or developed states. In contrast, the Palestinians are hungry for independence and liberation from the bonds of Israeli occupation. When established, Palestine will include only about 20 percent of the territory it aspired to and will be divided into two parts connected by a narrow corridor. At the present time, the economy of the Palestinian Authority already suffers from high unemployment, a low gross domestic product (GDP), a lack of physical infrastructure, a lack of advanced industry, and a lack of capital investment. Poverty is widespread, and the population is increasing at a dizzying rate, in particular exacerbating an already high population density in the Gaza Strip. Corruption pervades a not-insubstantial part of the Palestinian Authority's governing institutions, bureaucracy, and patron-client relationships. Refugee camps constitute a heavy burden on the economy and society, and there is great dependence on income from Israel. Finally, the religious opposition, Hamas, has established a countersociety whose aim is, in the long term, to replace the present ruling elite. These facts threaten to make Palestine a third-world state at the margins of the Arab world. Full control over the holy places of Islam and Christianity in Jerusalem and over the Old City would, however, grant Palestine a high symbolic status and make it a leading Arab and Islamic country. The symbolic importance of Palestine would compensate for its inferiority in real terms.

The fifth explanation holds that Arafat cannot concede in general, and on the Temple Mount in particular, before the option of the further use of force has been exhausted in another confrontation with Israel. Both sides have exhausted their potentials both demographically and geographically. These issues were the basis for the oral understandings discussed at Camp David. However, neither leader trusted the other. Furthermore, the Palestinian leadership felt angry, frustrated, and besieged at the conference itself and afterward, when the Western world, under U.S. guidance, blamed it for the failure of the talks. This, together with the pressures applied on it by radical wings of the Palestinian establishment and general public, pushed it toward violent confrontation. Two other factors also played a role. First, there was a Palestinian assumption that unilateral actions on the ground would bring better results at the negotiating table. Second, the Palestinians were not weary of violent conflict and did not feel that they had exhausted the potential of violent struggle and confrontation. On the contrary, they were charged with new energy, and this led to the al-Aqsa Intifada, which began on 29 September 2000. This explanation assumes that the violence was planned in advance by the Palestinian side and was employed as a means of gaining political advantage or of forcing an ar- rangement and causing Israel to surrender. Such was the understanding of the chief Israeli negotiators Barak, Ben-Ami, and Sher (see Susser 16 July 2001). However, this approach does not take into account that the use of force damages the image of the Palestinian side as a negotiator seeking peace and exacts a heavy price—in blood and in money—from Palestin- ian society. These are considerations that the political leadership takes into account, and, in keeping with this, the political leadership did not plan the violent acts in advance but rather surrendered to circumstances and to the pressure of the Tanzim (the Fatah organizational apparatus). Moreover, at the Barak-Arafat meeting at the prime minister's home on 23 September, six days before the Intifada broke out, the atmosphere was quite pleasant. Sher relates that, during the meeting, the two leaders "committed themselves to reaching an agreement within a few weeks" (Susser 16 July 2001). That night Barak flew to Washington to insert his views into the plan that Clinton was drawing up. Was Barak really blind to Arafat's true nature? Furthermore, this approach also ignores the fact that the confrontation with Israel was not planned in advance by the uppermost echelons of the leadership, and when it broke out, the Inti- fada was not directed by a headquarters that coordinated among the various armed groups that were directing violence against Israeli targets. As Yezid Sayigh concludes, "[Arafat's] behavior since the start of the Intifada has reflected not the existence of a prior strategy based on use of force but the absence of any strategy" (Sayigh 2001: 47). The political leadership tried its best to ride the tiger that had escaped from its cage on its own.

Finally, this explanation ignores the fact that, between the Oslo agree- ments of 1993 and 2001, support for the Oslo agreements never dropped below 60 percent in the surveys of the Palestinian public conducted by Khalil Shikaki. Expectations and confidence in the peace process eroded as a result of the election of Israeli Likud prime ministers Netanyahu and Sharon and Israeli settlement expansion. In July 2000, after Camp David but before the Intifada, support for violence had reached 52 percent. One year later, ten months into the Intifada, it had reached 86 percent. During that period Arafat's popularity dropped from 47 to 33 percent, while the Islamicists increased their support from 17 percent to 31 percent (Shikaki forthcoming).

The sixth explanation, accepted by many Israelis, assumes that the Palestinian state cannot be established without an armed conflict. It will not be established as an Israeli gift but will be forged by blood and fire. This explanation, first of all, ignores the change in the internal Palestinian discourse. Second, this explanation ignores the fact that the armed struggle commenced by the Fatah organization outside of Israel in January 1965, and the Intifada that broke out in the West Bank and the Gaza Strip in 1987, are perceived as a national symbol, as a resource of legitimization, and as a phenomenon thanks to which the political dialogue with Israel was made possible. According to the Palestinian view, Israel was brought to recognition of the PLO only because the PLO imposed itself on Israel by means of the armed struggle and the Intifada. Another problem concealed by this explanation is the assumption that the violent confrontation is independent of the negotiations that preceded it. The Palestinians are determined to take their independence by force, whether they get 100 percent of what they are demanding from Israel or only 10 percent.

An even more deterministic and pessimistic thesis holds that the Palestinian side was and remains totally uninterested in making peace with Israel and rather seeks to defeat and blame the Jewish state. Basically, the Palestinian side is not willing to accept Israeli sovereignty and Jewish self-determination in the land of Israel. The Palestinian concept of justice opposes the existence of another state on the Palestinian land, and the conflict over the Old City of Jerusalem and the Temple Mount signifies a wider disagreement. Historical Jerusalem symbolizes all of the land of Israel. The Palestinians will never present a counterproposal to Israel because the Palestinians want Israeli concessions without end. Shlomo Ben-Ami and Ehud Barak gave sharp expression to this approach (Shavit 14 September 2001; Morris 13 June 2002). Their profound personal disappointment with the failure to reach an agreement on the basis of their proposals to the Palestinians left them exuding contempt and disgust at Arafat and the Palestinian national movement. Ben-Ami characterized Barak as a rational leader. Arafat, in contrast, is a mythological leader who evades decisions and compromises and prefers to continue the conflict. Arafat, Ben-Ami concluded, is a strategic threat to peace in the Middle East and the world. This same view has been expressed by Israel's hawks who opposed the Oslo agreements from the start. Dennis Ross (*Ma'ariv* 17 September 2001) and Gilad Sher have spoken in the same tone, if less bluntly.

This is a problematic approach, as in this view Palestinian recognition of Israel, the amendment of the Palestinian National Covenant, and the agreements signed between Israel and the PLO since September 1993 do not express the Palestinians' strategic goal and in effect are opposed to it. Such moves are, according to this thesis, acts of fraud, mere tactics to improve the Palestinian position in their long-term struggle. If this is indeed the case, however, why did the Palestinian side not accept the Israeli proposals at the Camp David or Taba talks as a springboard for realizing its strategic goal? Those who accept this explanation view not just the Palestinian leadership but Palestinian society itself as being unprepared to make concessions. The Palestinian public is not willing to pay the minimal price demanded by Israel, and the Palestinian leadership will not be able to convince it to do so even if it itself accepts Israel's conditions. In other words, there are no ideological and political divisions within Palestinian society when it comes to Israel. Almost three decades of internal debate are no more than playacting.

As against these inclusive approaches, which are metahistorical and most of which cast the blame on the Palestinian side, there is another explanation—prosaic, concrete, and complex—that looks at all of the parties who took part in the negotiations and focuses on the dysfunctional process. This explanation assumes that a series of mistakes, misunderstandings, and lack of proper preparation prepared the ground for the failure or, at best, the only partial success of the Camp David summit. The dysfunctional process consisted of interactions between the two sides, interactions within each side, and the role played by the United States. Indeed, these components overlap in many aspects. Domestic and personal political considerations affected not only the internal interaction within each of the delegations but also the interaction with other sides participating in the process. The opposite is also true. The Israeli-Palestinian interaction influenced the domestic interaction and leadership of the two negotiating parties.

Noble Goal, Wrong Course: The Dysfunctional Israeli-Palestinian Interaction

In analyzing the Camp David summit and its aftermath, some people have concluded that it was a mistake to broach the issue of Jerusalem, or at least the subject of sovereignty over the Temple Mount and the Old City. Touching this sensitive religious-historical nerve caused a reaction of rage and made confrontation unavoidable. The representatives of Israel and the United States proposed, at various stages, to avoid these issues or defer them, but the Palestinian side, for its own reasons, demanded that they be discussed. After seeing how the Oslo agreements were implemented by Israel, the Palestinian side no longer had even a modicum of trust in partial or interim arrangements. The Palestinians were no longer willing to depend on Israeli goodwill and leave any subjects open for decision in the future. If this is the case, the defects in the preparations for the Camp David summit should be sought elsewhere.

One set of defects is the faulty preparations each side made for the talks in general and for the Camp David summit in particular. The following factors contributing to the failure also need to be kept in mind.

Barak's Tactics

Israel's prime minister did not want to follow the model of the Oslo agreement of September 1993—that is, he did not want to prepare the agreement in advance through secret bilateral contacts and arrive at the summit conference simply to sign it. Barak's directives regarding the Stockholm talks constrained Minister Ben-Ami on the subject of Jerusalem. He was permitted only to engage in a general and personal exchange of ideas. The taboo against discussing Jerusalem was so strong that Barak preferred that the heading "Jerusalem" not appear at all in the talking papers prepared for the Israeli delegation to Stockholm, even though a page had been left blank to indicate that this issue still had to be addressed (Shavit 14 September 2001). Fearing that his position might play into America's hands, Barak refused to reveal it to Clinton before the summit (Sher 2001: 135). The Palestinians were told that the subject of Jerusalem would be officially raised at the summit and that Israel would present an innovative position at that time. Minister Ben-Ami resigned himself to this and the manner in which Barak steered the talks. If he had any objections, they were expressed to Barak alone. In practice, the negotiators, including head negotiator Ben-Ami, did not deviate from the line dictated by Barak.

Israel Forces the Date

The Israeli side pushed for the conference even though it was told directly by Abu Mazen (secretary-general of the PLO Executive Committee) and indirectly by Yossi Beilin, Israel's minister of justice, and Yossi Ginossar, Barak's special envoy to Arafat, that the Palestinian side had not properly prepared for it (Abu Mazen to *al-Ayyam,* 28–29 July 2001; Horowitz 2001).

Poor Palestinian Preparation and Leadership

Although it estimated fairly accurately how the proposals defined by Israel as innovative would look (indeed, they were not much different from the formal and informal proposals made at Stockholm), the Palestinian side did not prepare attractive counterproposals on the eve of or during the Camp David summit or package its counteroffers in such a manner as to prevent Israeli and American misinterpretation. Unlike the Israelis, the Palestinians failed to market their concessions, as minimal and as unacceptable to Israel as they were. Also, the Palestinian side did not prepare its public opinion for concessions and did not build an internal coalition within the political elite for a concept other than the maximalist concept. The boundaries of Palestinian flexibility were not defined well enough, there was no agreed strategy, and within the Palestinian leadership several approaches were circulating, without Arafat's having indicated a goal and a direction, both in terms of content and on the personal level (*Jerusalem Post* 21 August 2000; Baskin 2001).

According to Shlomo Ben-Ami's 13 July diary entry, Muhammad Rashid and Muhammad Dahlan complained to him that Abu Mazen and Abu ʿAla (speaker of the Palestinian Authority Legislative Council) were shirking their historic responsibility and were too afraid of Arafat to press him to moderate his positions. Rashid and Dahlan said, however, that they were willing to do so (*Ma'ariv* 6, 13 April 2001).

According to the testimony of Gilad Sher, a number of ideas about compromise positions were circulating within the Palestinian leadership. But each senior leader had different priorities. Abu Mazen put the emphasis on solving the refugee problem; Abu ʿAla on the 1967 borders and full Palestinian sovereignty. Mohammad Dahlan emphasized security arrangements that would not detract from Palestinian sovereignty, and Erekat focused on having East Jerusalem under Palestinian sovereignty (Sher 2001: 155). Israel identified a moderate axis composed of Dahlan, Hassan ʿAsfour, and Mohammed Rashid, as against a hawkish axis consisting of Abu Mazen and Abu ʿAla. Sher says that at Camp David Dahlan and Abu Mazen almost reached the point of blows when the latter refused to convey an American proposal about Palestinian custodianship on al-Haram al-Sharif to Arafat (Sher 2001: 22, 26). Each one could find common language with Israel only on the one or two subjects that were important to him. On these subjects he was pragmatic, but on all others he was not.

The Israelis also discovered that understandings reached with members of the Palestinian delegation were not acceptable to Arafat and that his representatives did not always report to him accurately on the status of the negotiations and on the positions presented there. Each member of the Palestinian leadership, so the Israelis came to believe, had his own way of reporting to Arafat. One defamed his colleagues, another papered over differences, a third reported on the atmosphere at the talks. In general, it seemed to the Israelis, no one at all gave Arafat a precise and detailed report of what had transpired. (Sher 2001: 51–52; Benziman 23 March 2001). Several times during their talks with their Palestinian counterparts, the members of the Israeli delegation received the impression that this lack of concord forced the members of the Palestinian delegation toward their lowest common denominator and that the Palestinian demands were thus a bottomless pit. Here is how Sher summed up his experience:

> At Camp David the Palestinians acted dishonestly. They reiterated dogmatic positions, continued to make new demands even during advanced stages of the contacts, and refused to offer any proposals in place of the president's proposals that they had rejected. In contrast, at Camp David Israel displayed a willingness to discuss far-reaching proposals, with the goal of pursing to the fullest the opportunity to reach a permanent status agreement with the Palestinians. After Camp David there were another thirty-five or so additional negotiating meetings. During this period the Palestinians backed down from nearly all the positions they had presented at Camp David. In parallel, Palestinian preparations for an armed confrontation continued. At the end of September, in Washington, the contours of the package the Americans had formulated became clear to both sides. The Palestinians wanted to "upgrade" the package, and Sharon's visit to the Temple Mount fell into their hands like a gift from heaven. It was an opportunity to escape from the diplomatic road that they had been contractually obligated to since the signing of the Oslo agreements, and to try to obtain by physical force what they had not been able to achieve by negotiation. Arafat knowingly and deliberately led us into regional deterioration.
>
> The president's ideas mapped out the core of the agreement. . . . The government accepted these ideas as a basis for negotiation, and

submitted its reservations and qualifications. . . . The Palestinians' formal response to the president was positive, but for all practical purposes it was a negative response in every way. (Sher 20 March 2001)

Whether this impression reflects an objective or only a subjective reality, it left its mark on the Israeli delegation.

The Israeli impression derived in part from the contention within the Palestinian leadership about who would lead the negotiations with Israel. This was a contest both for the position of primary power directly below Arafat and at the same time for his inheritance after his death. Thus the Israeli-Palestinian problematic interaction met Palestinian internal leadership problems. It was Abu Mazen who raised, in his meeting with the Swedes in December 1999, the idea of establishing a secret channel in order to prepare the negotiations for a permanent arrangement. To his disappointment, Arafat chose Abu Mazen's rival Abu 'Ala to lead these back-channel contacts, together with Minister Hassan 'Asfour, who had been Abu Mazen's assistant in the formulation of the first Oslo agreement. 'Asfour had since deserted his patron, Abu Mazen, and their personal relations were disrupted. 'Asfour and Dahlan accused Abu Mazen of failure for having allowed Israel to evade freeing security prisoners. The Wye agreement, for which Abu Mazen had been the Palestinian negotiator, had not precisely defined which prisoners Israel would release, and the Netanyahu government had freed only criminal offenders. A full 1,894 Palestinian prisoners remained in Israeli jails. As a result of these accusations, Abu Mazen's home was stoned, and there was a campaign to discredit him. As will be seen below, the issue of the prisoners served as one of the axes around which the new Palestinian opposition coalesced (Sher 2001: 39, 44, 263; Beilin 2001: 94–95, 109, 130; Shavit 14 September 2001; Kershner 16 July 2001; Sontag 26 July 2001).

It was apparently Abu Mazen who gave out word about the Stockholm talks and severely criticized what he claimed were Abu 'Ala's huge concessions. Abu 'Ala consequently retreated from a few of the points he had raised in the Stockholm talks about the 1948 refugees, and he and Abu Mazen were back on good terms before the Camp David summit was convened. At the summit itself, Abu Mazen was, from the start, remote and uncooperative. Abu 'Ala became similarly withdrawn after Clinton yelled at him.

After Camp David, Abu Mazen and Abu 'Ala continued to cooperate. They created an axis against Erekat, who had, in their opinion, erred in agreeing in August–September 2000 to enter into a detailed discussion with Sher of some issues, without having reached an agreement acceptable to the Palestinians on principles (Sher 2001: 39, 44, 263; Beilin 2001: 94–95, 109, 130; Shavit 14 September 2001; Kershner 16 July 2001; Sontag 26 July 2001). To all this must be added the fact that, unfortunately, Israel and the United States were perceived by the Palestinians to be grossly interfering in their internal power struggles. Israel, they felt, was cultivating Muhammad Dahlan at Abu Mazen's expense (Pundak 2001). As will be shown, the members of the Israeli delegation at Camp David, as well as cabinet ministers, did not have identical opinions throughout the talks. However, in contrast to the Palestinian side, in the Israeli delegation the guiding and coordinating hand of Barak was apparent.

The personal interests and considerations of politicians are not primary shapers of events, but they can facilitate or hinder, reinforce or mitigate other factors. In the case of Camp David, the personal interests of the Palestinian negotiators—their backstage jockeying for position in the post-Arafat era and the tensions between the older and younger generations within the leadership—were detrimental to the successful conclusion of a peace agreement. Palestinian personalities who were insulted because they had not been included in the delegation, or because others had been chosen over them for key positions on the negotiating team, placed obstacles in the path of dialogue with Israel or did not make as great an effort as they could have to help advance the talks or to improve the public atmosphere on the Palestinian street. Prominent figures in the Palestinian leadership provided deliberate and distorted leaks from the talks. They initiated a process of public delegitimization of the negotiators. When difficulties arose they were passive and threw the entire weight of responsibility onto Arafat's shoulders. Those harmed by these moves could not, of course, let them go without response.

It should be noted that this is not a new phenomenon. The Israeli negotiators at the talks leading toward the Oslo agreement of 1993 were faced with similar phenomena. The Palestinians pursued a tactic of drawing the process out until the last minute, deliberately leaving issues open until the very moment of signing and sometimes even beyond. Like the Israelis at Camp David, one leading Israeli negotiator at Oslo came to the conclusion that the Palestinian habit of reneging on proposals that had been formally agreed to, or which the negotiators had understood as settled, was for the Palestinians a goal in and of itself and not a negotiating tactic (Pundak 2001). These flaws characterized the working methods of the Palestinian leadership in general and of Arafat in particular even before the Camp

David summit. Now, however, their effect was much greater than it had been in the past, and they were added to an accumulation of other faults.

Raising Expectations

Barak pushed not only to hold the summit conference but also to achieve the end of the historical conflict between the two peoples. It should be emphasized that the idea of terminating the conflict or ending the mutual claims was correct, because without it the agreement would have no real validity. Moreover, the peace process has been built on the assumption that the conflict between the two sides is no longer existential and is now over defined territorial property, the 1967 territories. The right of the other to exist, and the principle that the solution would not call into question the other's very being, formed the basis of the Oslo process and were reformulated in President Clinton's ideas. The problem arose because Barak brought in the historical dimension. He sought not just a solution on the ground but a resolution of the psychological divide between the two nations.

Setting such a goal raised expectations, particularly at the popular, public level, and more so in Israel than among the Palestinian public. Loading the burden of history onto the back of a political agreement made it more difficult to reach an understanding at Camp David. The end of the conflict will be a historical and social situation of reconciliation between peoples. A situation of reconciliation can arise only after the full implementation of a political agreement and on condition that the two peoples are wise enough to follow the path it lays out. In this respect, the experience accumulated by each of the sides that signed the Oslo accords was not encouraging. The manner in which the Oslo accords were implemented did not build confidence and did not prepare the way beyond interim agreements to permanent agreements, and certainly not for leapfrogging straight into an end of the historical conflict. Political agreements resolve violent conflicts but do not automatically bring their signatories to view history differently. They revise people's understandings of history ex post facto, as history is only seen in retrospect. In contrast, the statesman and the politician looks to the future. In the case of Camp David, the Israeli statesman marshaled history for his political needs. But he could not fill the high expectations with suitable content. The desire to arrive at the end of the conflict in its historic dimensions was accompanied by proposals that were unacceptable from the Palestinian point of view. Barak presented his proposals as a resolution of the historic conflict between the Israeli and Palestinian peoples. From the Palestinian point of view, however, his plan did not even offer a solution to the concrete aspects of the conflict. His proposals could serve to begin the negotiations but not to end them successfully, nor to end the historical conflict. As against Palestinian willingness to hear the Israeli proposals and bargain over them in a continuing process, Israel used a red-lines strategy. Israel issued an ultimatum: take it or leave it, because you will never have a better opportunity or a more generous prime minister than Barak. If you reject it, we will conclude that you are not ready for an arrangement and that we have no partner to talk to. Moreover, as Agha and Malley observe, Barak and Ben-Ami operated on the assumption that Arafat would reach the profound territorial compromise that Israel sought only after he had explored all other options. They asked the United States and the European Union to warn Arafat that he would bear the blame for the collapse of negotiations and would have to face the consequences. They urged the United States not to prepare any fallback position or to consider the possibility of ongoing negotiations if the summit failed (Agha and Malley 2001).

No Joint Text

At Camp David, the American and Israeli proposals were only relayed orally, so as not to lock their authors into a written text. The Americans had wanted to document the exchanges between the sides at the Camp David summit in order to prevent either side from reneging on agreements reached privately, but Barak sought to avoid being textually bound to any given position. For the same reason, Barak met with Arafat at Camp David only twice during the fifteen days of their stay there. At these meetings they exchanged neutral comments about the weather and American hospitality but did not deal with any substantive issue. Not a single Israeli position paper or map was passed on to the Palestinian side, and vice versa. Barak refused to reveal his final positions, even to the United States (Agha and Malley 2001). Barak's desire not to commit himself personally not only prevented him from holding substantial discussions with Arafat at Camp David but also led him to give his negotiators unspecific instructions during the Taba talks and to ask not to be fully briefed by them (Agha and Malley 27 June 2002).

Problematic U.S. Interaction and Functioning

The role of the United States, and President Clinton, presented another set of problems. The influence of the Jewish vote in the United States and the convening of the Camp David summit during the U.S. presidential elections prevented Clinton from pressuring Israel and from presenting balanced compromise proposals at Camp David. Clinton also refused to enable the Europeans to play a significant role as mediators, even in a temporary and limited manner, and to put pressure on Israel in his stead.

The Palestinians regarded the position of Secretary of State Madeleine Albright as being weak, and in general the status and authority of the American peace team was being eroded in the eyes of the Palestinians (Sher 2001: 130, 166). The American team was to a large degree overshadowed by the American president. Clinton played the role of an active mediator at Camp David, descending into the details of the negotiations, instead of acting as a supreme arbiter who would bring his full weight to bear only in times of crisis (Sher 2001: 169). Clinton listened, sometimes even shouted, and tried so hard to bridge over the differences that when he left for Japan the negotiators who remained at Camp David just sat there, waiting inertly for him to return (Susser 16 July 2001). By dealing with details and not formulating presidential ideas, Clinton left the Palestinians with the impression that he was fully coordinated with Barak. Three facts helped create this impression. First, it was Israel that raised and initiated most of the ideas, and President Clinton only passed them on to the Palestinian side. Second, from the substantive point of view the Americans were very close to the Israeli position on the question of sovereignty over the historical and religious heart of Jerusalem. Third, at least at certain stages, as Shlomo Ben-Ami documented in his diary, President Clinton was very aggressive toward Arafat and his delegation at Camp David. He put a great deal of pressure on them and spoke harshly in an attempt to impel them to accept his proposals for the division of sovereignty in the Old City and on the Temple Mount (*Ma'ariv* 6 April 2001). Clinton argued with Barak over his negotiating tactics, but he finally gave up and found himself "reluctantly acquiescing in the way Barak did things out of respect for the things he was trying to do" (Agha and Malley 2001). This increased even further the Palestinians' sense of siege, as well as their suspicion that an Israeli-American conspiracy had been concocted against them. When the summit ended Clinton ignored his commitment to Arafat and blamed him. This final accord helped Abu Mazen conclude that "Camp David was a trap from beginning to end, and we survived it. No one was ever subjected to pressures such as those applied to us" (*al-Ayyam*, 28–29 July 2001). Robert Malley admitted in retrospect that the administration leaned too much toward Israel, both in forcing the timing of the Camp David summit on the Palestinian side and in joining with Israel in pressuring Arafat. Barak's positions were viewed favorably by the American team, Malley has noted. The American team examined only the development of the Israeli position at Camp David relative to previous Israeli positions. The American peace team did not, however, measure the distance that Israel still had to go in order to arrive at a compromise agreement. When the positions of the two sides moved closest in December 2000, after President Clinton presented his ideas, the Palestinians lost faith in Barak and the United States. According to Robert Malley's testimony, at Camp David President Clinton took Barak's political constraints and coalition connections into consideration to too great an extent while ignoring Arafat's political problems. Moreover, President Clinton created a close relationship with Barak, which created an imbalance in his relations with Israeli and Palestinian leaders (Malley 7 March 2001; Agha and Malley 2001). In short, while Clinton helped Barak change his positions and provided him with support, he failed almost completely in inducing a parallel process on the Palestinian side. The Palestinian side felt that, were it to change its positions any further, it would lose its identity.

Internal Israeli Interaction and Leadership Problems

The Israelis made their own contributions to the lack of success of the negotiations.

(1) Barak's undertaking to bring the permanent status agreement before the Israeli people for their decision, thus circumventing the parliamentary political arena, created electoral constraints for him. Barak became the hostage of a taboo by which he had bound himself, such as his declaration at the Jerusalem Day ceremony on 31 May 2000. At the governmental memorial ceremony for the fallen of the 1967 war, Barak repeated his commitment to a whole and undivided Jerusalem under eternal Israeli sovereignty and declared that only a person who is cut off from Jewish history could cede any part of Jerusalem. Barak added the words "any part," which were not in the text produced by his speechwriter. Thus he was exposed to hawkish criticism when he was obliged to back down from his previous declarations, and his credibility was undermined.

(2) Another factor was the collapse of Barak's governing coalition on the eve of the Camp David summit, which limited his maneuverability. He faced an opposition coalition composed of the parties representing immigrants from the former Soviet Union, the religious community, and hawks who opposed what they viewed as excessive concessions to the Palestinians (Drucker 2002: 164–85). Acceptance or rejection of any agreement he brought back from Camp David was thus placed in the hands of an

amorphous political center. Barak sought to satisfy this constituency by signing an agreement ending the historical conflict and by insisting on Israeli sovereignty in the historical and religious heart of Jerusalem.

There was no uniformity of opinion within the Israeli delegation to the conference. Dan Meridor, the chairman of the Knesset's Foreign Affairs and Defense Committee, and Elyakim Rubinstein, the attorney general, were more hawkish than Barak and Sher. Barak included them in the delegation because of their intellectual capabilities, professional experience, and political stature. Yet they disagreed with Barak's positions and sometimes "voted with their feet," failing to show up for meetings. Barak himself sometimes removed them from the loop and did not invite them to consultations held by the Israeli delegation. On the opposite side, Ministers Amnon Shahak and Ben-Ami were somewhat more moderate than Sher and Barak. In December 2000, on the eve of Clinton's presentation of his ideas to the two sides, Ben-Ami even took private positions that caused considerable anger among his colleagues in the Israeli delegation (Sher 2001: 159, 190, 355–57). Such differences of opinion were not unique to Camp David. They existed at the top levels of the Israeli government. Yet despite these disagreements, Barak controlled the delegation and the government with a strong hand. While Barak was not always consistent in his positions (Sher 2001: 184–85), he always exercised his authority.

Barak himself limited the range of views he heard by choosing who would be physically present at Camp David with him. Oded Eran was allowed into Camp David only on the third day of the conference, whereas Israel Hasson, who worked under Eran, was there from the first moment. Similarly, Barak kept Minister of Education Yossi Sarid, leader of the dovish Meretz Party, away from Camp David on the pretext that there were not enough beds at the retreat—even though he easily found accommodations for Meridor and Minister of Tourism Amnon Shahak (Drucker 2002: 167). As noted, similar phenomena existed on the Palestinian side as well.

In comparison with the Israeli delegation to Camp David, the Israeli team that negotiated the first Oslo agreement was more unified and less concerned with personal and political tensions. According to participants in the Israeli delegation, interpersonal relations and the political and personal agendas of the senior Israeli participants at Camp David were detrimental to the unity of the Israeli delegation and encouraged competition among its members.

Indeed, the internal Israeli interaction and leadership problems affected the Israeli-Palestinian interaction. The Palestinians had doubts about

Barak's ability to get his party, governing coalition, and the public to accept whatever agreement he reached. Barak's coalition was unstable, and there were fundamental divisions within the cabinet between those who advocated a partial permanent arrangement (Peres, Ramon, and Sarid) and those who supported a full permanent arrangement (Beilin, Ben-Ami, and Barak himself). The Palestinian leadership wondered whether Barak could sign a full-fledged permanent status agreement. Would he be able to obtain a majority in his party and in the country for painful and difficult concessions by Israel, as the Palestinian position required? The Palestinian leadership was not enthusiastic about facing a leader whose sincerity and political position were, in their view, both open to doubt.

Israel's credibility in Palestinian eyes was also compromised by its delay in implementing some of the provisions of the Oslo accords during the period beginning with Netanyahu's accession to the premiership. Later, they were disappointed by the grueling negotiations conducted by Barak and Sher over the implementation of the Wye agreements signed by the Netanyahu government. The Palestinians were unsure whether Barak was Rabin's successor or another version of Netanyahu. This doubt was redoubled by the extensive construction in the settlements that took place under the Barak government. The Israeli army pulled back from major Palestinian population centers during the implementation of the second Oslo agreement, but the settlements remained in place and a large number of these are located in physical proximity to Palestinian residential areas. Their very existence, not to mention their expansion, gave rise to the feeling that nothing substantial had changed. From the Palestinian point of view, the occupation remained close at hand and continued to consume their territory. They met Israeli soldiers from afar on the outskirts of Zones A or B. But they saw the settlers up close every day in the settlements and on the extensive network of roads leading to them.

(3) Barak's personality, his long service in the army and lack of civilian and diplomatic experience, his individualism, centralized working habits, and way of thinking all contributed to the failure of the talks. Agha and Malley describe Barak as using a binary cost-benefit analysis and taking a single-minded approach. In his perception, the Palestinians were using a salami tactic—pocketing Israeli concessions and then using them as the starting point for the next round of talks. He concluded from this that it would be best to make the Palestinians what he saw as an attractive proposal, one they would have no choice but to accept (Agha and Malley 2001; Morris 13 June 2002). The Palestinians' negative reaction led the Israeli negotiating team to repeat the same approach, but with reduced

parameters. In doing so, Israel added an Oriental-bazaar negotiating style to its red-lines strategy. It should be added that Barak had been ambivalent toward the PLO and Arafat ever since the September 1993 Oslo agreement, an ambivalence that remained with him until his last day in office. On the one hand he recognized Israel's interest in reaching an agreement and knew what price would have to be paid for this. On the other hand, he had a deep emotional connection to the historical portions of the Land of Israel, and a deep skepticism of Palestinian willingness to compromise on the parameters that he, Barak, put before them. Even prior to the Camp David summit, Barak entreated the American administration to "expose" and "unmask" Arafat (Agha and Malley 2001), something he himself has endeavored to do ever since the summit ended. Barak thus did not hold working meetings with Arafat at Camp David, nor did he develop close and trusting personal relations with his counterpart. He had very few meetings with Arafat during the process, and most of those failed. He also failed to nurture a special relationship with Abu Mazen or Abu 'Ala. The lack of direct communication between the leaders negatively impinged on the process in general, and on the summit in particular. It also aroused Palestinian fears that Israel was setting a trap.

Furthermore, the Palestinians were confused by Barak's unwillingness to commit himself clearly to far-reaching measures, his concern to leave himself an escape hatch from every situation, and his insistence on testing the Palestinian side prior to each slow step toward it. The Palestinians complained that they were receiving mixed messages from Israel and that Israel was unwilling to pay the price required for a full and final permanent arrangement.

Internal Palestinian Interaction and Leadership Problems

The Palestinian response to Israeli actions, and dissension within the Palestinian leadership, caused further setbacks in the effort to achieve an agreement.

(1) Israel's unilateral withdrawal from southern Lebanon in May 2000 led to a consolidation of Palestinian opposition. The withdrawal from Lebanon came about as the result of public pressure, itself a reaction to the large losses of life suffered there by the Israeli army since the 1982 war. The withdrawal was perceived by a part of the Palestinian public, and by the new opposition within the Fatah, as proof that the Jews would respond only to force. These people believed that Israel had fled from Lebanon. They thus demanded that Arafat make no concessions to Israel in the

negotiations and that he allow them to carry out violent acts of protest against Israeli targets to counter Israel's actions and to force Israel to soften its positions.

At the same time, there was growing criticism within the Palestinian public of corruption among a part of the Palestinian political and economic elite, which was seen as collaborating with Israel in return for money and status. Palestinian pollster Khalil Shikaki found in 1996 that 43 percent of the Palestinian population in the territories had a positive opinion of Palestinian democracy and human rights and 64 percent gave positive marks to the Palestinian Authority. By 2001 these percentages had dropped to 21 and 40 percent respectively (Shikaki 2002).

This corruption was an important factor in shaping Palestinian public opinion. According to Dr. Shikaki's finding in 1996, 64 percent positively evaluated the performance of the Palestinian Authority institutions. In 2001 this percentage dropped to 40 percent (Shikaki 2002). Senior figures in the Palestinian Authority and in its security services controlled the border crossings with Egypt and the crossings to Israel and took a percentage of the revenues from the commerce that passed through. Muhammad Dahlan, the head of the preventative security force in the Gaza Strip, controls all movement between the Gaza Strip and Israel from the north and east and between the Strip and Egypt from the west. Jamil Tarifi, minister of civil affairs in the Palestinian Authority, controls the Allenby Bridge crossing. The regime of monopolies in the Palestinian Authority placed the import of gasoline, cement, and tobacco, for example, under the control of Jibril Rajoub, head of the preventative security apparatus in the West Bank, Muhammad Rashid, Arafat's economic adviser, Jamil Tarifi, and Abu 'Ala, the head of the Palestinian Legislative Council. To this must be added the large profits from the operation of the casino in Jericho, which were divided between the Austrian investors and Muhammad Rashid, the representative of the Palestinian Authority (*Ha'aretz* 4 January 2001). A number of retired Israeli security personnel were also involved in running this economic regime. The cooperation between them and personnel of the Palestinian Authority added fuel to the fire of criticism raised by members of the Fatah apparatus, members of the Legislative Council, and intellectuals who were not included in the executive branch.

The Palestinian Authority was built on symbiosis among a security elite, an academic-professional elite, a political elite, and a local propertied and social elite of notables. This symbiosis eroded the status of the historical leadership of the PLO and the Fatah, most of which arrived "from the outside." The status of this leadership was based on the historical "armed struggle," a concept personified charismatically by Arafat. It was also based on the achievement of managing the transition from war to political dialogue with Israel and on the transition from representation from afar, from outside of Palestine, to direct elections in 1996 and the establishment of governing institutions in the West Bank and the Gaza Strip (Klein 2001: 214–46; Schultz 1999: 102–5, 119–43; Klein 1997). However, a large number of factors eroded the standing of the ruling elite and brought young Fatah leaders to prominence. These factors included Arafat's loss of direct contact with the Palestinian Authority's citizenry and the PLO rank and file and the limited effectiveness of governmental institutions. Another factor was the way in which Palestinian Authority military and police forces operated, with patronage going from Arafat's office down through his powerful gatekeepers and uncoordinated ministers. There was also a high degree of deinstitutionalization of the political and administrative systems (Sayigh 2001: 47–60), corruption of a magnitude that could hardly be ignored, and the fact that the average Palestinian's quality of life did not change much under the Oslo accords. This echelon of young leaders, around forty years of age, had been admired field activists in the 1987 Intifada, during which many of them were wounded, arrested, or deported. The passage of the PLO and the Fatah from the "outside" to the "inside" from 1994 to 1996 left some of these activists, such as Marwan Barghouthi from Ramallah or Sami and Jamal Abu-Smahadana, two brothers from Rafah in the Gaza Strip, outside the supreme institutions of the movement, the Central Council, and the Revolutionary Council. These two bodies were controlled by Arafat loyalists and the historical veteran leadership that arrived from Tunis. In contrast, some prominent activists from the young, local generation of the Fatah, such as Jibril Rajoub, Muhammad Dahlan, Sufian Abu-Zaydeh, and Hisham Abd al-Raziq, were placed in key positions in the executive authority (respectively, chief of preventative security, West Bank; chief of preventative security, Gaza Strip; head of the Israel desk in the Ministry of Planning and International Cooperation; minister of detainees and freed detainees). Others of their generation, such as Qadura Fares of Ramallah, Hussam Khader of Balata refugee camp, and Khatim 'Eid of Jerusalem, were chosen for the Legislative Council in the Fatah elections.

At the end of 1997 the members of the young leadership of the Fatah who were left outside of the establishment decided to breathe life into the movement and to establish their power base by conducting elections to Fatah's local branches, mainly in the West Bank (the Gaza Strip was controlled more closely by the veteran leadership). By 1999, a total of 122

such elections had been held, in which more than 85,000 people participated (Baskin 2001).

One of the power bases of the new opposition was the West Bank refugee camps. Despite the entry of the Palestinian Authority into the West
Bank and Gaza Strip, the residents of the refugee camps retained local
loyalties. Local loyalty to the camp was stronger than the loyalty to the
National Security Agency, for which many residents of the refugee camps
worked. The primacy of local identity and loyalty was due to more than
the refugees' protracted residence in the camps, beginning after the 1948
war. It was also a product of the role played by the residents of the camps
in the 1987 Intifada, producing a much-admired local leadership; the
weapons that had since that time come into the hands of the residents; and
animosity toward the traditional, conservative, wealthy notables. National factors were also involved: the weakness of the processes of institutionalization, centralization of power, and nation building since the establishment of the Palestinian Authority; and the beginning of the imprinting
of the patron-client relationship that characterized the PLO "outside"
onto the institutions of the Palestinian Authority as well. A situation was
created whereby personal loyalty, loyalty to the residential quarter and to
the refugee camp, and loyalty to the political organization represented by
the local leader in the refugee camp all converged. The Palestinian Authority penetrated the camps only in a limited way. It was perceived as corrupt,
or overly conciliatory with Israel, or, most often, both. The opposition
that organized itself among the rank and file of the Fatah succeeded in
establishing itself in the camps and in competing with the national intelligence agencies to a great extent thanks to the local leadership—"the field
leadership"—that joined it (Regular 28 January, 4, 11, 18, 25 February
2000; Shikaki 2002; Hass 21 August 2001).

The veteran leadership tried to deal with the new organization in a
variety of ways, including attempts to confiscate the weapons of the members of the Fatah apparatus (the Tanzim). In October 1998, military intelligence forces under the command of Colonel Musa Arafat attempted to
confiscate weapons from the Tanzim in Ramallah but were met with gun-
fire. After several tense days, the military intelligence forces withdrew
from the city. A similar incident took place in the Balata refugee camp near
Nablus a month later, when general security forces under the command of
Haj Isma'il Jabr tried to collect illegal weapons there (Baskin 2001; Regular 28 January, 4 February 2000).

Alternatively, the veteran leadership tried to co-opt the young local
leaders into the agencies of the authority. The residents of refugee camps

such as Balata and al-'Amari were drafted into the security apparatus of Jibril Rajoub or the Tawfiq Terawi security forces, but this was not very helpful. Violent confrontations broke out at the beginning of 2000 between the Palestinian police and security apparatuses under the command of the veteran leadership, on the one side, and on the other, local forces in the refugee camps that had joined together in the new opposition. The spark that set off the confrontations was in many cases some minor issue, but one behind which more serious matters lurked (Hass 27 March 2000; Regular 28 January, 4 February 2000). To mark two events on the Palestinian calendar in May 2000, Prisoners Week and Naqba Day (marking the Palestinian catastrophe that resulted from the establishment of Israel in 1948), Arafat ordered that Marwan Barghouthi and Jibril Rajoub be reconciled. Rajoub was accused by Barghouthi of collaboration with Israel and with handing over five Palestinians arrested by his people. The five were wanted by Israel (Baskin 2001). Finally, at the beginning of September 2000, the veteran leadership initiated a coup in the Tanzim, bringing about the election of Hussein al-Shaykh as secretary-general of the Fatah in the West Bank, in place of Barghouthi. Al-Shaykh is of Barghouthi's generation but, unlike the latter, was close to the veteran establishment. The number of members of the body that elects the secretary-general was enlarged, and loyalists of the veteran leadership were included.

These brought about a formal change that lasted only a short time (*Kol HaIr* 8 September 2000). The outbreak of the Intifada three weeks later united the ranks of the Tanzim. Barghouthi led the confrontation with Israel and represented the Tanzim to the outside world, with Hussein al-Shaykh subordinate to him. Thus, internal Palestinian processes and personal and institutional factors mixed with the problems in the dialogue with Israel. The members of the Tanzim demanded that the national leadership take hawkish positions in the negotiations with Israel—total evacuation of the settlements, the establishment of a Palestinian state in all the territories of the West Bank and the Gaza Strip, Israeli recognition of the right of return of the 1948 refugees, and fulfillment of all of the agreements signed by Israel. The first pressure tactic employed by the Tanzim was raising the continuing detention of some 1,894 Palestinian prisoners in Israeli prisons. The Palestinian leadership demanded the release of the majority of these in accordance with its interpretation of the Oslo accords, but Israel refused, claiming that at issue were people with "blood on their hands." The prisoner question affected many Palestinian families across the political spectrum; around it, public and organizational support could crystallize. Through the issue of the prisoners, the new opposition brought out the powerlessness of the leadership and at the same time backed up that leadership in its demand to release the prisoners. The events of Prisoners Week and Naqba Day (a week of violent demonstrations, 8–15 May 2000) were organized by the new opposition and expressed the connection between the actual problem of the prisoners and the powerful symbolic issue of the right of return of the 1948 refugees. The bitterness and protest over the nonimplementation of some of the provisions of the interim agreement (the Oslo agreement) were attributed to the negotiations over a permanent arrangement.

Arafat's leadership style blends anarchy and lack of supervision with exaggerated centralism. He encourages people and institutions to fight over positions of power and influence at the highest echelons of the executive authority. Furthermore, he has delayed the processes of institutionalization and nation building in order to continue employing the system of personal loyalty and patronage that characterized the PLO in Beirut and Tunis (Rubinstein 2001; Sayigh 1997: 447–63, 663–92). His style has created foci of protest and agitation within the Palestinian leadership. The decline in the legislature's activity and the ongoing contention between the members of the Legislative Council and Arafat over the council's powers and the laws that it has enacted or sought to enact over Arafat's disapproval (Abu Amr 1999: 25–29) have helped create a focus of opposition based around the Fatah organization and Fatah members on the Legislative Council. In contrast to some of the members of the ruling elite who came from "outside" after many years as part of the PLO apparatus in Tunis, the members of this echelon lived in the West Bank or were expelled by Israel only in the 1980s. The new opposition drew legitimacy from the previous Intifada and from the new issues in the public discourse. It made claims in the name of the "values of the Intifada"; called for "building institutions"; and desired "democratic legitimacy," "transparency and supervision of the activities of the Palestinian regime," "the separation of powers," "proper working procedures in the executive authority," and "struggle against the despotism and arbitrariness" (Schultz 1999: 163–67; Jayyusi 1998: 189–211; Klein 31 July 1994).

This opposition within the establishment is an opposition of a new kind, completely different from the opposition of the leftist organizations who had previously been Arafat's antagonists within the PLO. The leftist organizations have not been a significant factor on the Palestinian political map since the collapse of the Soviet Union and the Fatah movement's decision to conclude agreements with Israel according to parameters that were unacceptable to them. The left failed to convince the Palestinian public at large to oppose the Fatah's policies. Radical Islam's rise in the 1980s also hurt the Left, leaving its organizations with neither an agenda nor public support. The new internal Fatah opposition differs no less from Hamas and Islamic Jihad than from the left. Besides subscribing to a different ideology—national-conservative rather than religious-radical—it has a different attitude toward the Palestinian establishment. Between 1987 and 1994, Hamas and Islamic Jihad were antiestablishment organizations, seeking to replace the PLO, but since the establishment of the Palestinian Authority in 1994, they have been extraestablishment but not antiestablishment. Moreover, some Hamas operatives have joined, on an individual basis, the religious establishment of the Palestinian Authority, and others ran in the elections for the Legislative Council and were elected. However, as organizations, Hamas and Islamic Jihad are extraestablishment and are waiting for the public to call on them to assume the leadership mantle now worn by the current ruling elite (Klein 1996). Their position outside of the establishment has made it difficult for them to operate their institutions and has prevented them from using national institutions as a source of legitimacy. The Fatah, in contrast, is the movement of the government, the spine of the Palestinian Authority. This opposition from within the establishment has greater standing in the public and in the government system. The members of the new opposition enjoy both a direct line to the establishment and political strength based on unmediated contact with and attentiveness to the population. In this way, they differ from the executive establishment and the ruling elite, which have maintained power through coercive enforcement.

As noted, the Palestinian ruling elite did not succeed in bringing about Israeli withdrawal from the territories during the seven years following the Oslo accords. There was also protracted public bitterness over the violence perpetrated by the Palestinian security apparatuses and their haughtiness toward Palestinian civilians. The new opposition identified the Palestinian government's modes of operation with its policies, in particular with its negotiations with Israel, and sought to change these fundamentally. This brought the internal Fatah opposition together with some of the members of the Legislative Council and the intellectual and academic elite who were not included in the ministries of the Palestinian Authority. Although one homogenous body challenging the leadership was not created, a common critical denominator was formed that continued to gain strength as it transpired that the negotiations were not yielding the hoped-for results.

The internal Fatah opposition took advantage of the elites' distress in the face of the reality of interim agreements. The interim agreements created an ambiguity both in relations with Israel and on the internal Palestinian scene. Without a permanent status arrangement, the future remained unclear and the struggle for independence had not ended. The leadership could not paint the future in concrete colors and did not bring about a sharp and full transition from the revolutionary ethos of the Fatah to the building of political institutions. This lack of clarity assisted the Fatah opposition. They demanded permission to engage in attacks on Israel as the negotiations sputtered on. When the talks on a permanent arrangement reached a crisis, the ground had been prepared. All that was missing was the spark that would set off the conflagration.

The rocky progress and delays in the implementation of the Oslo accords made the Palestinians suspicious and raised doubts even among those negotiating with Israel and senior members of the Palestinian security establishment. It should be recalled that the heads of the Palestinian security apparatuses had, since 1995 (and even more since 1998), been coordinating their antiterrorist activities with Israel. During the years in which the Oslo accords guided their activity, the Palestinian security apparatuses considered the struggle against terror by the Hamas and the provision of security to Israel as a national Palestinian interest, a condition for the end of the occupation. They could thus deny that they were collaborators, as Hamas accused them of being. During this period the self-image of the Palestinian security apparatuses changed, as did their view of Israel. Israel's dependence on Palestinian security cooperation weakened Israel's image as a power and strengthened the Palestinian self-image (Usher 1998: 146–61). This was productive for as long as both sides were talking and reaching agreements. However, when the peace track was disrupted, it contributed to the outbreak of the Intifada, in which Palestinian security personnel of all ranks participated in violent attacks against Israeli soldiers and civilians on both sides of the Green Line. This allowed members of the security organizations to cleanse themselves of the "guilt" of military collaboration with Israel imputed by Hamas and Islamic Jihad. This course succeeded from their point of view. With the Intifada being run by members of Fatah and the ruling establishment, the masses did not turn to Hamas to replace the ruling elite. On the contrary, the public image of the ruling establishment and of the Palestinian security agencies improved, as public opinion polls conducted on behalf of Bir Zeit University in November 2000 and February and June 2001 demonstrate (www.birzeit.edu/dsp).

The mixture of limited centralized oversight by Palestinian institutions and their chaotic operational methods could be seen in the Intifada that broke out in late 2000, both in the lack of general strategy or central command and by the methods used by armed units or individuals. A paper published by Yazid Sayigh, as well as Palestinian documents confiscated by the IDF, clearly show the lack of a political or military strategy and the absence of planning and operational coordination on a level higher than local midlevel commanders. There was a shortage of basic logistical supplies, and confrontations broke out between some security units and Fatah militiamen. The documents published by Israel show also that at the first stage of the Intifada the different parts of the new opposition played an active role in its operations. As the conflict with Israel escalated after the end of 2001, they began to cooperate in the field with Palestinian Authority units (Sayigh 2001; www.idf.il; Ze'ev Schiff, "Peeping into Captured Documents," *Ha'aretz* 24 May 2002).

(2) The Palestinian leadership made little effort to present its case to the Israeli public and to convince Prime Minister Barak of the justice of its position. Instead, the Palestinian delegation withdrew into itself in the face of what it perceived as the arrogance of the Israeli conqueror and its attempt to dictate a solution by force.

Moreover, according to Robert Malley, President Clinton's adviser for Middle East affairs, the Palestinian delegation was unable to conduct a dialogue with the United States in language that the Americans could understand and in accordance with the operative code of the American administration. The Palestinians assumed that there was an Israeli-American intrigue afoot, whereas there was no more than close coordination between the representatives of the two states. The belief that they were facing a conspiracy of major dimensions caused the Palestinians to develop a siege mentality and to take refuge in an emotional bunker. Their goal was survival, rather than exploration of opportunities to progress toward additional achievements. The Palestinian delegation did not present counterproposals to those put forward by Israel, proposals that the American government could not ignore. According to Malley, instead of taking an open approach and engaging in give-and-take, the Palestinians were suspicious, unimaginative, and closed-off, both at Camp David and later, in December, when they were presented with President Clinton's ideas (Malley, 7 March, 12 April 2001). What the Palestinian delegation did not know is that throughout the entire process, and at Camp David in particular, Israel feared even the shadow of any American document that seemed about to be placed on their table. They were concerned that their position would be whittled away by the United States before it was presented to the Palestinians and that the end result would be very different from what Israel had planned. Barak tried to guess what the American document would contain, and he held consultations about how to prevent its submission, or at least how to shape it in accordance with Israel's positions. He also began to plan how to respond to it if it were to be submitted (Sher 2001: 159–63, 168, 191–92, 260, 315). This fear was built into the redlines strategy that Israel used in conducting the permanent status negotiations with the Palestinians.

Thus the Palestinians concluded that the American government's positions were close to those of Israel and that the United States was therefore not an honest broker. In their opinion, the American administration displayed too much sympathy for Barak's coalition and public problems and was not considerate enough of Palestinian and Muslim feelings toward the Temple Mount and the Old City and of Arafat's internal problems. The American position, concluded the Palestinians, was coordinated with Israel, and the Americans put pressure on the Palestinian side only (Haniyya 2000).

The sense of siege and the absence of an atmosphere of equal partnership—because of the language of hegemony adopted by Israel—led the Palestinians to cast themselves into rigid positions and to perceive Israel as taking similar positions. The Palestinian side saw its interlocutors as arrogant, seeking to dictate a solution that suited them. The Israelis, the Palestinians believed, were the prisoners of their own myths about the creation of the refugee problem in 1948 and were influenced by internal Israeli political considerations rather than by the necessity of finding paths to the heart of its negotiating partners (Haniyya 2000). Gaps in expectations, in behavior, in culture, and in religion grew ever larger during the course of the conference. The United States did not succeed in bridging these and creating a dialogue between them and a dynamic of compromise.

More than anything else, Israel's claims regarding the Temple Mount, and the reasoning it employed, shocked the Palestinian delegation. Israel demanded that its sovereignty over the site be recognized; it also wanted a synagogue built at its periphery, in a place that, according to the calculations of several rabbis, was outside the historical area of the Temple. The Israeli claim was based on the holiness of the site where the Jewish temples had been located. This was the first time that Israeli representatives officially raised these claims and presented them as a red line over which they were prepared to break the agreement. It was also the first time that the representatives of Israel based their claim to sovereignty on manifestly religious grounds. The connection between the religious issue and the national issue was self-evident to the members of the Israeli delegation with regard to their own position, but they did not consider that same connection to be legitimate on the Palestinian side (Diaries of Shlomo Ben-Ami, *Ma'ariv* 6 April 2001). The Palestinian side had trouble understanding how a government that had declared a civil-secular revolution could adopt the position and language of a nationalistic and Messianic group in Israel. The introduction of the topic of the Temple into the center of the Israeli discourse and onto the negotiating table touched a sensitive Palestinian point—it gave credence to the Palestinian belief, widespread since the mid-1920s, that Zionism sought to erect a third Temple on the ruins of the Islamic holy places.

The Israeli delegation presumably did not raise these claims because it envisioned the construction of a temple. It rather sought to prove to the Israeli public that the negotiations had led to a change in the existing situation. This was in order to reduce the criticism voiced by the majority of the religious and hawkish public against the course taken by the Israeli government. The Israeli delegation was thus motivated by public relations considerations and not the fear that it would not be possible to attain an agreement once the Israeli claims concerning the Temple Mount had been raised.

In raising these claims, the Israeli delegation also ignored the problem of fulfilling the agreement over time and preventing damage to the Islamic holy places on the Temple Mount should the Israeli claim be accepted. The change that would take place on the Temple Mount in Israel's favor could be too small and very frustrating for the Jewish extremists who wanted to build the temple and not have to see before them, beyond their small synagogue at the periphery of the area, hundreds of thousands of Muslims praying in majesty, splendor, and glory, with Arafat at their head hosting the heads of the Arab and Muslim states. The huge gap that would exist between their dream of building the Jewish temple and the reality in which they would find themselves could arouse severe frustration and lead them to harm the Muslim holy places at the site.

Thus, faulty Israeli preparation for the talks left its mark on the religious issue as well. The lack of a religious discourse within the Israeli establishment that prepared for the summit and the failure to initiate a religious dialogue between the Israeli and Palestinian representatives were critical once the question of the Temple Mount was raised in the way it was raised. The religious issue seems to have deterred the Israeli decision makers. They were afraid to deal with it because they themselves were not religious and lacked familiarity with the philosophical and legal world of Judaism. They did not foster an internal Israeli religious discourse, and in its absence they perceived the religion of Israeli nationalist extremists as the authentic expression of Jewish religion. Judaism's attachment to the Temple Mount was thus seen through the eyes of these religious extremists (Sher 2001: 247). The religious extremist always takes absolute positions and claims that he expresses the absolute truth. In contrast, the believer stands *before* the Absolute. To the outside observer it seems, mistakenly, that the authentic religious person is the one who speaks *in the name of* the Absolute. Only a deep religious discourse will lay bare this optical illusion (Fruman 2001; Gorenberg 2001).

Because the Temple Mount was symbolically and historically charged, the issue of its control easily became one of principle. The Palestinian side could not free itself from the impression that Israel was looking after the interests of a small and extreme religious group. On the other hand, they also failed to estimate correctly the change that would occur in the symbolic status of the Temple Mount among the Israeli public once the dispute came out into the open. Until then, the status of the Temple Mount in the Israeli public consciousness had been fairly marginal. However, the dispute, and the Palestinian denial of any religious or historical Jewish connection to the site, turned the Temple Mount, in the eyes of the majority of the Israeli public, into a symbol of the Jewish people's historical connection to the city of Jerusalem and the Land of Israel. For the majority of Israelis, the Temple Mount does not symbolize the Temple ritual but rather the historical and religious roots of the Jewish people there, and in this the majority differs from the marginal groups that wish to rebuild the Temple.

In order to balance the picture, the Palestinian delegation fortified itself behind UN resolutions ("international legitimacy" and "the full rights of the Palestinian people"). In response to the historical claims of Israel in the matter of the Temple Mount, Arafat answered with his own historical narrative and denied any possibility of the location of the ruins of the Jewish Temple beneath the Temple Mount area.

(3) A third factor contributing to the lack of success of the negotiations was the unwillingness of both Arafat and Barak to report directly to their publics about the concessions made by the other side. Each side feared that doing so would worsen its own position as the talks proceeded, harm its bargaining position, and undermine its standing before its electorate. The Israeli public received its information largely from deliberate leaks and from protests by the opposition against the major concessions made by the

Israeli delegation. The leaks were intended to portray the Israeli government as desiring peace more than the Palestinian delegation and to preserve public support during the Camp David summit. This, the government hoped, would bring about a softening in the Palestinian position and lower the level of opposition protest activity from Israeli hawks. On the other hand, the Palestinian delegation sought to portray their Israeli interlocutors as obstinate and to preserve their internal unity.

Both parties ended up leaving the negotiations feeling they had not found much common ground with the other side. Instead, the atmosphere was one of all-out competition and arm twisting in a zero-sum game. When, on the first day of the conference, Arafat and Barak politely pushed each other into the doorway of Clinton's cabin and then both tried to fit through together, it symbolized not only the opening of the conference but also its course. The manner in which the Camp David conference was conducted prevented each side from publicly revealing the concessions of the other side.

Poor Negotiating Strategies

Conceptual inventiveness does not derive from the establishment but rather from extraestablishment factors, according to Yair Hirschfeld (Hirschfeld 2000: 276–77). That is what happened in the process that created the Oslo agreement and in the first stages of the negotiations over Jerusalem. The back channels and the work done in some think tanks contributed to the shaping of Israel's positions at the initial stage of the negotiations over Jerusalem. However, in contrast to the Oslo process and the formulation of the Beilin–Abu Mazen document, in which the team that created the conceptual innovation was also directly involved in the negotiations, in the official talks over the final status agreement, and at Camp David in particular, the negotiator was the establishment itself. Some experts who were involved in developing new concepts were called upon to assist, but only on occasion. Their contribution was limited to intermittent supplementary consultation. It was establishment thinking that proved decisive.

In addition, the establishment rejected a proposal of assistance from some academic experts, who indeed possessed practical experience in the field of negotiation and its accompanying processes, and not just with the Palestinians. Furthermore, in total contrast to Oslo, at Camp David and thereafter no "win-win" spirit, respect, personal friendship and trust, dialogue among equals, or sense of partnership was created. These factors, which so characterized the negotiators of the first Oslo agreement (Hirschfeld 1998: 278), affected as well the persons who did not actually negotiate but rather stood behind the scenes and guided the delegations: Arafat, Abu Mazen, Rabin, Peres, and Beilin. During the peace process of the year 2000, of which the Camp David was the peak, the opposite occurred. Tempers heated up during the arguments and instead of being calming and unifying, the atmosphere quickly became explosive and wrenching. The members of the delegations returned from Camp David disappointed, mistrustful, frustrated, bitter, and angry. The more the disagreement between them deepened, the more each side lost the ability to see things from the other side's perspective. It seems, moreover, that the involvement of extraestablishment persons in the negotiations over the 1993 Oslo agreement gave the Israeli team experience in introducing new ways of thinking and finding ways of changing positions during negotiations. To a lesser degree, these qualities characterized the contacts before, during, and after Camp David. The dominant approach in these contacts was the establishment's approach.

The American management of the conference allowed both sides to steer the discussions to the question of sovereignty over the Temple Mount and the Old City and to concentrate on a top-down approach. The concept that guided all of those involved in the conference was that the appropriate formula for sovereignty regarding the Temple Mount would serve as a locomotive. Attainment of a settlement in this territory would lead to the attainment of a settlement in the Old City and subsequently an agreement on the inner arc of Palestinian neighborhoods near the Old City. The resolution of the question of Jerusalem would bring in its wake agreement on the rest of the issues in the permanent arrangement. The adoption of this approach turned Jerusalem into the benchmark issue. Jerusalem was not the last subject on which the entire compact would stand or fall, as Begin, Sadat, and Carter assumed at the first Camp David summit. On the contrary: Jerusalem blocked all progress on the other subjects. The failure to reach agreement on the Temple Mount and the Old City affected the agreements that emerged at Camp David on the other issues on the agenda.

The focus on the search for a concept of sovereignty that would suit the conflicting claims over the Temple Mount and the Old City caused the discussion on the question of Jerusalem to be cut off from other issues. It thus became impossible to engage in barter among the core issues in the permanent arrangement. The ability of the negotiators to maneuver was restricted, and neither side wanted to give in. This was also the opposite of the traditional American approach, which was to proceed from the easier to the harder issues. The idea was to first resolve those issues that could be agreed upon and then subsequently to create tools for finding a real or imagined solution to difficult questions. An imagined solution is, for example, one in which deliberate vagueness allows each side to think that it has attained what it desired.

However, even without this it was not appropriate to deal only with the search for a definition of sovereignty that would save the talks. In parallel with the top-down approach, it was necessary to employ a bottom-up method and examine carefully, in work teams and by means of professional experts, the questions of the basic powers in various areas and the principles of an arrangement with respect to which there is no practical disagreement between the sides. The bottom-up approach was tried for a short period in August–September 2000 at Israel's initiative (Sher 2001: 253) However, the Israeli position was shaped by the parameters that had been fixed since the Stockholm talks, rather than by maximal openness to examining opposing possibilities. The move was perceived by the Palestinian leadership as a trick way of marketing, in a different way, principles it had already rejected. A different use of the bottom-up approach would have mitigated the deep Palestinian suspicion that Israel intended to perpetuate the existing situation. The area of agreement would have increased, and perhaps the Palestinian side would have recoiled less from accepting the proposal to defer the decision on the question of supreme sovereignty on the Temple Mount and in the Old City.

The opposite possibility also exists: it could have become clear to Israel that its supreme sovereignty would not be meaningful in practical terms and that it could relinquish sovereignty in exchange for practical arrangements. The bottom-up system is self-evident with regard to many areas in which there is close, intensive contact between Israelis and Palestinians: some of the areas of the holy basin and part of the city center of East Jerusalem. From this point of view the question of supreme sovereignty in these areas is largely symbolic because reality requires the establishment of special arrangements in the areas of law, policing and security, currency, transportation, infrastructure, and holy places, without connection to the question of who is the formal sovereign. Working together on the principles of the special arrangements would have lessened the sting of the question of sovereignty and opened the possibility of barter among various symbols or within the symbolic dimension of the Temple Mount.

Dealing with the practical level in parallel to the discussion of symbols would have provided a response to an important question presented by the Palestinian delegation: how would life look in the eastern city if the city were under Israeli sovereignty and Palestinian management? Wouldn't division and the complicated arrangements referred to by the Israeli delegation make daily life unbearable for the residents (Haniyya 2000)? This is a claim that is not to be taken lightly, and the delegations should have dealt with it in parallel with the discussion of a concept of sovereignty that would suit the interests of the two sides.

In order to succeed, the discussion of both subjects should have been based on egalitarian dialogue. Unfortunately, this was not the case. A similar question arose in the Israeli public and among professional experts after President Clinton presented his ideas, which included the division of sovereignty and of management between the two states and the two cities. In particular the Israeli question related to the Old City: how might President Clinton's ideas be implemented in the contentious territory of the Old City?

In the official negotiations on the permanent settlement, Israel was the leading force. It initiated and submitted proposals and made suggestions. The Palestinian side replied with its own proposals, but, as noted, the Palestinians failed to stress and market them to Israel and to the American mediator. Furthermore, Israel was the dominant force, the conductor of the orchestra. The Palestinian side, as was its custom, lacked a guiding and coordinating hand. This left the stage vacant for Israel.

Israel's key player was Ehud Barak. He set Israel's position, and with Gilad Sher's help he shaped its negotiating strategy. Barak's fundamental assumption was that time was working against Israel in the region. Iran was striding toward nuclear capability, and Islamic fundamentalism among Israel's neighbors threatened the stability of moderate Arab regimes and Israel itself (Sher 2001: 21; Morris 13 June 2002). But the assumption that time was against Israel was not applied to the Palestinian territories. The Israeli leadership viewed the territories as an asset. In part, this was because of the territories' historical status as "the land of the Patriarchs" and in part because the territories were important to the Palestinians and were thus a good bargaining card in the negotiations. At no point were they perceived as an ever-increasing burden for Israel. At no point did the Israeli leadership grasp that in the long run it could not control, indirectly and at a distance, the fate of more than three million Palestinians, while nibbling away at its land and water reserves and striking out at the power and legitimacy of the Palestinian establishment with which Israel had to negotiate a permanent settlement.

Believing that time was working against Israel put the leadership in a defensive position. The Israelis felt they had to fortify themselves, to defend their country from threats and enemies both distant and within Palestinian society. Peace seemed like a kind of fortification against war. In this spirit, in the permanent status negotiations Israel demanded oversight of the Palestinian state's borders and air space. It wanted to leave Israeli army bases in the Jordan Valley and allow the construction of the Gaza port only under its supervision. The Palestinian side, with which Israel demanded to achieve an end of hostilities and mutual claims, was expected to accept these security requirements in the context of war and to provide a solution for Israel's coalition and ideological problems. These latter problems had shaped Israel's red-lines strategy and formed its negotiating positions. Regrettably, this strategy, along with a negotiating style resembling that of a Levantine bazaar, was an important cause of the failure to achieve a permanent settlement in the negotiations that took place during 2000.

The red-lines strategy is based on a unilateral, ultimatum-style statement of the limits of one's concessions. It suits the ethos of Israeli heroism, Israel's self-image, and the Israeli concept of how best to conduct negotiations with the Arabs. It also suited the personal position of Barak, who had declared more than once his deep connection to the historical parts of the Land of Israel. The cultural component of this strategy may be stronger than its utilitarian considerations: toughness at the beginning in order to restrict the dimensions of the concessions and the flexibility that would come later. However, the red-lines strategy exacts a price. It encourages disagreement and crises and prods each side to take actions that will illustrate in the field just how important it regards its red lines to be. This may explain why Barak permitted the expansion of the settlements during the negotiations. This strategy leads the other side to draw its own red lines. And once both sides have done so, they will be lucky if the crisis remains only political and plays out only at the negotiating table. The al-Aqsa Intifada proves how explosive and uncontrollable this method is.

A red-lines strategy is very much a zero-sum game—whatever lies beyond the red line is dangerous. Any benefit to the other side would be a loss for Israel. No wonder that Gilad Sher liked to depict the permanent status negotiations as a match in his favorite sport—Far Eastern martial arts. For Sher, the critical elements of negotiation are the need to attack and keep the initiative, the need to avoid the traps set by one's rival, and the need to bring one's opponent to the position that one, or the leader whom one is representing, has determined. The mindset is an athletic or legal one based on a binary concept of win and lose. There can be no win-win situation—which is what characterizes the blue-lines strategy (see p. 175).

The approach is also a hierarchical one in which relations are always between inferior and superior; Israel must thus always be in the superior position. Naturally, this approach is rejected by the Palestinians, who see this as the continuation of occupation by other means. From the start they worked to create a dialogue of equals with Israel with regard to the 1967 territories. They could not ignore Israel's superiority and power, just as they could not ignore the fact that Israel covers 82 percent of Mandatory Palestine. But they conditioned their consent to a two-state compromise on the achievement of full sovereignty and status equal to that of Israel in its 1948 borders.

When Israel operates according to a red-lines strategy it concentrates on itself. It wants to establish its red line by itself, according to its own needs. One of these needs, and not the least important of them, is the position of its own internal opposition and Israeli public opinion. Only after the red lines are determined by taking these factors into account is the other side considered and any consideration given to its positions. At the time the red line setting the parameters of the permanent arrangement is established, the other side is but a secondary presence. Characteristically, in the lead-up to the Stockholm talks the Israelis assumed that the security issue would be easy to resolve because it was a technical-professional matter devoid of emotions. Furthermore, Israel's security position was so clear and rational that it was obvious that the opposite side would accept as logical the arrangements that Israel was proposing. The Israeli negotiators never imagined that control of air and land space, and the deployment of Israel forces deep in Palestinian territory and on its borders, contradicted a central Palestinian value—the desire to end the occupation (Sher 2001: 113–16). When Israel's negotiators came to realize this, it was difficult for them to retreat from their previous positions because of the unyielding framework of the red-lines strategy.

Furthermore, the Israeli leadership did not correctly estimate the influence of pressure groups, various elites (the local economic elite, foreign investors, the academic elite, groups of political activists of various types), nationalist spirit, and public opinion. The Israeli leadership preferred to concentrate most of the time on a single decision maker, Yasir Arafat, and invested a major effort in attempting to comprehend his way of thinking.

The Palestinian leader was not seen by official Israel as standing at the center of an insufficiently institutionalized political coalition, or even of a state of partial anarchy. Israel saw before it a single decision maker, with ranks of irrelevant people below him. In keeping with this assumption, Barak wanted to come to a summit where leaders would make decisions, rather than to a summit where an agreement would be signed after most of its major points had already been agreed on. Even after Camp David, and perhaps especially then, ministers and advisers urged Barak to invite Arafat to a meeting, to open up to him personally, and to improve the bad communication between them. It was argued that only he, Barak, could get Arafat to make the concessions that he expected (Sher 2001: 197, 276, 280).

In fact, for a time Israel took Abu 'Ala and Abu Mazen into account. One of the conclusions that Israel's negotiators drew from Camp David was that these two men had the ability to stymie any compromise that other members of their delegation might try to present to Arafat (Sher 2001: 242–43). Israel tried to market its preferred settlement to them, rejecting their proposal to base the contacts on a different strategy and thus reach a different kind of settlement (see chapter 1 and Sher 2001: 312–13). In response, Israel's principal negotiators expressed profound disappointment with the two men and used undiplomatic language in speaking of them and with the Palestinian leadership as a whole (Sher 2001: 11, 193; Ben-Ami in a published interview with Ari Shavit, Ha'aretz 14 July 2001).

From within "Fortress Israel," the view of the Palestinians was obscured. This structural failure in the Israeli strategy prevented the Israeli negotiators from properly identifying fundamental flaws in its own position. It led the Israelis to project Israeli characteristics onto the Palestinians and to blame the other side for the talks' failure. Israel's leaders interpreted Palestinian responses in accordance with Israel's strategy and conceptual world and thus viewed them as tactical evasion and an attempt to raise the ante (Sher 2001: 113–30). Israel projected onto the Palestinian side the inevitable result of the use of the red-lines strategy that Israel itself had formulated. The red lines were necessarily smudged, and Israel thus attributed to the Palestinians the use of a salami strategy intended to slice away at Israel's core positions. The Israelis simply did not understand the fundamental principles guiding the other side.

As a result, it took the rejection of its proposals at Camp David to mean that there was no Palestinian partner for a peace agreement. From the end of the Camp David summit through the end of Barak and Clinton's terms, the American government kept trying to persuade Israel that the Palestinians were indeed interested in a settlement, in contradiction to what Barak said. Barak told the Americans that the Palestinians wanted America to take a position very close to that of the Palestinians. The American stand, Barak argued, would then become the starting point for further erosion of Israel's position. According to Barak, Arafat was avoiding a decision, and he had to be pinned against the wall and left with no choices. Only then would he make the decision that Barak expected of him (Sher 2001: 326; Morris 13 June 2002).

The truth is that Barak's post–Camp David position was based on a profound contradiction. On the one hand, he expected to reach a settlement with Arafat and pressured Clinton to push Arafat to the wall and leave him with no alternatives. On the other hand, he complained to Clinton that Arafat was a liar and that the Palestinian position was irresponsible (Sher 2001: 328).

No less importantly, the red-lines strategy painted Israel's relations with the United States red, just as it did Israel's relations with the Palestinians.

Israel's objective was to construct relations with the United States that would help Israel force the Palestinians to accept Israel's red lines. Any American deviation from the red lines drawn by Israel—whether the deviation was real or only imagined—was perceived by Israel's leader as a strategic threat. The Israeli leadership was quick to coordinate its every move with Washington, and when it did not succeed in averting the submission of an American working paper, it began presenting maximalist positions to the United States as well. Israel assumed that some of its red lines would be smudged during bilateral talks with the United States, followed by continued smudging when the Palestinians entered the talks (Sher 2001: 260). As the direct talks with the Palestinians ran aground, Israel increasingly expected, and sometimes hoped, that an American paper would be presented to both sides. On the assumption that this would indeed happen, Israel took a tougher position. This intensified the crisis with the Palestinians and made it even more difficult to achieve a breakthrough.

Israel's view was that peace would be attained when the United States gave its backing to Israel's red lines and helped achieve them. The peace would be preserved and guaranteed by strengthening and upgrading Israeli's defense relationship with the United States. Even in a state of peace, Israel's relations with the United States would be on a much higher level than its relations with Palestine. American security guarantees were not just a way of persuading the Israeli public to cede the territories. They were a fundamental conception that was a corollary of the red-lines strategy and the view that time was working against Israel. Upgraded relations with the United States would compensate Israel for what it defined as a loss of defense assets.

Furthermore, Israel's strategy did not take into account the effect that an armed peace would have on the Palestinian public and its leaders. Like the other Arab nations, they had difficulty understanding Israel's profound existential insecurity. Feeling the weight of its military might on their backs every day, they could not conceive that Israel's government and people truly feared for their country's future. For the Palestinians, it was a conundrum that a strong country could feel insecure and therefore need to become even stronger in order to prove to itself how strong and secure it is. For Middle Eastern peoples who have lived in their lands for hundreds and thousands of years, this is incomprehensible. Israel's striving for power is interpreted by them as lack of confidence in peace and as preparation for another round of conquest and control of its immediate neighbors.

In the red-lines strategy, a close American-Palestinian relationship is perceived as negative. Any approach between the two is perceived as being at Israel's expense. Israel was indeed concerned about such closeness and worked successfully to prevent it. Negotiations were conducted according to the outline and pace set by Israel. The timing of the Camp David summit and its operational model were established in keeping with this line, which was accepted by the American administration.

With the outbreak of the Intifada, the red-lines policy caused even more damage. The central principle established by Israel was that there would be no prize for violence. Israel would not change its negotiating positions as a result of violence against it, and in any case it would not open negotiations until there was quiet. Israel did not properly discern the real reasons for the outbreak and continuation of the Intifada. A typical expression of Israel's attitude was Barak's statement to international leaders that Arafat could have ended the Intifada with two telephone calls (Sher 2001: 293, 301, 303). Israel assumed that the Intifada had been planned in advance by Arafat or that it was being run by him in order to make political gains that Israel had prevented at Camp David. While exploiting Palestinian violence for its own political purposes, Israel tried to impose on the Palestinians positions they had rejected during negotiations. The Palestinian violence eroded what remained of the trust each side had in the other, and Israel's condition that talks would continue only when violence ceased brought an end to the negotiations. Every act of violence, every gratuitous murder, every violation of orders by military, intelligence, or police forces, each attack by Israeli civilians and or by Palestinian terrorists simply placed more and more obstacles in the way of a negotiated settlement.

Israel's red-lines strategy also harmed U.S.-Palestinian relations. It led Clinton to attempt to sell Israel's red-lines positions to the Palestinians instead of putting forward a plan of his own that neither side could reject. Furthermore, one Israeli red line was often replaced by another (Agha and Malley 2001).

The political strategy of the Palestinian side at most of the stages of the negotiations was a strategy of passivity. It left the initiative to Israel, which the world perceived as taking greater steps toward the Palestinians than the Palestinians did toward Israel. Instead of catching the attention of Israel and the United States by marketing their own initiatives and taking a single, united, and coordinated stand, the Palestinians instead drew their own countervailing red line. The battle of the red lines then took precedence over the search for a compromise. When the Palestinians softened their position somewhat and proposed, for example, the division of the Old City according to a formula of 3:1, or agreed to the annexation to Israel of 4 percent of the area of the West Bank, it was hard for Israel to perceive this as a positive development. Both sides kept declaring in public what they would not concede, strengthening the perception that the negotiations had reached a dead end.

Bazaar-bargaining strategies found expression in the maps that Israel submitted during the course of the negotiations in three main areas—the dimensions of the Palestinian state as compared to the territory that would be annexed to Israel; the territorial exchange offered by Israel; and Jerusalem. In January 2000 Israel had spoken of ceding 66 percent of the West Bank to the Palestinian state. From March to December 2000, the official figure was 88 percent, and orally Israel had stated its willingness to add another 2 to 4 percent under certain circumstances. In December 2000, Israel submitted a map in which the Palestinian state included 92 percent of the West Bank, while orally Israel expressed a willingness to add another 2 percent if the Palestinians would in turn cut 2 percent off their demand. The territory that Israel demanded to annex was consequently smaller, and even the idea of leasing the Jordan Valley and retaining military control of it was dropped—although Israel still demanded that it be allowed to maintain forces on the Palestine-Jordan border at all times and to deploy Israeli troops elsewhere in the Palestinian state in times of emergency. Second, Israel had not offered an exchange of territories during the Stockholm talks. Its first expression of willingness to consider an exchange came at Camp David, under pressure from the Americans. At that time Israel expressed a willingness to exchange 9 percent of the West Bank for a piece of sovereign Israeli territory adjacent to the Gaza Strip equivalent to 1 percent of the West Bank. At the Taba talks in December the ratio was already down to 2:1 in Israel's favor. The Jerusalem question developed in a similar way.

During the period that the Israeli representatives were prohibited from negotiating over Jerusalem and Israeli willingness to withdraw on the West Bank was limited, Israel sought to establish Greater Jerusalem. In the map submitted by Israel to the Palestinian delegation in May 2000, the boundaries of Israeli Jerusalem were greatly expanded, stretching from the settlements north of Ramallah (Ofra and Beit El) toward the Jordan Valley and the shores of the Dead Sea (Beit Ha'arava and Kalia), and east from there to Ma'aleh Adumim and Jerusalem. From there the line moved south toward the settlements in Gush Etzion. In July 2000, at the opening of the Camp David summit, Barak warned the Americans that he could not accept Palestinian sovereignty over any part of East Jerusalem other than a purely symbolic foothold (Agha and Malley 2001). But shortly thereafter, Israel agreed to transfer the peripheral neighborhoods to Palestinian sovereignty. After that came President Clinton's proposals concerning the internal neighborhoods and the Old City. Furthermore, Israel had initially agreed to grant the Palestinians only functional sovereignty in the Old City. But then it agreed to the 2:2 formula that Clinton proposed toward the end of the conference; in other words, it agreed to divide sovereignty in the Old City between the two sides.

The aggressive Palestinian "no" brought about the creation of a new Israeli red line, tension with the Palestinian Authority, and additional erosion of a position that had no chance of being accepted in the first place and in fact contradicted Israel's most significant interest: preserving a significant Jewish majority in the Israeli capital.

It should be noted that the red-lines strategy and the Middle-Eastern-market bargaining method were not unique to the Barak government. They were adopted by the Likud government under Netanyahu in the negotiations over the Israeli withdrawal in the framework of the Oslo accords. In March 1997 Israel wanted to withdraw from only 2 percent of the area of the West Bank, later claimed that a withdrawal from about 9 percent would endanger the security of Israel, and, finally, in the October 1998 Wye agreement, agreed that the withdrawal would turn 13.1 percent of Zone C into Zone B and 14.2 percent of Zone B into Zone A.

It would have been more appropriate for Israel to employ a different strategy, that of the "common good" or "blue lines." The blue-lines strategy seeks common interest and understanding and is built on openness and dialogue. Necessary conditions for the success of this approach are mutual trust and viewing the other side as having equal rights. Usually there is also a need for the involvement of a third party as a mediator and referee of the rules of the game. However, these did not exist in the process in which the Barak government and the Palestinian Authority participated. The concept of the common good is characterized by the existence of channels of communication, and it cultivates trust and understanding, whereas the red-lines strategy is built on dictates and moves from crisis to crisis. At the basis of the concept of the "common good" lies the assumption that the creation of a situation of mutual gain will ensure the resilience of the agreement. The mutual understanding also cultivates each side's sensitivity to the other's red lines. The blue-lines strategy does not ignore the red lines but gets to them in a different way.

Furthermore, the blue-lines strategy prevents the consistent erosion of red lines by friction with the other side's red line. On the contrary, as trust and communication grow, so will the credibility of adhering to one's red lines. But the red lines must be restricted to the utter and absolute necessities. As the negotiations develop there is a new definition of the vital and the substantive. The vital and the substantive are defined not only in and of themselves but also in terms of external influences of public opinion, interest groups, and lobbies and considerations of marketing the agreement to the general public. This strategy requires conceptual flexibility, creativity, and the ability to make broad and unconventional gestures. In contrast, the red-lines strategy is built on minimal deviation from convention and on conservatism and caution.

The blue-lines strategy served Israel in its negotiations with Egypt (1977–79) and Jordan (1994), both of which resulted in peace agreements. It was also the basic strategy in the negotiations toward the Oslo accords in 1993 and 1995. Only the blue-lines strategy could, at the time, have brought about Palestinian agreement to defer the core issues of the conflict to future negotiations on a final setetlement. The same is true with respect to the second Oslo agreement of September 1995, which provides that Israel may decide unilaterally on the extent of the three withdrawals to be implemented in accordance with the agreement. Previous understandings were upset by changes of Israeli government and policy, the expansion of the settlements, the massacre by Baruch Goldstein of Muslim worshippers in the Cave of the Patriarchs in February 1994, terrorist attacks by the Hamas and the Palestinian Islamic Jihad, and the Palestinian attitude toward such terrorist attacks. Abu Mazen, the Palestinian architect of the Oslo agreement, was supposed to and indeed wanted to be the Palestinian figure who would lead the negotiations for his side. He recommended to Israel that it table its set of principles for the agreement, in particular on territorial questions, from the beginning. But Barak rejected his proposal and sent Ben-Ami to speak with Abu 'Ala (Pundak 2001). At the end of quarrelsome bargaining, Barak laid down a territorial proposal at Taba that was similar to the one Abu Mazen had expected to be laid down already at the opening of the negotiations. However, at the Taba talks Barak was perceived by the Palestinians as politically weak and untrustworthy.

The above analysis indicates that the factors that prevented the conclusion of a permanent status agreement between mid-1999 and mid-2000 developed during that same period. Barak and his government did not properly comprehend what was happening in Palestinian society, nor the growth of the new opposition there. They focused their gaze on Syria instead of on Palestine. They gave too much weight to the positions of Israel's religious and hawkish parties on the Palestinian question when they put off changing the status of Abu Dis, al-'Azariya, and Sawahreh al-Sharqiyya. They also approved the expansion of Israeli settlements in the territories and the paving of roads for the use of the settlers. No less important, the Israeli approach to the negotiations was influenced by a profound conviction that it was necessary to compromise on the territories occupied in 1967 but not to touch the borders established in 1949. This was why Israel did not want to carry out the territorial sections of the Oslo II and Wye agreements that it had signed. In other words, political pressures and the preference given to Syria on Israel's diplomatic agenda were only accessory factors. It was Barak's personal position that led him to reject the approaches made by Yossi Beilin and Abu Mazen, each on his own, in October and December 1999 respectively, and also to miss more than one opportunity to discuss a permanent agreement with contours much like that of the Beilin–Abu Mazen agreement in January and June 2000. The same reason led to the rejection of Abu 'Ala's proposal during the Stockholm talks of April–May 2000. Barak's position and the public taboo against the partition of Jerusalem, and other taboos relating to the permanent status negotiations, all fed into one another. The result was that the Israeli leadership did not act to neutralize the taboo and to prepare public opinion for new ideas. It was only during the negotiations that the taboo was shattered, in an unnecessarily painful way.

It must be emphasized that this was not an inevitable failure resulting from a deterministic process. Elites and broad social groups on both sides were prepared for compromise and a sincere pursuit of a permanent status agreement. The Palestinian side preferred to construct its state and live in coexistence alongside Israel. Israel had undergone a gradual transformation from a mobilized society with a frontier ethos to a society with an ethos of normality and the establishment of a civil society. The permanent status talks passed through many points of decision. At each of these points there were a number of realistic possibilities to be chosen from, among them the possibility of reaching a permanent settlement. The turn toward confrontation was not predetermined. A complex historical fabric of considerations and factors stood before the leaders at each of these turning points. In retrospect it turns out that not just Israel but also the United States and the Palestinian leadership made mistaken judgments and incorrectly weighed different factors. Each side contributed to the failure when it chose which considerations to give preference to. One mistaken discussion does not necessarily dictate a similar decision at the next stage. But that is in general what happened, though not always. The potential for confrontation was built up gradually and then changed from potential to real. The complexity of the situation continued even after the Intifada broke out, but then the correct choice was even more difficult.

Although the negotiations were conducted in a manner that encouraged disagreements, there were a number of oral agreements during the process, including at the Camp David summit. After the summit the focal points of dispute in Jerusalem were the Temple Mount/al-Haram al-Sharif; the Old City; the crescent of Palestinian neighborhoods adjacent to the Old City that constitute the historical and religious cores of Jerusalem; and the city as defined by the Jordanians between 1949 and 1967. The dispute focused less on the management of these areas and more on the symbolic and political issue of sovereignty. In contrast, the two sides reached understandings about a significant number of questions of principle. These understandings are based on irreversible geographic and demographic reality and on the national interests of each side. On a fundamental level, then, this was a win-win situation.

First of all, it was understood, as Israel demanded, that there was no returning to the reality of Jerusalem prior to the war of 1967. At the same time, it was understood that the municipal boundary unilaterally established by Israel as Jerusalem could not remain.

Second, all agreed that Jerusalem would grow in both directions. The Jewish city would be larger than that defined by Israel immediately after the 1967 war, and the Palestinian city would also grow to include the suburbs of Jerusalem that, in 1967, were villages not physically connected to the city. The two parts of the city would be larger than its current territory.

Third, this enlarged Jerusalem was seen to be a single metropolitan unit with common characteristics and needs and would remain open. An international border, in the common sense of the word, would not run through it. In order to avoid damaging the common fabric of the city and the two-way flow between the two parts of the city, appropriate security measures would have to be taken that would keep Jerusalem from turning into a focus of terror, crime, and violence. Furthermore, a series of agreements would have to be reached to lay out the day-to-day functioning of the metropolitan area. Some of these arrangements would apply to the entire zone and require coordination between the two sides in solving problems that span the administrative borders, such as air pollution and sewage. Another kind of special arrangement grows out of the need to preserve common interests such as the appearance of the Old City and its sites. Legal and economic arrangements would be required because of the freedom of movement between the eastern and western cities. These special arrangements would apply largely to the seam where the two populations are in intensive contact.

Fourth, both sides agreed to the establishment of two municipalities in the enlarged territory of Jerusalem. A Palestinian municipality would be established as a separate administrative unit under full Palestinian sovereignty. It would serve as the capital of the Palestinian state (Barak to the *Jerusalem Post* 28 September 2000). The debate at the Camp David summit centered on the powers of the Palestinian municipality in the historical and religious heart of the city, the municipal commercial center, and the adjacent neighborhoods. Everyone agreed, however, that the Palestinian municipality would have full powers in most parts of metropolitan East Jerusalem. Agreement on the principle of establishing two municipalities and an open municipal space requires, in turn, agreement on whether it is a coordinating committee or umbrella municipality.

Fifth, both sides realized that an exchange of neighborhoods is necessary. Israel would exclude from its sovereign territory neighborhoods in its outer belt, such as Sur Baher in the southeast and Sho'afat and Bait Hanina in the north. These would be joined to the suburbs that now lie outside the municipal boundary drawn by Israel in 1967.

In exchange, Israel would receive sovereignty over settlements adjacent to Jerusalem—Ma'aleh Adumim, Givat Ze'ev, and Gush Etzion. Israel could decide whether Gush Etzion would remain an independent entity or be integrated into the Jewish Jerusalem municipality. In addition, the Palestinians would officially recognize the Jerusalem neighborhoods that Israel built after 1967 on former Jordanian territory. As far as the Palestinians are concerned, these neighborhoods are illegal settlements just like any others in the West Bank and Gaza Strip. It will be hard for the Palestinians to make the distinction between the Jerusalem neighborhoods and other settlements, but, realistically, this is what they must do. About half of the residents of the former Jordanian zone are Israeli Jews, and their inclusion in the Palestinian city, even if they were to remain Israeli citizens, would give the eternal capital of Palestine a binational character. The same is true in Israel's case. As hard as it would be for Israel to retract its unambiguous and determined statements about Jerusalem with its 1967 borders being the united Israeli capital forever, the fact that a third of the city's residents are Palestinian Arabs makes such rhetoric hollow.

In short, both sides reached the conclusion that it is people, more than anything else, who determine the identity of the land on which they live. In this sense, the foundation laid at Camp David will constitute a reference framework for all future agreements, since its base is solid. While guns are blasting and people dying, it is hard to see how the two sides can begin to negotiate again and complete what they began at Camp David. The Camp David summit closed a period in which Jerusalem was discussed through slogans. The national agenda of Israel and the Arabs now includes the understanding that on the subject of Jerusalem mutual concessions must be made. Without a resolution of the Jerusalem question and the inclusion of an arrangement for Jerusalem in the general Israeli-Palestinian agreement, there can be no peace.

Whether it was a political gesture toward both of the new governments or an angry reaction against the Palestinian side, the clearing of the political table by Ehud Barak and Bill Clinton before handing over the reins of power to Ariel Sharon and George W. Bush did not make the reality on the ground disappear. Now, more than ever in the past, it is clear that the status quo does not shape the relations between West and East Jerusalem. The taboo on dealing with the question of Jerusalem was broken during the course of the negotiations, and this may not be erased from the memory and collective consciousness of the two sides.

Afterword

Inevitability versus Intangibility

Try to imagine this: A Palestinian municipality is operating in Arab East Jerusalem. The Israeli municipality is no longer responsible for the affairs of East Jerusalem's Arab neighborhoods. The school system is Arab, as are the health, legal, water, and road systems, gardening services, and tourism affairs. Israeli drivers receive parking tickets from the al-Quds municipality. The change is largely symbolic, but it is a slap in the face for Israelis. There are emblems of Palestinian sovereignty and administration all over the place. The language used to run the city is different. The dominant colors are those of the Palestinian flag. Public ceremonies and the calendar are also Palestinian. Palestinian sounds and hues replace the thin but salient Israeli veneer that once covered Arab Jerusalem. Palestinian policemen direct traffic. They give out orders to Israeli drivers and reprimand Israeli cabbies from Jewish Jerusalem who cause traffic jams by letting out tourists on Sultan Suleiman Street. Al-Quds University has moved from the suburbs into the center of the city and has become a national symbol as well as an institution of higher education. It competes both with the Hebrew University of Jerusalem and the Palestinians' own Bir Zeit University outside Ramallah.

The Temple Mount is administered by the Palestinian Waqf. This is brought home by the Waqf uniforms and assertiveness of the officials there and their pride at having liberated the site from "the claws of occupation." The Temple Mount becomes the main focus of Palestinian national and religious identity. In order to enhance his own political and personal status, as well as that of the state of Palestine, Arafat makes a point of officially receiving every visiting head of state on al-Haram al-Sharif. During their visits he also accompanies them on a visit to Christian holy sites. The Palestinian Parliament sits in Abu Dis, and one of the president's offices is located in the Old City's Muslim Quarter, next to al-Haram al-Sharif. A huge wave of Arab and Muslim heads of state comes to visit the new country and pray at its Islamic holy sites. The speeches made at these ceremonies reek of national pathos and hostility to the previous Israeli regime. In the early years of Palestinian independence, a special emphasis is placed on the liberation. Contrast with the recent past is at the center of public life. The future seems new and promising and papers over the dreariness of normal, nonrevolutionary life, something the Palestinians have trouble coping with.

Even in the past the average Israeli did not move freely through the eastern city. The Intifada dictated a geography of fear and prevented him from strolling through the Muslim Quarter's narrow roads. Then, however, he was the one deciding not to visit those places, while now he thinks he is prevented from doing so because the Palestinians don't want him to. Even in those parts of Arab Jerusalem he does feel free to visit, the Israeli visitor must take into account Palestinian law and the special arrangements that prevail there. What happens if he or his car gets hit by a Palestinian driver? Still, Israelis have unimpeded access to the Western Wall and the Mount of Olives via sovereign Israeli territory. Israeli policemen guard the route and are stationed at these holy sites.

The establishment of the state of Palestine, with al-Quds as its capital, has ended East Jerusalem's isolation. Many Palestinians come to visit the city. Most of them have not been there for years. For others, especially the Gazans, this is their first visit ever. The influx of national and religious pilgrims is especially notable during the Muslim holy month of Ramadan and on other Islamic holidays. These crowds of visitors create traffic jams on the binational roads—Route 1, which leads from the Old City walls to the city's north; Hebron Road, from the Old City to Jerusalem's southern entrance, near Bethlehem; and the eastern ring road and the road from Ma'aleh Adumim to Jerusalem. Israel has instituted special security arrangements in Jewish Jerusalem and on the city's boundaries, in order to prevent the visitors to al-Quds from Palestine and from other countries from entering Israel freely.

Israeli Jerusalem has always been unique among the country's cities, and this uniqueness is enhanced after the permanent settlement. Before the settlement the difference was attributed to the conflict and tension that prevailed there. Yet it is now clear that the settlement has not turned Israeli Jerusalem into just another Israeli city.

The establishment of the Palestinian capital has removed all obstacles to Palestinian construction. The Palestinians make a special effort to make up for lost time in housing construction. Construction and development accelerate in the neighborhoods distant from the city's historical and religious center. Multistory buildings are being built to the north of al-Quds, like those built since 1996 in Ramallah and al-Bireh. A contiguous Palestinian urban area stretches from Bethlehem in the south to Ramallah and al-Bireh in the north, skirting to the east the Jewish neighborhoods of Tzameret HaBirah, Pisgat Ze'ev, and Neveh Ya'akov. A similar process takes place in the south. Abu Dis and Sur Baher join up with Bethlehem, surrounding the Jewish neighborhood of Har Homa on three sides. Israel has trouble getting people to move to Har Homa, and there are those who call for the country to cancel future construction plans there. Kalandia, formerly Atarot, airport reopens, at first providing air service between Palestine and Jordan.

Al-Quds becomes a center of employment and source of income and attracts Palestinian internal immigration. Not only the building trades are providing new employment opportunities—there is also tourism, the Palestinian civil service, and small businesses. The establishment of embassies and consulates in the Palestinian capital makes northern al-Quds desirable and exclusive. The momentum of Palestinian development and migration into the city raise fears among the Israelis. They remember that for years they ran a demographic race with the Palestinians in Jerusalem, and one of their major motives for reaching a permanent settlement was the matter of demography. "Don't the Palestinians intend to change the city's identity by encouraging migration to it?" they ask themselves.

The Jewish neighborhoods built in the eastern part of the city after 1967 are recognized as part of West Jerusalem. This includes the Jewish Quarter, which has been expanded slightly to include Jewish-owned homes in the Armenian Quarter. It also includes the road running just inside the city wall that leads from the Jaffa Gate, which points to Jewish Jerusalem, to the Jewish Quarter, and from there to the Dung Gate, which points to the Western Wall.

The Israeli settlers remaining in Ras al-'Amud, Shaykh Jarah, the Muslim Quarter, and Silwan have tense relations with their Arab neighbors and the Palestinian municipality. The settlers are subject to harassment and severe treatment from those who for years had wanted to act against them but could not. Previously the settlers were arrogant and condescending; now it is the Palestinians. The political settlement allowed the settlers to remain Israeli citizens while living in Arab neighborhoods, but they are anomalies in the municipal fabric. Jerusalem is divided into ethnic-national units. The atmosphere in East Jerusalem is not national-liberal and pluralistic to the point of being reconciled with having Israeli settlers living in Palestinian neighborhoods. Some of the settlers are obliged to leave; others continue to run the seminaries and synagogues established there without actually living in the Arab neighborhood. A small extremist minority insists on remaining, and their presence rankles the Palestinians. On the other side, Israel is having to cope with the demands of some Jerusalem Arabs who want to live in the Jewish part of the city in homes they owned before the 1948 war. This problem is more acute than it is in other Israeli cities because the entire city space is open and there is geographical proximity between the West Jerusalem homes these Palestinians are demanding and their current residences in East Jerusalem.

The political settlement has not resolved East Jerusalem's social problems. The establishment of the embassies, the arrival of waves of tourists, and the resulting cosmopolitan and international atmosphere have intensified the tension between Jerusalem's sanctity and its attraction for foreign visitors. Furthermore, the social and economic gap between the Sho'afat refugee camp and the wealthy Shaykh Jarah neighborhood has grown. The social, economic, and political elite is the main beneficiary of the building boom, economic development, tourism, and the arrival of embassies in the Palestinian capital. The less well-off get only what is left over. In other places the disadvantaged find their solace in radical religion. A similar process is underway in Israeli Jerusalem.

Two social groups have come into being in al-Quds. One is that of new arrivals, the second that of the residents of East Jerusalem, who, under Israeli rule, bore Israeli identity cards and thus enjoyed freedom of movement and Israeli social benefits. In order to ease East Jerusalem's social plight, Israel has agreed that the residents of the Arab city will continue to enjoy freedom of movement in the Israeli city and will continue to receive social security payments and benefit from Israeli national health insurance. This is, however, a temporary measure, since these beneficiaries are not Israeli citizens and do not vote in Israeli municipal elections. The special arrangement makes West Jerusalem hospital services available to the residents of East Jerusalem, and East Jerusalem medical and support professionals work in the hospitals on the Jewish side of the city.

The city is not divided physically by a wall, but it is quite obvious who is in charge and where. It is obvious because it is important to both sides that it be so. Israel's municipal and national administration must coordinate a number of its activities with a Palestinian administration that does not view itself as inferior to its Israeli counterpart in any way. A metropolitan coordinating committee has begun to deal with joint problems such as infrastructure (electricity, water, communications, major roads), metropolitan planning, water reservoirs, environmental quality, jurisdiction, and employment. The two bureaucracies have trouble getting used to each other. The Palestinian system is run inefficiently and suffers from lack of coordination between its different branches; furthermore, personal loyalties are more important on the Palestinian side than institutional ones, both on the municipal and national levels. Sometimes a Palestinian official takes it upon himself to demonstrate to the Israelis that things are not as they once were and that the Palestinian side has power. This makes it difficult to work together. But the Israeli side also has trouble cooperating. Not long ago the Palestinians were its subjects, and now Israeli officials must treat them as equals. Moreover, it is hard for the Israeli side to accept that decisions made, or not made, by the Palestinians have implications for West Jerusalem. In the past the Israeli administration decided when, for whose benefit, and to what extent it would operate in East Jerusalem. Israel's decisions not to act in certain areas had in fact left many vacuums in East Jerusalem, vacuums the Palestinian Authority filled cautiously and partially. In other words, the failure is also an Israeli one. Israel must now accustom itself to a different situation, one in which the Palestinian side has a status equal to that of the Israeli side and can directly affect the Israeli side through its actions, or lack of action, because the two cities are open to each other.

Unlike the other West Bank cities that the Palestinian Authority took charge of gradually in the years 1994–96, its entry into Jerusalem was hesitant and was on occasion blocked by Israel. Al-Quds never existed before as a Palestinian administrative-municipal unit subordinate to a central Palestinian government. In the period of the British Mandate there was a Jewish-Arab municipal government headed by a Palestinian. In the Jordanian period, the Palestinian municipality was subject to the central government in Amman. More than a generation has gone by since Israel's dissolution of the Jordanian-Palestinian municipal government in 1967. The Palestinian national and local establishment has had difficulty adjusting instantly from having no municipal institutions to having a functioning municipality that both represents and provides services and infrastructure to the local population. The Palestinian population is also having a hard time getting used to the new situation. As much as they admire their national achievement, on the personal level they are apprehensive about the Palestinian central government's mode of operation. Years of living at the margins of the social and political systems in the West Bank and in Israel, and a high level of exposure to Israeli norms, have had their effect. For many years the Palestinians of East Jerusalem specialized in maneuvering between the Palestinian and Israeli systems in order to survive as a unique social and political entity. They lived in a frontier city for more than a generation, on the margins of the West Bank's social and political system. It is hard for this population to become accustomed to a reality in which it must govern itself and construct its own governing institutions. It is also difficult for it to accept the authority of the central government. But the central power does not give in. The establishment of al-Quds as the capital means that the Palestinian regime has moved in and established its authority. The central authority wants to turn Jerusalem from a frontier city into a center of national life.

It is not only East Jerusalem that has changed in the wake of the settlement. With foreign embassies moving from Tel Aviv to Jerusalem, the Israeli capital has taken on a universal and cosmopolitan character, and tourists have again appeared in the city. As a city whose economy and income is based on services and tourism, the settlement has given West Jerusalem a big push forward. Since West Jerusalem is open to the eastern side of the city, it has become attractive to tourists, who can enjoy the west side's more numerous and better hotels. Taxi drivers, restaurateurs, and tour guides are up to their necks in work, the exact opposite of the situation that had prevailed since the beginning of the Intifada in 2000. Jerusalem's status as Israel's capital has become stronger thanks to government and Jewish initiatives. The Israeli government is pouring lots of resources into Jerusalem as a counterweight to al-Quds's status as the Palestinian capital. World Jewry is also participating in the efforts to emphasize Jerusalem's importance to the Jewish people. Numerous plans that had previously been left on paper now become reality—for example, the capital finally gets its high-speed train line to Tel Aviv via Ben-Gurion Airport.

Jerusalem has an Israeli-Palestinian seam that snakes from west to east and from south to north. This seam is of double significance: first, it separates the Jewish-Israeli neighborhoods from the Arab-Palestinian ones; second, it is the area in which the two populations encounter each other. At first the seam is characterized by uncertainty and apprehension. The residents of the Jewish neighborhoods in East Jerusalem fear not only that their Palestinian neighbors will snipe at them but also that Palestinians will steal their property and harass their young women and children. Some of the Jewish neighborhoods decide to fence themselves off and have demanded that the Israeli government provide them with security guards 24 hours a day. On the second seam, that of encounter, there is fear of the special arrangements that govern the daily contact between the two populations. How will personal security be guaranteed? How will the economic and financial arrangements ensure that business will be profitable and the labor market efficient? What bureaucratic agonies will each side need to undergo in order to guarantee its rights against injury or dispute with the other side?

Jerusalem and al-Quds are two cities in which police forces are highly visible. Unobtrusive oversight by plainclothes agents is not sufficient, nor are the observation posts and television cameras whose signals are sent into the joint operations room at the Jaffa Gate. The large number of policemen must provide for the psychological needs of the two populations and express with their uniforms the sovereignty of their countries.

Jerusalem and al-Quds do not have a hard border, but policemen from the joint Israeli-Palestinian unit patrol the seam. From time to time they erect unannounced roadblocks and seek out people suspected of criminal acts or of being in the city without a permit. This salient police presence tells thieves that there is a lacuna here, a problematic place. Checkpoints are scattered throughout the metropolitan area, meant to prevent Jerusalem from becoming an uncontrolled entry point for people and goods into the hinterland of each country. Palestinian citizens and tourists are permitted to enter the rest of Israel only after producing an appropriate document. The same is true of an Israeli citizen who wants to enter Palestine via al-Quds. The residents of the former settlements that have now been annexed to Israel (Ma'aleh Adumim, Givat Ze'ev, and Gush Etzion) travel freely to and from Jerusalem on roads that are under Israeli sovereignty. Israelis who want to drive to Eilat via the northern Dead Sea, and to Tiberias via the Jordan Valley, can do so by paying a toll at the entry point and exit points from Palestinian territory.

Those who have read this scenario as one of inflexible partition of the city along the 1967 border, in which there is a Palestinian capital with full territorial sovereignty over the city's Arab neighborhoods, have done so of their own volition. In other words, this scenario does not necessarily have to be read as a depiction of daily life in a city organized according to former President Clinton's ideas. It can also reflect the model that Israel proposed at Camp David—a soft partition with reduced Palestinian powers in the Old City and adjacent Arab neighborhoods. One who reads the scenario in this way must remember that not just Palestinian powers will be restricted in these areas. Israel will also have reduced powers in the Old City and nearby places. In short, the reality that the planners of the Israeli annexation of 1967 sought to create has not been realized. Jerusalem has been moving in a different direction from that of the dream of 1967.

This is not the only possible scenario. There are others that are rosier, and still others that are blacker. The goal of presenting the above sketch is not to predict the future. It uses one possibility among many for the future, as hypothetical as it might be, to get a sense of where the two sides are today.

The distance between the current Israeli-Palestinian reality and the reality of a peace settlement is very large. First, there is a distance of consciousness. Public and institutional discourse has not developed to the point of being able to comprehend the full significance of a political settlement in Jerusalem. At the inspiration of the discussions between political leaders at Camp David, public discussion in Israel and the Palestinian territories has centered largely on the issue of sovereignty. As important as this issue is, the settlement in Jerusalem cannot focus entirely on this single point. The spectrum of issues at the center of the public and institutional discussion must be broadened. Along with the discussion of sovereignty, there must be a bottom-up discussion aimed at formulating programs and solutions for a range of subjects having to do with daily life in the city under a permanent settlement. The scenario presented above is meant to draw attention to these issues, which have been neglected so far. Until now these issues have been addressed only by task forces outside the establishment, such as the Jerusalem Institute for Israel Studies. In contrast with the past, today these political scenarios must be molded into programs that address daily life. The taboo was broken during the year 2000. The current Intifada has pushed off the achievement of the settlement but has not revived the old taboo.

Second, in order to imagine a settlement in Jerusalem and progress toward it, joint Israeli-Palestinian groups must prepare plans for the shaping of the city's day-to-day life. They must boldly sketch out a political settlement, as difficult as this might be. Each side must see its counterpart as being of equal status and enjoying equal rights, and as representing legitimate interests and aspirations. Instead of playing a zero-sum game— either I win everything and you lose everything, or vice versa—both sides must win. As was proved by the negotiations that took place during 2000, this is difficult for establishment people to do. It is thus necessary to include people and institutions from outside the establishment in this activity, people who have experience in speaking with the other side as an equal.

It looks as if there is no avoiding the difficulties that an arrangement in Jerusalem would present. The assumption that the existing state of affairs in Jerusalem is stable and that Israel should maintain it is an illusion. Israel's position in East Jerusalem is constantly eroding, and its presence there is firm only in places where it is founded on large masses of Jewish population. In those parts of the eastern city populated by Arabs, Israel's presence is, for the most part, symbolic. In the absence of a municipal status quo and a solid separation between the territory under Israeli sovereignty and the territory outside it, there is no way of making Jerusalem an island of tranquility in the midst of a turbulent sea. Faisal Husseini's death in the spring of 2001 left a leadership vacuum in Arab East Jerusalem. The leader who knew how to maneuver between constraints and extremes and to talk with all the actors in East Jerusalem is gone. The vacuum may draw in extremists and the inexperienced (on both sides) who are liable to act with destructive force. There is thus no small chance that tensions will escalate. Furthermore, in the absence of a status quo, it is impossible to guarantee full and uninterrupted control of the confrontation in Jerusalem. The potential for escalation has, in fact, begun to be actualized—yet this may still be prevented by an agreement. A permanent settlement will not create paradise in Jerusalem. But continuation of the Israeli-Palestinian conflict as a whole, and specifically its full-force incarnation in Jerusalem, will be very costly. As attorney Daniel Zeidman has put it, the problem of an agreement on Jerusalem today pits the inevitable against the unthinkable. Many people now only see the unthinkable side, but that is not the full picture that they must see. The full picture includes the inevitable, and a way must be found to overcome the serious tension between these two elements. Such a way is proposed here.

As I have noted, East Jerusalem is not cut off from the rest of the Palestinian lands. The question of the price to be paid for a settlement on the status of Jerusalem is connected to the price that will be paid if, instead of a settlement, there is large-scale Israeli-Palestinian conflict in the West Bank. An Israeli-Palestinian agreement cannot be reached without addressing at least some of the aspects of the Jerusalem problem. Jerusalem is the soft underbelly of any settlement. Any settlement that neglects it will implode.

Jerusalem is also an impediment to any Israeli plan to withdraw unilaterally from the West Bank, since the existing city boundary cannot be the Israeli redeployment line. It is impossible to establish a buffer zone that literally crosses residential neighborhoods, runs through buildings, and divides families in two. Nor is it possible to withdraw to the 4 June 1967 lines unilaterally and thus endanger that half of Jerusalem's Jewish population that lives outside those lines.

On the other hand, drawing an impermeable border beyond the present lines and within the Palestinian territories will not make things easy for Israel, even if it is presented as temporary. The expansion of the municipality's jurisdiction will increase Jerusalem's Palestinian population from some 210,000 to approximately 330,000. Israel cannot live long with this demographic situation, even if it annexes the Jewish settlements in the metropolitan zone and ensures that they are linked to the capital with roads that may be traveled safely. Such an annexation would become intolerable if the Palestinian population crossed over into hostile forms of protest. Israel would then be doubly under pressure, in the area in which it had redeployed and outside it as well. It is not credible that the Palestinian state that will be established in the territories Israel vacates will give up the 10 percent of its population that will find itself under Israeli rule. Neither will it give up its goal of "liberating" al-Haram al-Sharif and the Old City. It is also difficult to believe that the Palestinians in East Jerusalem will agree to sever their social and political ties to the Palestinian interior. The Intifada of 1987 marked the Palestinian public's metamorphosis from passive to active. Turning the clock back hardly seems to be an option.

Furthermore, expanding the territory that Israel rules directly to beyond the suburbs of East Jerusalem would present Israel with serious problems in terms of the city's day-to-day life. What will be the status of the 120,000 Palestinians who will become city residents? Will they be permanent residents in the city? Will the Jerusalem municipality be able to supply them with the standard services and infrastructure that it has found difficult to supply to the 220,000 Arabs who have lived in the city since 1967? And if it succeeds, will that not contradict its declaration that the borders established by the unilateral withdrawal are temporary?

The reality created by the al-Aqsa Intifada and the failure of the previous permanent status talks on Jerusalem is instructive. It is impossible to move in an instant from the current state of latent confrontation in the heart of the city and of active confrontation at its fringes into a reality created by a comprehensive and permanent settlement in Jerusalem. The transition must be done gradually. Yet it is also clear that it is no longer possible to reach an Oslo-style agreement that leaves the Jerusalem question open, to be decided at a later date. The Oslo accords broke down in their interim stage because the future was left indeterminate. It is now necessary to lay out the future sharply and to direct the interim steps toward the achievement of that end result.

The evaporation of the Oslo accords left each side believing that the other side was seeking to establish facts in the field that would tip a future agreement in its favor. It is thus necessary to determine the principles of the Israeli-Palestinian permanent settlement in advance, including the resolution of the Jerusalem question. Along with this, there must be a decision in advance about the various stages that will gradually lead to the implementation of these principles. Each interim stage will address Jerusalem and will implement an agreement regarding the city. Each transitional stage will have to address a range of the subissues that make up the Jerusalem question. It would be incorrect to have the interim stages deal only with the easy and inconsequential issues. They must relate—with all due caution—to the most problematic issues and areas, those that are at the heart of the conflict. Along with this, trust should be created between the two sides as they advance from one stage to the next. This trust will grow through the implementation of agreements, and it will grow because during the interim stages it will be possible to correct errors made in the initial stages. Alongside the correction of errors, a mechanism for resolving disputes must be created and used to resolve conflicts over the implementation of the different stages and their relation to the permanent agreement at the conclusion of the process. The Oslo process dissolved in part because it did not have a mechanism that could review each side's numerous complaints about the other side's violations of the agreements. The agreement was worn down until it fell apart. The gradual process, along with mechanisms to build confidence, correct errors, and resolve disputes, will mitigate the difficulties I have noted above in the implementation of the permanent status agreement. So, for example, the al-Quds municipality will be established and gradually begin to function, and cooperation between it and the Jerusalem municipality on the local and metropolitan level will progress in stages. The gradual process is also important for the Jewish and Arab populations in East Jerusalem, since it will allow them to become accustomed to the new reality. It must be reiterated and reemphasized: the gradual process must lead to a destination that is known to and agreed upon by the two sides.

The oral understandings that took form at Camp David were set on the foundations of Jerusalem's reality. The future permanent status agreement in the city must likewise be formulated on realistic foundations that the two sides establish together. The key to the permanent status agreement in Jerusalem is already in the door, and during the second half of the year 2000 the two sides began turning the key. All who hope for a better, more promising reality should help turn that key all the way so that the Israelis and Palestinians can step through the door.

Appendixes

A. Table of Dates

Oslo Accords

September 1993	Oslo I accord.
September 1995	Oslo II accord.
October 1997	Target date for completion of Israeli redeployment in accordance with Oslo II accord. Postponed to July 2000, not yet implemented.
May 1999	Target date for the permanent settlement agreement to take force, according to the Oslo treaties.
October 1998	Wye memorandum, which established a new timetable for the implementation of the Oslo accords.
September 1999	Sharm al-Sheikh memorandum, which established a new timetable for the implementation of the Wye memorandum.

The Palestinian Authority

May 1994	Establishment of the Palestinian Authority.
January 1996	Elections for the Legislative Council and presidency.

Permanent Status Agreement

May 1996	First opening ceremony for the permanent status talks.
October 1999	Second opening ceremony for the permanent status talks.
December 1999	Ceremony for actual beginning of talks.

January 2000	Target date for reaching a declaration of principles for the permanent status agreement (May 2000 was the alternate date chosen).
September 2000	Target date for reaching a detailed permanent status agreement.
April 2000	Stockholm talks.
July 2000	Camp David summit.
December 2000	President Clinton submits to the Israelis and Palestinians his ideas to serve as a basis for a declaration of principles for a permanent status agreement.
January 2001	The Taba talks on the Clinton principles.

B. Old City Data for the Year 2000

Area

The city's area is approximately 900 dunams (225 U.S. acres, 0.9 sq. km.), consisting of the Muslim Quarter, 461 dunams; the Christian Quarter, 192 dunams; the Armenian Quarter, 126 dunams; and the Jewish Quarter, 122 dunams.

The Old City occupies 0.8 percent of Jerusalem's municipal area as defined by Israel in 1967.

Population

The city has a population of 33,542, including 23,692 Muslims (about 70 percent); 5,203 Christians (about 18 percent); and 3,842 Jews (about 12 percent). The average Muslim household has 5.3 people, Jewish 4.0, and Christian 3.7. The distribution of the ethnic groups does not exactly match the quarters. The number of Muslims in the Christian Quarter has doubled since 1967, reaching approximately 1,000. The number of Jews in the Jewish Quarter grew by only 22 people between 1983 and 1995, reaching 2,800. But the number of Jews living in the Muslim, Christian, and Armenian Quarters grew by 1,100 during the same period, reaching 400 in the Muslim Quarter, 100 in the Christian Quarter, and 600 in the Armenian Quarter adjacent to the Jewish Quarter. Some 500 Muslims live in the Jewish Quarter, mostly on the edges, in apartments that were designated for expropriation after the 1967 war as part of the plan for the Jewish Quarter, but they were never taken from their owners.

The Old City's population constitutes about 5 percent of the population of the city as a whole. The Old City is a much-sought-after place of residence, particularly for weaker segments of the Arab population. The population grew 42 percent between 1967 to 1995, or an additional 9,870 people. While that is only a quarter of the overall growth of the Arab population of East Jerusalem, it is still more than would be expected in a profoundly overcrowded area.

When the Jewish Quarter was first repopulated by Jews after 1967, 60 percent were religious and 40 percent were secular. Over the last decade the numbers have changed dramatically. Some 70 percent are Haredim, 25 percent are religious-nationalist, and only 5 percent are secular. Since religious and especially Haredi Jews tend to have many children, the average Jewish family in the Old City is very large. There has also been a rise in the number of Jewish religious schools in the Old City.

Population Density

Population growth within a territory that cannot be modified has created a high average density of 58.7 people per dunam as opposed to 26.0 people per dunam in 1972. The highest population density is in the Muslim Quarter, where the average is 171 people per dunam. Population density in the Old City is probably the highest in the country. But if only the residential area is counted, and public spaces—religious, schools, markets, and other open areas—are discounted, the net density rises much more, making it one of the most densely populated places in the Middle East. In contrast, the density in the Christian Quarter is 16.0 people per dunam; in the Armenian Quarter, 13.0 people per dunam; and in the Jewish Quarter 12.5 people per dunam.

The Old City has some 5,600 housing units, representing 3.5 percent of all Jerusalem's housing units, filling an area of about 250,000 square meters. The Muslim Quarter is the largest, with 3,300 units. The Christian Quarter has 1,150 units, the Armenian 600, and the Jewish Quarter 550. The average size of an apartment in the Old City is smaller than the overall average for the city. Jews have the largest apartments on average—75 square meters. In the Muslim Quarter the average size of an apartment is 40 square meters, 42 in the Christian, and 54 in the Armenian.

Landownership

There are four types of landownership in the Old City: church-owned, Muslim Waqf–owned, Jewish-owned (meaning state-owned), and privately owned Arab property. Landownership in the Old City is extremely complex. In effect, most of the property is not registered but rather owned by virtue of possession. There are many reasons for this—no organized land registry, overcrowded construction, no listings in the Tabu (registration office), population movement from area to area inside the Old City, wars and various other events, and of course hundreds of years spent under a variety of rulers. The division of ownership is not precise, but nonetheless the picture shows that of the 879 dunams of the Old City, 271 dunams (31 percent) are owned by the churches, 200 dunams (23 percent) are privately owned by individual Arabs, the Waqf owns 223 dunams (25 percent), and Jews, through the state, own 185 dunams (21 percent). Nearly half the land is owned by Muslims, whether through religious trusts or privately, and nearly all the land in Jewish hands is owned by the state—152 dunams in the Jewish Quarter, 21 dunams at and around David's Tower, 2 dunams at Herod's Gate, and the rest along the northern wall of the Old City.

In most Middle East countries, the waqf, as an institution, is in decline, and has even faded away in some. But in Jerusalem, and in the Old City in particular, it is flourishing. The waqf's revival in Jerusalem is a result of the government's granting autonomy to the Muslim community, making the waqf a unifying factor for the community in dealing with a non-Muslim government, and the utilization of the waqf as an alternative to Palestinian authority in Jerusalem after 1967. The Islamic Trust has 65 mosques in East Jerusalem, two colleges, two high schools, and an elementary school, and it conducts night schools for teaching the Qur'an. And some 61 percent of the ninety religious trusts formed between 1967 and 1990 are family owned and operated.

Holy Places

In 1949, a list of 30 holy sites was given to the UN. Fifty years later, in 2000, a team of three—a Jewish Israeli, an Armenian Christian, and a Muslim Palestinian—prepared a list with no fewer than 326 holy sites. Leading the list are the sites named in various international treaties (such as bilateral treaties between Israel and Jordan and the Palestinian Authority), as well as holy sites designated by the Israeli government ministries and holy sites with world recognition, like the Temple Mount. Included are graves and other memorials. In September 1981, UNESCO's World Heritage Center accepted the Kingdom of Jordan's request to list the Old City and its walls in the list of sites of worldwide cultural heritage, even though Jordan was no longer in control of the city by then. During the debate on Jordan's request, the commission refused to hear the Israeli side.

In December 1982, at Jordan's request, Jerusalem was listed as an endangered cultural-heritage site because the Old City's growing population was causing grave damage. In the 1995 list of world cultural-heritage sites, Jerusalem was no longer listed as Jordanian. Instead, Jerusalem was listed as an independent entity, without a state. On October 1999, Israel joined the UNESCO treaty for the protection of world cultural heritage, providing a list of 23 such sites in Israel. The list included Jerusalem, but without any details.

Sources: The data on population and landownership are from Israel Kimhi's appendixes in Ruth Lapidoth with Amnon Ramon, ed., *The Old City: A Summary Following Think Tank Discussions* (Jerusalem: Jerusalem Institute for Israel Studies, 2002) and Nadav Shragai, "The Bubbling Volcano of Teeming Old Jerusalem," *Ha'aretz,* 9 May 2002. Kimhi provided updated figures to the author in September 2002.

C. The Clinton Proposal

Meeting with President Clinton, White House, 23 December 2000

Attendance

United States: President Bill Clinton, Secretary Madeleine Albright, John Podesta, Samuel Berger, Steve Richetti, Bruce Reidel, Dennis Ross, Aaron Miller, Rob Malley, Gamal Hilal.
Palestine: Sa'eb Erekat, Muhammad Dahlan, Samih Abed, Ghaith Al-Omari.
Israel: Shlomo Ben-Ami, Gilad Sher, Penny Medan, Shlomo Yanai, Gidi Greenstein.

Minutes

President Clinton:
Territory:
  Based on what I heard, I believe that the solution should be in the mid-90%'s, between 94–96% of the West Bank territory of the Palestinian State.
  The land annexed by Israel should be compensated by a land swap of 1–3% in addition to territorial arrangements such as a permanent safe passage.
  The Parties also should consider the swap of leased land to meet their respective needs. There are creative ways of doing this that should address Palestinian and Israeli needs and concerns.
  The Parties should develop a map consistent with the following criteria:

- 80% of settlers in blocks.
- Contiguity.
- Minimize annexed areas.
- Minimize the number of Palestinians affected.

Security:

The key lies in an international presence that can only be withdrawn by mutual consent. This presence will also monitor the implementation of the agreement between both sides.

My best judgment is that the Israeli presence would remain in fixed locations in the Jordan Valley under the authority of the International force for another 36 months. This period could be reduced in the event of favorable regional developments that diminish the threats to Israel. On early warning stations, Israel should maintain three facilities in the West Bank with a Palestinian liaison presence. The stations will be subject to review every 10 years with any changes in the status to be mutually agreed.

Regarding emergency developments, I understand that you will still have to develop a map of the relevant areas and routes. But in delineating what is an emergency, I propose the following definition:

Imminent and demonstrable threat to Israel's national security of a military nature that requires the activation of a national state emergency. Of course, the International forces will need to be notified of any such determination.

On airspace, I suggest that the state of Palestine will have sovereignty over its airspace but that two sides should work out special arrangements for Israeli training and operational needs.

I understand that the Israeli position is that Palestine should be defined as a "demilitarized state" while the Palestinian side proposes "a state with limited arms." As a compromise, I suggest calling it a "non-militarized State."

This will be consistent with the fact that in addition to a strong Palestinian security force Palestine will have an international force for border security and deterrent purposes.

Jerusalem and Refugees:

I have a sense that the remaining gaps have more to do with formulations than practical realities.

Jerusalem:

The general principle is that Arab areas are Palestinian and Jewish ones are Israeli. This would apply to the Old City as well. I urge the two sides to work on maps to create maximum contiguity for both sides.

Regarding the Haram/Temple Mount, I believe that the gaps are not related to practical administration but to the symbolic issues of sovereignty and to finding a way to accord respect to the religious beliefs of both sides.

I know you have been discussing a number of formulations, and you can agree on one of these. I add to these two additional formulations guaranteeing Palestinian effective control over the Haram while respecting the conviction of the Jewish people. Regarding either one of these two formulations will be international monitoring to provide mutual confidence.

(1) Palestinian sovereignty over the Haram and Israeli sovereignty over the Western Wall and the space sacred to Judaism of which it is a part (the Western Wall and the Holy of Holies of which it is a part). There will be a firm commitment by both not to excavate beneath the Haram or behind the Wall.

(2) Palestinian sovereignty over the Haram and Israeli sovereignty over the Western Wall and shared functional sovereignty over the issue of excavation under the Haram and behind the Wall, as that mutual consent would be requested before any excavation can take place.

Refugees:

I sense that the differences are more relating to formulations and less to what will happen on a practical level.

I believe that Israel is prepared to acknowledge the moral and material suffering caused to the Palestinian People as a result of the 1948 war and the need to assist the international community in addressing the problem.

An international commission should be established to implement all the aspects that flow from your agreement: compensation, resettlement, rehabilitation, etc. . . . The US is prepared to lead an international effort to help the refugees.

The fundamental gap is on how to handle the concept of the right of return. I know the history of the issue and how hard it will be for the Palestinian Leadership to appear to be abandoning this principle.

The Israeli side could not accept any reference to a right of return that would imply a right to immigrate to Israel in defiance of Israel's sovereign policies and admission or that would threaten the Jewish character of the state.

Any solution must address both needs.

The solution will have to be consistent with the two-state approach that both sides have accepted as a way to end the Palestinian-Israeli conflict:

the state of Palestine as the homeland of the Palestinian people and the state of Israel as the homeland of the Jewish people.

Under the two-state solution, the guiding principle should be that the Palestinian State would be the focal point for Palestinians who choose to return to the area without ruling out that Israel will accept some of these refugees.

I believe that we need to adopt a formulation on the right of return that will make clear that there is no specific right of return to Israel itself but that does not negate the aspiration of the Palestinian people to return to the area.

In light of the above, I propose two alternatives:

(1) Both sides recognize the right of Palestinian refugees to return to Historic Palestine, Or,

(2) Both sides recognize the right of Palestinian refugees to return to their homeland.

The agreement will define the implementation of this general right in a way that is consistent with the two-state solution. It would list the five possible homes for the refugees:

(1) The state of Palestine.

(2) Areas in Israel being transferred to Palestine in the land swap.

(3) Rehabilitation in host country.

(4) Resettlement in third country.

(5) Admission to Israel.

In listing these options, the agreement will make clear that the return to the West Bank, Gaza Strip, and areas acquired in the land swap would be a right to all Palestinian refugees. While rehabilitation in host countries, resettlement in third countries and absorption into Israel will depend upon the policies of those countries.

Israel could indicate in the agreement that it intends to establish a policy so that some of the refugees would be absorbed into Israel consistent with Israel's sovereign decision.

I believe that priority should be given to the refugee population in Lebanon. The parties would agree that this is [in order to] implement resolution 194.

The End of Conflict:

I propose that the agreement clearly mark the end of the conflict and its implementation put an end to all claims. This could be implemented through a UN Security Council Resolution that notes that Resolutions

242 and 338 have been implemented and through the release of Palestinian prisoners.

Concluding remarks:

I believe that this is the outline of the fair and lasting agreement.

It gives the Palestinian people the ability to determine their future on their own land, a sovereign and viable state recognized by international community. Al-Quds as its capital, sovereignty over the Haram, and new lives for the refugees.

It gives the people of Israel a genuine end to the conflict, real security, the preservation of sacred religious ties, the incorporation of 80% of the settlers into Israel, and the largest Jewish Jerusalem in history recognized by all as its capital.

This is the best that I can do. Brief your leaders and tell me if they are prepared to come for discussions based on these ideas. If so, I would meet them next week separately. If not, I have taken this as far as I can.

These are my ideas. If they are not accepted, they are not just off the table, they also go with me when I leave office.

Source: Verbatim transcript (slightly edited to correct obvious spelling errors) as published by *jmcc.org/documents/clintonprop.htm*.

D. The Taba Nonpaper

Background Note

Accepted by the parties on August 2001, the following document reflects the issues discussed at the Taba talks eight months earlier. It outlines both the understandings reached by the two sides and their remaining disagreements. Since Taba was the last link in a chain, one can backtrack and identify in the document the footprints of previous negotiations and debates. Nevertheless, it is worth noting that the document was discussed and composed when the sides were engaged in hostilities. Israel and the United States had withdrawn their proposals, and a hawkish government led by Prime Minister Ariel Sharon had replaced Ehud Barak's coalition. Under these circumstances former negotiators who were asked to approve the nonpaper were highly cautious. They not only looked back in time but also over their shoulders, where their respective constituencies stood.

Taba, January 2001

Introduction

This EU nonpaper has been prepared by the EU special representative to the Middle East Process, Ambassador Miguel Moratinos, and his team after consultations with the Israeli and Palestinian sides, present at Taba in January 2001. Although the paper has no official status, it has been acknowledged by the parties as being a relatively fair description of the outcome of the negotiations on the permanent status issues at Taba. It draws attention to the extensive work undertaken on all permanent status issues such as territory, Jerusalem, refugees, and security in order to find ways to come to joint positions. At the same time it shows that there are serious gaps and differences between the two sides, which will have to be overcome in future negotiations. From that point of view, the paper reveals the challenging task ahead in terms of policy determination and legal work, but it also shows that both sides have traveled a long way to accommodate the views of the other side and that solutions are possible.

1. Territory

The two sides agreed that in accordance with the UN Security Council resolution 242, the 4 June 1967 lines would be the basis for the borders between Israel and the state of Palestine.

1.1 West Bank

For the first time both sides presented their own maps over the West Bank. The maps served as a basis for the discussion on territory and settlements. The Israeli side presented two maps, and the Palestinian side engaged on this basis. The Palestinian side presented some illustrative maps detailing its understanding of Israeli interests in the West Bank.

The negotiations tackled the various aspects of territory, which could include some of the settlements, and how the needs of each party could be accommodated. The Clinton parameters served as a loose basis for the discussion, but differences of interpretations regarding the scope and meaning of the parameters emerged. The Palestinian side stated that it had accepted the Clinton proposals but with reservations.

The Israeli side stated that the Clinton proposals provide for annexation of settlement blocks. The Palestinian side did not agree that the parameters included blocks and did not accept proposals to annex blocks. The Palestinian side stated that blocks would cause significant harm to the Palestinian interests and rights, particularly to the Palestinians residing in areas Israel seeks to annex.

The Israeli side maintained that it is entitled to contiguity between and among its settlements. The Palestinian side stated that Palestinian needs take priority over settlements. The Israeli maps included plans for future development of Israeli settlements in the West Bank. The Palestinian side did not agree to the principle of allowing further development of settlements in the West Bank. Any growth must occur inside Israel.

The Palestinian side maintained that since Israel has needs in Palestinian territory, it is responsible for proposing the necessary border modifications. The Palestinian side reiterated that such proposals must not adversely affect the Palestinian needs and interests.

The Israeli side stated that it did not need to maintain settlements in the Jordan Valley for security purposes, and its proposed maps reflected this position.

The Israeli maps were principally based on a demographic concept of settlement blocks that would incorporate approximately 80 percent of the settlers. The Israeli side sketched a map presenting a 6 percent annexation, the outer limit of the Clinton proposal. The Palestinian illustrative map presented 3.1 percent in the context of a land swap.

Both sides accepted the principle of land swap, but the proportionality of the swap remained under discussion. Both sides agreed that Israeli and Palestinian sovereign areas will have respective sovereign contiguity. The Israeli side wished to count "assets" such as Israel's "safe passage/corridor" proposal as being part of the land swap, even though the proposal would not give Palestine sovereignty over these assets. The Israeli side adhered to a maximum 3 percent land swap as per Clinton proposal.

The Palestinian maps had a similar conceptual point of reference, stressing the importance of a nonannexation of any Palestinian villages and the contiguity of the West Bank and Jerusalem. They were predicated on the principle of a land swap that would be equitable in size and value and in areas adjacent to the border with Palestine and in the same vicinity as that annexed by Israel.

The Palestinian side further maintained that land not under Palestinian sovereignty—such as the Israeli proposal regarding a safe passage/corridor—as well as economic interests are not included in the calculation of the swap. The Palestinian side maintained that the "no man's land" (Latrun area) is part of the West Bank. The Israelis did not agree.

The Israeli side requested an additional 2 percent of land under a lease arrangement, to which the Palestinians responded that the subject of lease can only be discussed after the establishment of a Palestinian state and the transfer of land to Palestinian sovereignty.

1.2 Gaza Strip

Neither side presented any maps over the Gaza Strip. It was implied that the Gaza Strip will be under total Palestinian sovereignty, but details have still to be worked out. All settlements will be evacuated. The Palestinian side claimed it could be arranged in six months, a timetable not agreed upon by the Israeli side.

1.3 Safe Passage/Corridor from Gaza to the West Bank
Both sides agreed that there is going to be a safe passage from the north of Gaza (Beit Hanun) to the Hebron district, and that the West Bank and the Gaza Strip must be territorially linked. The nature of the regime governing the territorial link and sovereignty over it was not agreed.

2. Jerusalem
2.1 Sovereignty
Both sides accepted in principle the Clinton suggestion of having Palestinian sovereignty over Arab neighborhoods and Israeli sovereignty over Jewish neighborhoods. The Palestinian side affirmed that it was ready to discuss Israel's request to have sovereignty over those Jewish settlements in East Jerusalem that were constructed after 1967, but not Jebal Abu Ghneim and Ras al-'Amud. The Palestinian side rejected Israeli sovereignty over settlements in the Jerusalem Metropolitan Area, namely of Ma'ale'h Adumim and Givat Ze'ev.

The Palestinian side understood that Israel was ready to accept Palestinian sovereignty over the Arab neighborhoods of East Jerusalem, including part of Jerusalem's Old City. The Israeli side understood that the Palestinians were ready to accept Israeli sovereignty over the Jewish Quarter of the Old City and part of the Armenian Quarter.

The Palestinian side understood that the Israeli side accepted to discuss Palestinian property claims in West Jerusalem.

2.2 Open City
Both sides favored the idea of an open city. The Israeli side suggested the establishment of an open city whose geographical scope encompasses the Old City of Jerusalem plus an area defined as the holy basin or historical basin.

The Palestinian side was in favor of an open city provided that continuity and contiguity were preserved. The Palestinians rejected the Israeli proposal regarding the geographic scope of an open city and asserted that the open city is only acceptable if its geographical scope encompasses the full municipal borders of both East and West Jerusalem.

The Israeli side raised the idea of establishing a mechanism of daily coordination, and models were suggested for municipal coordination and cooperation (dealing with infrastructure, roads, electricity, sewage, waste removal, etc.). Such arrangements could be formulated in a future detailed agreement. It proposed a "soft border regime" within Jerusalem between al-Quds and Yerushalaim that affords them "soft border" privileges. Furthermore the Israeli side proposed a number of special arrangements for Palestinian and Israeli residents of the open city to guarantee that the open city arrangement neither adversely affects their daily lives nor compromises each party's sovereignty over its section of the open city.

2.3 Capital for Two States

The Israeli side accepted that the city of Jerusalem would be the capital of the two states: Yerushalaim, capital of Israel, and al-Quds, capital of the state of Palestine. The Palestinian side expressed its only concern, namely, that East Jerusalem is the capital of the state of Palestine.

2.4 Holy/Historical Basin and the Old City

There was an attempt to develop an alternative concept that would relate to the Old City and its surroundings, and the Israeli side put forward several alternative models for discussion, for example, setting up a mechanism for close coordination and cooperation in the Old City. The idea of a special police force regime was discussed but not agreed upon.

The Israeli side expressed its interest and raised its concern regarding the area conceptualized as the holy basin (which includes the Jewish cemetery on the Mount of Olives, the City of David, and the Kidron Valley). The Palestinian side confirmed that it was willing to take into account Israeli interests and concerns provided that these places remain under Palestinian sovereignty. Another option for the holy basin, suggested informally by the Israeli side, was to create a special regime or to suggest some form of internationalization for the entire area or a joint regime with special cooperation and coordination. The Palestinian side did not agree to pursue any of these ideas, although the discussion could continue.

2.5 Holy Sites: The Western Wall and the Wailing Wall

Both parties have accepted the principle of respective control over each side's respective holy sites (religious control and management). According to this principle, Israel's sovereignty over the Western Wall would be recognized, although there remained a dispute regarding the delineation of the area covered by the Western Wall and especially the link to what is referred to in Clinton's ideas as the space sacred to Judaism of which it is part.

The Palestinian side acknowledged that Israel has requested to establish an affiliation to the holy parts of the Western Wall, but maintained that the question of the Wailing Wall and/or Western Wall has not been resolved. It maintained the importance of distinguishing between the Western Wall and the Wailing Wall segment thereof, recognized in the Islamic faith as the Buraq Wall.

2.6 Al-Haram al-Sharif/Temple Mount

Both sides agreed that the question of al-Haram al-Sharif/Temple Mount has not been resolved. However, both sides were close to accepting Clinton's ideas regarding Palestinian sovereignty over al-Haram al-Sharif notwithstanding Palestinian and Israeli reservations.

Both sides noted progress on practical arrangements regarding evacuations, construction, and public order in the area of the compound. An informal suggestion was raised that for an agreed period such as three years, al-Haram al-Sharif/Temple Mount would be under international sovereignty of the P5 [the five permanent members of the UN Security Council] plus Morocco (or other Islamic presence), whereby the Palestinians would be the "guardians/custodians" during this period. At the end of this period, either the parties would agree on a new solution or agree to extend the existing arrangement. In the absence of an agreement, the parties would return to implement the Clinton formulation. Neither party accepted or rejected the suggestion.

3. Refugees

Nonpapers were exchanged that were regarded as a good base for the talks. Both sides stated that the issue of the Palestinian refugees is central to Israeli-Palestinian relations and that a comprehensive and just solution is essential to creating a lasting and morally scrupulous peace. Both sides agreed to adopt principles and references that could facilitate the adoption of an agreement.

Both sides suggested, as a base, that the parties should agree that a just settlement of the refugee problem in accordance with UN Security Council resolution 242 must lead to the implementation of UN General Assembly resolution 194.

3.1 Narrative
The Israeli side put forward a suggested joint narrative for the tragedy of the Palestinian refugees. The Palestinian side discussed the proposed narrative and there was much progress, although no agreement was reached in an attempt to develop a historical narrative in the general text.

3.2 Return and Repatriation, Relocation and Rehabilitation
Both sides engaged in a discussion of the practicalities of resolving the refugee issue. The Palestinian side reiterated that the Palestinian refugees should have the right of return to their homes in accordance with the interpretation of UNGAR 194. The Israeli side expressed its understanding that the wish to return as per wording of UNGAR 194 would be implemented within the framework of one of the following programs:

A. Return and Repatriation
1. to Israel
2. to Israel's swapped territory
3. to the Palestine state

B. Rehabilitation and Relocation
1. Rehabilitation in host country
2. Relocation to third country

Preference in all these programs shall be accorded to the Palestinian refugee population in Lebanon. The Palestinian side stressed that the above shall be subject to the individual free choice of the refugees and shall not prejudice their right to their homes in accordance with its interpretation of UNGAR 194.

The Israeli side, informally, suggested a three-track, 15–year absorption program, which was discussed but not agreed upon. The first track referred to the absorption into Israel. No numbers were agreed upon, but a nonpaper referred to 25,000 in the first three years of this program

(40,000 in the first five years of this program did not appear in the non-paper but was raised verbally). The second track referred to the absorption of Palestinian refugees into Israeli territory to be transferred to Palestinian sovereignty, and the third track referred to the absorption of refugees in the context of a family reunification scheme.

The Palestinian side did not present a number but stated that the negotiations could not start without an Israeli opening position. It maintained that Israel's acceptance of the return of refugees should not prejudice existing programs within Israel such as family reunification.

3.3 Compensation

Both sides agreed to the establishment of an international commission and an international fund as a mechanism for dealing with compensation in all its aspects. Both sides agreed that "small-sum" compensation shall be paid to the refugees in the "fast-track" procedure; claims of compensation for property losses below a certain amount shall be subject to "fast-track" procedures.

There was also progress on Israeli compensation for material losses, land and assets expropriated, including agreement on a payment from an Israeli lump sum or proper amount to be agreed upon that would feed into the international fund. According to the Israeli side the calculation of this payment would be based on a macroeconomic survey to evaluate the assets in order to reach a fair value. The Palestinian side, however, said that this sum would be calculated on the records of the UNCCP [the UN Conciliation Commission for Palestine established under UN General Assembly Resolution 194 to provide protection and facilitate a durable solution for the 1948 Palestinian refugees] and the Custodian for Absentee Property and other relevant data with a multiplier to reach a fair value.

3.4 United Nations Relief and Works Agency

Both sides agreed that UNRWA should be phased out in accordance with an agreed timetable of five years, as a targeted period. The Palestinian side added a possible adjustment of that period to make sure that this will be subject to the implementation of the other aspects of the agreement dealing with refugees, and termination of Palestinian refugee status in the various locations.

3.5 Former Jewish Refugees
The Israeli side requested that the issue of compensation to former Jewish refugees from Arab countries be recognized, while accepting that it was not a Palestinian responsibility or a bilateral issue. The Palestinian side maintained that this is not a subject for a bilateral Palestinian-Israeli agreement.

3.6 Restitution
The Palestinian side raised the issue of restitution of refugee property. The Israeli side rejected this.

3.7 End of Claims
The issue of the end of claims was discussed, and it was suggested that the implementation of the agreement would constitute a complete and final implementation of UNGAR 194 and therefore end all claims.

4. Security
4.1 Early Warning Stations
The Israeli side requested to have three early warning stations on Palestinian territory. The Palestinian side was prepared to accept the continued operations of early warning stations, subject to certain conditions. The exact mechanism has therefore to be detailed in further negotiations.

4.2 Military Capability of the State of Palestine
The Israeli side maintained that the state of Palestine would be nonmilitarized as per the Clinton proposals. The Palestinian side was prepared to accept limitation on its acquisition of arms and be defined as a state with limited arms. The two sides have not yet agreed on the scope of arms limitations, but they have begun exploring different options. Both sides agree that this issue has not been concluded.

4.3 Airspace Control
The two sides recognized that the state of Palestine would have sovereignty over its airspace. The Israeli side agreed to accept and honor all of Palestine's civil aviation rights according to international regulations, but it sought a unified air control system with overriding Israel control. In addition, Israel requested access to Palestinian airspace for military operations and training.

The Palestinian side was interested in exploring models for broad cooperation and coordination in the civil aviation sphere but was unwilling to cede overriding control to Israel. As for Israeli military operations and training in Palestinian airspace, the Palestinian side rejected this request as inconsistent with the neutrality of the state of Palestine, saying that it cannot grant Israel these privileges while denying them to its Arab neighbors.

4.4 Timetable for Withdrawal from the West Bank and Jordan Valley

Based on the Clinton proposal, the Israeli side agreed to a withdrawal from the West Bank over a thirty-six-month period, and an additional thirty-six months for the Jordan Valley in conjunction with an international force, maintaining that a distinction should be made between withdrawal in the Jordan Valley and elsewhere.

The Palestinian side rejected a thirty-six-month withdrawal process from the West Bank, expressing concern that a lengthy process would exacerbate Palestinian-Israeli tensions. The Palestinian side proposed an eighteen-month withdrawal under the supervision of international forces. As to the Jordan Valley, the Palestinian side was prepared to consider the withdrawal of Israeli armed forces for an additional ten-month period. Although the Palestinian side was ready to consider the presence of international forces in the West Bank for a longer period, it refused to accept the ongoing presence of Israeli forces.

4.5 Emergency Deployment (or emergency locations)

The Israeli side requested to maintain and operate five emergency locations on Palestinian territory (in the Jordan Valley), with the Palestinian response allowing for a maximum of two emergency locations conditional on a time limit for the dismantling. In addition, the Palestinian side proposed that these two emergency locations be run by an international presence and not by the Israelis. Informally, the Israeli side expressed willingness to explore ways that a multinational presence could provide a vehicle for addressing the parties' respective concerns.

The Palestinian side declined to agree to the deployment of Israeli armed forces on Palestinian territory during emergency situations but was prepared to consider ways in which international forces might be used in that capacity, particularly within the context of regional security cooperation efforts.

4.6 Security Cooperation and Fighting Terror
Both sides were prepared to commit themselves to promoting security cooperation and fighting terror.

4.7 Borders and International Crossings
The Palestinian side was confident that Palestinian sovereignty over borders and international crossing points would be recognized in the agreement. The two sides had, however, not yet resolved this issue, including the question of monitoring and verification at Palestine's international borders (Israeli or international presence).

4.8 Electromagnetic Sphere
The Israeli side recognized that the state of Palestine would have sovereignty over the electromagnetic sphere and acknowledged that it would not seek to constrain Palestinian commercial use of the sphere, but the Israeli side sought control over it for security purposes.

The Palestinian side sought full sovereign rights over the electromagnetic sphere but was prepared to accommodate reasonable Israeli needs within a cooperative framework in accordance with international rules and regulations.

Source: Akiva Eldar, "The Peace That Nearly Was at Taba," *Ha'aretz*, 15 February 2002.

Bibliography

Books and Articles in Hebrew

B'tselem. December 2000. *Imaginary Restraint: The Violation of Human Rights during the Events in the Territories*. Jerusalem: B'tselem.

———. 2002. *Land Grave: Israel's Settlement Policy in the West Bank*. Jerusalem: B'tselem.

Beilin, Yossi. 1997. *To Touch Peace*. Tel Aviv: Yedioth Aharonoth.

———. 2001. *Guide for a Wounded Dove*. Tel Aviv: Yedioth Aharonoth.

Ben-Ami, Shlomo. 1998. *A Place for All*. Tel Aviv: Ha-Kibbutz Ha-Me'uchad.

———. 6 April 2001. Shlomo Ben-Ami's Diaries. *Ma'ariv*.

Ben Dov, Meir. 19 June 2001. Dust Has No Significance. *Ha'aretz*.

Benziman, Uzi. 26 January 2001. The Jerusalem Syndrome. *Ha'aretz*.

———. 23 March 2001. What Is to Be Done with Arafat. *Ha'aretz*.

Cohen, Hillel. 29 April 1998. Shake-up in the Territories. *Kol HaIr*.

Drucker, Raviv. 2002. *Harakiri Ehud Barak: The Failure*. Tel Aviv: Yedioth Aharonoth.

Efrat, Elisha. 31 May 2001. The Spatial Village Wins Out Over the Linear Road. *Ha'aretz*.

Eldar, Akiva. 27 September 2000. God Does Not Pay Municipal Taxes. *Ha'aretz*.

———. 31 May 2001. The Monster of the Right of the Return. *Ha'aretz*.

———. 15 February 2002. The Peace that Nearly Was at Taba. *Ha'aretz*.

Fruman, Menachem. 2001. Lecture, study day on religion and conflict resolution, 3 January, at Davis Institute, Hebrew University of Jerusalem.

Galili, Lili. 4 August 1996. Enlarging the Cake Instead of Dividing It. *Ha'aretz*.

Gorenberg, Gershom. 2001. Lecture, study day on religion and conflict resolution, 3 January, at Davis Institute, Hebrew University of Jerusalem.

Hass, Amira. 27 March 2000. Eighty-one Wounded Including 12 Children. *Ha'aretz*.

———. 25 July 2000. Willing to Cede Katamon, Malha, and Ein Karem. *Ha'aretz*.

———. 28 September 2000. The Temple Mount Is in Our Hands. *Ha'aretz*.

———. 21 August 2001. Palestinian Wanted Man: In the End You'll Have to Ask Why It Was Necessary. *Ha'aretz*.

Hasson, Shlomo. 1993. *The Municipal Organization of Metropolitan Jerusalem:*

Alternative Ideas. Jerusalem: Jerusalem Institute for Israel Studies. Published in English as "Local Politics and Split Citizenship in Jerusalem," *International Journal of Urban and Regional Research* 20 (1996):116–33.

Herman, T., and A. Ya'ar, eds. 1999. *Integration or Separation: An Examination of the Future of the Relations between Israel and the Palestinian State.* Tel Aviv: Tami Steinmetz Center for Peace Research, Tel Aviv University.

Hirschfeld, Yair. 2000. *Oslo, a Formula for Peace.* Tel Aviv: Yitzhak Rabin Center for Israel Studies and Am Oved.

Horowitz, U. 2001. *The Second Camp David Conference and President Clinton's Bridging Proposals, the Palestinian Version—Strategic Update.* Tel Aviv: Jaffe Center for Strategic Studies, Tel Aviv University.

Kaspit, Ben. 17 September 2001. How Oslo 1993 Peace Hopes Ended in 2001 with War and Despair. *Ma'ariv.*

Klein, Menachem. 31 July 1994. Straight Forward in One Line to Our Homeland Soil. *Ha'aretz.*

———. 1999. *Doves over Jerusalem's Sky.* Jerusalem: Jerusalem Institute of Israel Studies.

———. 23 January 2002. South Africa's Lesson. *Ha'aretz.*

Kra, Baruch. 2 July 2000. How Could He—He Is the Chief Rabbi of Israel. *Ha'aretz.*

Matz, David. 8 February 2002. The Failure Has Two Fathers. *Ha'aretz.*

Mazar, Eilat. 28 June 2000. An Opening to Irreparable Destruction. *Ha'aretz.*

Porath, Yehoshua. 1974. *The Emergence of the Palestinian-Arab National Movement, 1918–1929.* Tel Aviv: Am Oved.

———. 1978. *From Riots to Rebellion: The Arab-Palestinian National Movement, 1929–1939.* Tel Aviv: Am Oved.

Regular, Arnon. 28 January 2000. A State within a Non-State. *Kol HaIr.*

———. 4 February 2000. Palestine's Altalena. *Kol HaIr.*

———. 11 February 2000. A Model Camp. *Kol HaIr.*

———. 18 February 2000. The End of the World. *Kol HaIr.*

———. 25 February 2000. The Wheel of Fortune. *Kol HaIr.*

———. 30 June 2000. The Temple Mount Is in His Hands. *Kol HaIr.*

Rubinstein, Dani. 27 May 1996. Jerusalem Outside of Jerusalem. *Ha'aretz.*

———. 2001. *Arafat.* Tel Aviv: Zmora Bitan.

Shavit, Ari. 14 September 2001. The Day Peace Died. *Ha'aretz* weekly magazine.

Sher, Gilad. 2001. *Just Beyond Reach: The Israeli-Palestinian Peace Negotiations, 1999–2001.* Tel Aviv: Yedioth Aharonoth.

———. 20 March 2001. *The Peace Process: Vision versus Reality.* Tel Aviv: Tami Steinmetz Center, Tel Aviv University.

Shilhav, Y. 2001. *The Sound of Doves or Gathering Clouds: An Internal Jewish Debate on the Future of Jerusalem.* Jerusalem: Jerusalem Institute for Israel Studies.

Shragai, Nadav. 18 January 1998. How Much Are They Really Building Settlements. *Ha'aretz.*

———. 13 June 2000. Thus Will Jerusalem Be Redivided. *Ha'aretz.*

Sokol, Sami. 4 August 1996. The Cards Have Been Shown and Reshuffled. *Ha'aretz.*

Statistical Yearbook for Jerusalem. 1998. Jerusalem: Jerusalem Institute for Israel Studies.

Think Tank on the Issue of Jerusalem in the Political Negotiations. 2000. *Peace Arrangements in Jerusalem.* Jerusalem: Jerusalem Institute for Israel Studies.

Books and Articles in Arabic

Abdul Hadi, Mahdi. 2000. Reading in Jerusalem's File. In *Jerusalem: Palestinian, Islamic, and Christian Research,* edited by Jiries Sa'ad Khuri, 'Adnan Mussalam, and Musa Darwish. Jerusalem: Al-Liqa.

Abu Mazen (Mahmoud Abbas). 2000. Speech at the meeting of the PLO Central Council, 9 September. *Al-Quds.* www. pna.org/negotiations

Ahmad, 'Aisha. 1997. The Building of the Palestinian Legislative Council. In *The First Palestinian Elections: Political Context, Electoral Behavior, and Results,* edited by Khalil Shikaki. Nablus: CPRS.

Haniyya, Akram. 29 July–10 August 2000. Camp David Papers. *Al-Ayyam.*

Husseini, Faisal. 2000. The Israelis Should Terminate Their Occupation of the City of Jerusalem. In *Jerusalem: Palestinian, Islamic, and Christian Research,* edited by Jiries Sa'ad Khuri, 'Adnan Mussalam, and Musa Darwish. Jerusalem: Al-Liqa.

Books and Articles in English

Abdul Hadi, Mahdi, ed. 1998. *Dialogue on Jerusalem.* Jerusalem: PASSIA.

———. 2000. *Awakening Sleeping Horses and What Lies Ahead.* Jerusalem: PASSIA.

Abu Amr, Z. 1999. The Palestinian Legislative Council. In *Dialogue on Palestinian State Building and Identity,* edited by Mahdi Abdul Hadi. Jerusalem: PASSIA.

Agha, Hussein, and Robert Malley. 9 August 2001. Camp David: The Tragedy of Errors. *New York Review of Books.*

———. 13 June 2002. Camp David and After: An Exchange. 2. A Reply to Ehud Barak. *New York Review of Books.*

———. 27 June 2002. Camp David and After, Continued. Reply by Hussein Agha and Robert Malley. *New York Review of Books.*

Baskin, Gershon. 1994. *Jerusalem of Peace.* Jerusalem: IPCRI.

———. May 2000. The Agreement on Jerusalem and Its Price. *www.ipcri.org*

———. 2001. What Went Wrong. *www.ipcri.org*

———, ed. 1994. *New Thinking on the Future of Jerusalem.* Jerusalem: IPCRI.

Baskin, Gershon, and R. Twite, eds. 1993. *The Future of Jerusalem.* Jerusalem: IPCRI.

Bir Zeit University, Development Studies Programme. November 2000, *Survey 2;* February 2001, *Survey 3;* June 2001, *Survey 4. www.birzeit.edu/dsp*

Cingoli, Janiki, ed. 2001. *Israeli, Palestinian Coexisting in Jerusalem.* Milano: Centro Italiano per la Pace in Medio Oriente.

Chazan, N. 1991. *Negotiating the Non-negotiable: Jerusalem in the Framework of an Israeli-Palestinian Settlement.* Cambridge, Mass.: Occasional Papers of the American Academy of Arts and Sciences, no. 7 (March).

Darby, John, and Roger MacGinty. 2000a. Introduction: Comparing Peace Process. In *The Management of Peace Processes,* edited by John Darby and Roger MacGinty. London: Macmillan.

———. 2000b. Northern Ireland: Long Cold Peace. In *The Management of Peace Processes,* edited by John Darby and Roger MacGinty. London: Macmillan.

Du Toit, Pierre. 2000. South Africa: In Search of Post-settlement Peace. In *The Management of Peace Processes,* edited by John Darby and Roger MacGinty. London: Macmillan.

Erekat, Sa'eb. 2000. Speech at conference, New Thinking about Jerusalem: Life after Camp David, 5 September, Washington, D.C. *www.centerpeace.org*

Gorenberg, G. 2000. *The End of Days: Fundamentalism and the Struggle for the Temple Mount.* New York: Free Press.

Haniyya, Akram. 2000. Camp David Diary. *Al-Ayyam,* 29 July–10 August 2000. English translation at *http://www.nad-plo.org*

Hassassian, Manuel. 2001. Final Status Negotiations on Jerusalem: An Inside Look. Presentation 13 March at PASSIA. *www.passia.org*

Hirschfeld, Yair. 1998. Keeping Oslo Alive: Developing a Non-governmental Peace Strategy. In *Is Oslo Alive?* Jerusalem: Konrad Adenauer Foundation.

Hroub, Kheled. 2000. *Hamas: Political Thought and Practice.* Washington, D.C.: Institute for Palestine Studies.

IPCRI (Israel/Palestine Center for Research and Information). 1992. *A Model for the Future of Jerusalem, Draft Version.* Jerusalem: IPCRI.

———. 1999. *Jerusalem Maps.* Jerusalem: IPCRI, May.

Israeli Private Response to the Palestinian Refugee Proposal of 22 January 2001, Non-Paper, Draft 2, 23 January 2001, Taba. *Journal of Palestine Studies,* no. 123, 31 (3): 148–50.

Javetz, Eylon. 2002. Deficiencies in the Israeli "Permanent Status" Peace Strategy and Some Initial Recommendations. Forthcoming paper.

Jayyusi, L. 1998. The Voice of Palestine and the Peace Process: Paradoxes in Media Discourse after Oslo. In *After Oslo: New Realities, Old Problems,* edited by George Giacaman and Dag Jorund Lonning. London: Pluto Press.

JMCC (Jerusalem Media and Communication Center). 1996. The Palestinian Council. Jerusalem: JMCC.

Kassisiyyeh, Issa. 2002. Second Track Negotiations: The Jerusalem File. *Jerusalem Quarterly* no. 15. *www.jqf-jerusalem.org*

Kershner, Isabel. 16 July 2001. The PA's Abu 'Ala': I Warned of Catastrophe. *Jerusalem Report.*

Klein, Menachem. 1996. Competing Brothers: The Web of Hamas-PLO Relations. *Terrorism and Political Violence* 8: 11–132.

———. 1997. Quo Vadis? Palestinian Authority Building Dilemmas since 1993. *Middle Eastern Studies* 33 (2): 189–211.

———. 2001. *Jerusalem: The Contested City.* London: C. Hurst; New York: New York University Press, in association with the Jerusalem Institute for Israel Studies.

Malley, Robert. 2001. Briefs to the Center for Policy Analysis on Palestine. 7 March, *www.nad-plo.org* and at *www.palestinecenter.org,* 12 April 2001.

Macleod, Stuart. 26 February 2000. Waiting for History to Happen. *Time.*

Maoz, Moshe, and Sari Nusseibeh. 2000. *Jerusalem: Points of Friction and Beyond.* London: Kluwer.

Moore, John N., ed. 1974. *The Arab-Israeli Conflict.* Vol. 3, *Documents.* Princeton, N.J.: Princeton University Press.

Morris, Benny. 13 June 2002. Camp David and After: An Exchange. 1. An Interview with Ehud Barak. *New York Review of Books.*

———. 27 June 2002. Camp David and After, Continued. *New York Review of Books.*

Mussalam, Sammi F. 1996. *The Struggle for Jerusalem: A Programme of Action for Peace.* Jerusalem: PASSIA.

Palestinian Proposal on Palestinian Refugees, 22 January 2001, Taba. *Journal of Palestine Studies,* no. 123 (spring 2002) 31 (3): 145–48.

Peace Now. 3 December 2000. Facts on the Ground since the Oslo Agreements. *www.peacenow.org.il*

Pundak, Ron. 2001. From Oslo to Taba, What Went Wrong. *Survival* 43 (3): 31–45.

Rothstein, Robert, Maoz Moshe, and Khalil Shikaki, eds. 2002. *The Israeli-Palestinian Peace Process, Oslo, and the Lessons of Failure: Perspectives, Predicaments, and Prospects.* Brighton: Sussex Academic Press.

Sayigh, Yazid. 1997. *Armed Struggle and the Search for State: The Palestinian National Movement, 1964–1993.* Oxford: Clarendon.

———. 2001. Arafat and the Anatomy of a Revolt. *Survival* 43 (3): 47–60.

Schultz, Helen L. 1999. *The Reconstruction of Palestinian Nationalism: Between Revolution and Statehood.* Manchester, U.K.: Manchester University Press.

Shatayyeh, Muhammad, ed. 1998. *Scenarios on the Future of Jerusalem.* Al-Bireh: Palestinian Center for Regional Studies.

Shikaki, Khalil. 2000. Speech at conference, New Thinking about Jerusalem: Life after Camp David, 5 September, Washington, D.C. *www.centerpeace.org*

———. 2002. Palestinians Divided. *Foreign Affairs* 81 (1): 89–105.

Sontag, Deborah. 26 July 2001. Quest for Mideast Peace: How and Why It Failed. *New York Times.*

Susser, Lesely. 16 July 2001. Israel's Ben-Ami: Disillusions from Day One. *Jerusalem Report.*

Usher, Graham. 1998. The Politics of Internal Security: The Palestinian Authority's New Security Services. In *After Oslo: New Realities, Old Problems,* edited by George Giacaman and Dag Jorund Lonning. London: Pluto Press.

Yuchtman-Ya'ar, Ephraim, and Tamar Hermann. 2000. Shas: The Haredi-Dovish Image in a Changing Reality. *Israel Studies* 5 (2): 32–77.

Web Sites

www.birzeit.edu
www.centerpeace.org
www.idf.il
www.jmcc.org
www.mfa.gov.il
www.pna.org
www.palestinercs.org
www.tau.ac.il
www.arabrights.org

Periodicals in Hebrew

Ha'aretz
Yedioth Aharonoth
Kol HaIr
Ma'ariv
Iton Yerushalayim

Periodicals in Arabic

Al-Ayyam
Al-Quds
Al-Sharq al-Awsat
Kol al-Arab

Periodicals in English

Jerusalem Post
Jerusalem Report
Newsweek
Time

Index

Menachem Klein is a senior lecturer in the Department of Political Science at Bar-Ilan University, Israel, and a senior research fellow at the Jerusalem Institute for Israel Studies. He is the author of *Jerusalem: The Contested City* (2001).